Monograph 54
The American Ethnological Society
Robert F. Spencer, Editor

THE AINU ECOSYSTEM

Environment and Group Structure

by

HITOSHI WATANABE

University of Washington Press
Seattle and London

Library of Congress Cataloging in Publication Data

Watanabe, Hitoshi, 1919–
  The Ainu ecosystem.

  (American Ethnological Society. Monograph [s] 54)
  Originally published July 1964 in the Journal of the
Faculty of Science, University of Tokyo, section 5,
Anthropology, v. 2, pt. 6, under title: The Ainu: a
study of ecology and the system of social solidarity
between man and nature in relation to group structure.
  1. Ainu. I. Title. II. Series.
DS832.W37   1973   915.2'06'946   73-5690
ISBN 0-295-95292-X

CONTENTS

LIST OF TEXT ILLUSTRATIONS

PREFACE

In my introduction to the first edition of this study, written eight years ago and based on data gathered from 1952 to 1959, I pointed out the problems involved in trying to reconstruct a unified picture of the traditional pattern of life of the Ainu. Today the situation is even more serious. These aboriginal inhabitants of Japan, whose culture, language, religion, and economy once set them off as distinctly different from the Japanese, are now virtually indistinguishable from the majority among whom they live. For all practical purposes, the Ainu language has been dead for a long time; it lives only in the memory of a few old Ainu who will themselves soon be gone. The clothing habits of the Ainu have changed completely, such that today no Ainu ever wears traditional dress and even traditional objects of personal decoration have disappeared from daily life. The Ainu religion too has been radically transformed: the *kamui* cult which was its core has rapidly collapsed, and its formal aspect has been only partially retained in the ancestor ritual. The so-called bear ceremony of the Ainu in its traditional form is only barely preserved among present-day Ainu hunters, with whom the event has ceased to function socially as it did in the past. In short, fragmentary remnants of the old Ainu customs are maintained only precariously; they may be completely lost in a few years. Informants who know the old Ainu way of life will cease to exist in the very near future, if they have not already.

Like language, dress, and religion, the physical life and livelihood of the Ainu have also changed considerably. Traditional Ainu structures have nearly completely disappeared. Present-day Ainu live in wooden houses of the Japanese style popular in Hokkaido, although occasionally a traditional Ainu-style roof can be seen. Even the furniture and utensils are Japanese. The only exceptions are Ainu baskets made of local plant fibres, which are still in use in some localities, but the younger Ainu tend to dislike using them.

Sites for Ainu dwellings were traditionally chosen with a view to proximity to sources of drinking water and fishing and hunting grounds, since the Ainu economy was based on hunting and fishing. The most important factor in this respect was usually the spawning ground of dog salmon. Thus the houses were usually situated on or near the edge of a river terrace close to the spawning grounds. They were especially arranged according to cosmological principles. These patterns of arrangement of houses were quickly discarded, however, with the Ainu's conversion to agricultural life, which started in 1883 at the behest of the Japanese Government. The Ainu were moved to more favorable areas in order to bring their hitherto scattered settlements together into smaller areas for

convenience of supervision and instruction in farming. The introduction of
agriculture by the Japanese Government thus resulted in a considerable displacement of the territorial groupings of the Ainu and began the process of change
that has resulted in the dilution of their culture described above.

Another result of this policy was a radical change in the Ainu food habits.
The traditional staple foods, salmon and deer, were replaced by cultivated food
plants as the Ainu became farmers. All their animal food supplies now come
from local dealers. The quantity of animal foods consumed by present-day
Ainu seems to be very small, comparable to that of the Japanese farmers around
them. Wild plants have also ceased to be of importance to the Ainu. Cultivation and stock farming have devastated patches of edible plants once so important in their daily diet. Their food habits, in short, differ little from those of
neighboring Japanese.

No reservation system such as seen among the American Indians has been
applied to the Ainu, and no legal or administrative distinction has been made between the Ainu and the Japanese. There is, however, a tendency for the present-
day Ainu to maintain their own communities and to live in settlements more or
less separated from those of the Japanese. Some of these Ainu settlements
have become popular tourist centers where Ainu are engaged in commercial
activities related to tourism, but most Ainu have nothing to do with tourists in
general. Their occupations vary from stock farming to local transportation,
but the most common occupation appears to be agriculture or agriculture sup-
plemented with seasonal wage-labor in an industry such as forestry. There
seem to be many unmarried Ainu working in towns and cities in Hokkaido and
for various industrial enterprises in places distant from their homes. The only
opportunity for homecoming comes at the *bon* season in summer, the traditional
Japanese holiday season for observing an ancestor ceremony based on Buddhism.
It is in this season that the present-day Ainu observe their own ancestor ritual,
although the form seems to have been more or less influenced by Buddhism. At
present, there is a shortage of Ainu who are able to observe the festival properly.
I once saw an old male Ainu acting as a kind of professional priest for the ancestor
ritual.

The standard of living among the Ainu varies greatly from household to
household, but in general the Ainu seem to be poorer than their Japanese neigh-
bors. The current educational system makes no distinction between the Ainu
and the Japanese. By 1909 twenty-one primary schools had been established
exclusively for Ainu children, but from 1910 onward these were gradually
abolished. In spite of educational and administrative efforts, however, there
remains a socio-psychological barrier between the Ainu and the local settled
Japanese. Intermarriage between the two peoples has taken place rather
frequently, but there remain nonetheless many Ainu of " pure blood." Thus
we find the paradox that, while the Ainu as a racial group are still very much in

evidence in Japan and are perceived by the Japanese as being a different people, the Ainu culture is on the brink of extinction.

This being the case, studies like the present one, which attempts to reconstruct the past, are no longer possible. There are no longer living Ainu who have personally experienced traditional Ainu life. Studies of the distribution of Ainu culture elements or historical reconstructions based on what present-day Ainus have heard from their parents or grandparents as part of the oral tradition of the people are still possible, but a great many questions concerning the Ainu culture will inevitably remain unsolved. There is, however, another aspect of Ainu studies that remains largely unexplored, and this is the arena of current social relations between living Ainu groups. Such studies might examine, for instance, the social function of the remnants of the old Ainu traditions, or the interrelationships between the Ainu and the Japanese. It is my hope, in preparing the second edition of this study, that the research reported herein may help to further Ainu studies both by clarifying the traditional framework against which the present-day Ainu can be observed, and by raising pertinent questions about the nature of the relationship that exists between men and their environment.

Finally, I would like to express my sincere thanks to Mr. Shigeo Minowa and Mrs. Elizabeth Kodama, both of the University of Tokyo Press, for their help in preparing this edition for publication.

H. W.

Tokyo
March 1972

I

INTRODUCTION

The Ainu in Hokkaido.

The Ainu are an aboriginal people living in Hokkaido, southern Sakhalin, and the southern part of the Kurile Islands (Teikoku Gakushi-in, ed., 1944a, p. 7). They have been noted for their hirsute bodies, wavy hair and narrow heads. They number about 17,000 (ibid., p. 7). The Ainu population of Hokkaido was estimated in 1940 at about 16,300 (NATORI, 1945, p. 280), a figure which has remained almost stable since 1854[1].

Hokkaido is an island of about 77,900 square kilometres (Tokyo Temmon-dai, ed., 1954, Sect. Geogr., p. 7), situated north of the Japanese mainland between circ. 41°30'N and 45°30'N and circ. 140°E and 146°E. The northern tip of the island is about 40 kilometres away from Sakhalin and to the northeast of the island the Kurile Islands stretch away towards Kamchatka. The annual means of temperature for the years 1921–1950 vary from 5.2°C. to 8.5°C. in different areas in Hokkaido (ibid., Sect. Meteor., p. 8). There is a long season of snowfall from October to May (ibid., Sect. Meteor., p. 34 and pp. 36–42) (in Obihiro on the middle Tokapchi, from November to May). The monthly mean temperatures in the island for the years 1921–1950 indicate below 0°C. for the four months from December to March[2]. Apart from some local differences, at least in Obihiro on the middle Tokapchi, this is roughly the period of base snow which covers the ground through the winter (Obihiro Sokkō-sho, 1959, p. 8 and p. 24). The island is well wooded: the southwestern part is rich in latifoliate trees represented by beech while the northeastern part abounds in coniferous forests, the representative species being firs, Abies sachalinensis and Picea jezoensis (MIURA, 1933, p. 275 and p. 278)[3]. From north to south through the centre of the island runs a range of hills and mountains the highest of which is Mt. Taisetsu, 2290 metres above sea-level and in which the main rivers of Hokkaido have their sources. Among these rivers, the longest is the Ishikari (365 km), followed by the Teshio (306 km) and the Tokapchi (196 km) (Tokyo Temmon-dai, ed., 1954, Sect. Geogr., p. 27). In most of these rivers there are successive runs of salmon, Oncorhynchus masou and O. keta, from early summer to early or mid-winter (OYA, 1954; MIHARA et al., 1951). Among larger land mammals in Hokkaido are brown bear, Ursus arctos, and deer, Cervus nippon (HATTA, 1911; INUKAI, 1933, 1934 and 1952)[4]. The Ainu exploited these resources by hunting and fishing, and also collected wild plants.

Contact between the Ainu and the Japanese, their southern neighbours, is of long standing[5], and for a considerable period the life of the Ainu had been subject to Japanese influence through what was called the "basho" or district system that lasted from before 1789 to 1869[6]. In 1868, Hokkaido came under the administration of the Japanese Government: the island became a part of the territory of Japan and colonization was started[7]. With this began a process which greatly changed Ainu life, so that today the Ainu language is rarely spoken and then only by the aged; full-blood Ainus are about to be extinct; and the whole system of their subsistence has been profoundly altered. The most sudden and significant change in their mode of life happened in 1883 when the new Government started carrying out its programme of encouraging the Ainu to take up farming[8]. The object of this study is the Ainu as they lived their autonomous life in the last phase of the intermediate period between the abolishment of the "basho" system and the introduction of new life based on agriculture[9].

The Aim and Method.

The Ainu have interested many students concerned with the origins of this ethnic group, their customs and artifacts as well as their bodily features. The result has been listings of patterns of those elements and mappings of their distributions, but little has been known about the process of their life, that is, how the Ainu have lived and are still living in the field. To take an example, although the Ainu have been described as a gathering people with no need for nomadic wanderings (HABARA, 1937, pp. 73-74, quoted from The Aborigines of Hokkaido published by Hokkaido Government; Note 40), scarcely anything has been investigated about how they maintained a settled life and in what conditions and with what effects, even the ascertainment alone of which may be of theoretical significance.

Man is a unique animal with unique properties; yet he remains part of the biotic world and his life process at any level of organization, whether at that of the cell, the individual or the group, is nothing but a part of nature. This study deals with the Ainu in terms not of the types of implements and customs but of a life process functioning in a system of activities incorporating these means and mechanisms. The life process as such should be understood in the context of habitat, the place of abode, because no organisms can function apart from it. On the other hand, their activities should be understood in terms of the contribution to maintainance of the individual, the group and the species because this is what the students of organisms consider as the end or purpose of the life process in general. From this point of view the present writer has attempted to analyse the modes and arrangement of Ainu activities with reference to their habitat and group structure.

The relationship between organisms and environment is usually understood in terms of ecology. Ecology in this sense is the relationship between
organisms and environment as recognized objectively by scientists, i. e. objective environment. Animal ecology reveals, however, that objective environment alone is not sufficient to account for animal behaviour, and that subjective environment as perceived by the animal itself plays a significant role in
limiting its behaviour (ELTON, 1953, p. xvi; MIYAJI and MORI, 1957, pp. 24-
28). The Ainu have their own view of nature: their activities react to and
are limited by nature as seen by them. This implies that workings of
the Ainu in relation to their habitat should be understood not only in terms
of ecology in the narrower sense but also in terms of the relationship between
man and nature as perceived by the Ainu themselves. This is the subject of
the present study. It aims to ascertain the reciprocal adjustments of both
systems of relations between the Ainu and nature and their group structure.

Field trips were made to collect data in the following areas in Hokkaido:
Saru valley in August 1951; Azuma, Mukawa and Chitose, or formerly Shikot,
valleys in August and December 1952; upper Tokapchi, middle Tokapchi,
Otopuke and Tushipet valleys during August and September 1953; upper
Tokapchi and Otopuke valleys in August 1954; upper Tokapchi, Otopuke,
Kushiro, formerly Kusuri, and Saru valleys in September 1957; upper Tokapchi
and Otopuke valleys in July 1958 and February 1959.

The main portion of the original data incorporated in this study were
collected in the upper Tokapchi, Otopuke and Azuma valleys, which form the
objective areas of this paper. Data from other areas are only referred to on
necessary occasions, because the time horizon of these data is, as will be
explained later, a little newer than that of the data from the upper Tokapchi,
Otopuke and Azuma areas. Except for references cited, the whole text of
this study is based on original data, while the notes are devoted to such
original data as can not be given in the text and to citations from and discus-
sions on published materials.

The data for the present study were obtained by the interview technique.
This method, which is usually employed in ethnographical or historical studies
of anterior cultures for collecting the culture elements or traits of a given
group, has seldom been applied to functional or conjunctive studies of
group life. Such attempts as made by STEWARD (1938) and DRUCKER (1951),
for instance, might be classed as exceptions.

The intention of the author was to understand the make-up and working
of the Ainu groups of an anterior generation in relation to their habitat;
accordingly, some special caution in handling the technique was necessary,
viz., determination of a time horizon and indirect observation.

The date chosen for the study is that immediately preceding the period of great changes brought about in their group life by Japanese interference or the introduction of a new farming system under Japanese guidance and superintendence, following the agricultural-land allotment programme and the free distribution of farming tools and plant seeds by the Japanese government. Although varying to some extent in different localities in Hokkaido, the period dates from 1883 (TAKAKURA, 1942, pp. 486–488; Note 10); in the Tokapchi valley it dates from 1886 (YOSHIDA, 1955, p. 6) and in the Azuma valley from 1888 (A Chronological Chart of Azuma Village History, compiled by the village office). With this date as dividing line, there occurred throughout Hokkaido wholesale migrations of settlement groups with attendant dispersions and aggregations. As far as the present study is concerned, for instance, the Nitmap group on the river Tokapchi moved from their old home to a new site allotted downstream; the Ainu on the Otopuke, tributary of the Tokapchi, were suddenly transformed from their entire gathering life to a new farming life. This visible and sudden change brought on the Hokkaido Ainu was imprinted in the memory of those who experienced it as an epoch-making event in their life histories, a fact which enabled the writer to segregate data pertaining to the Ainu groups prior to the transition. As a necessary procedure to studying groups at the given time horizon, it was important to get into contact with informants who have both experienced the life of the groups themselves as members thereof and also are competent to supply information of that life. Three Ainu informants satisfying these conditions were made available to the author: Ushintasan (Yoshimura by Japanese family name; female, native resident of Tonika on the river Azuma; died in 1954), Ushino (Kachikawa by Japanese family name; female, native of Nitmap on the river Tokapchi and resident of Memroputu) and Kazari (Hosoda by Japanese family name; female, native of Rucha on the river Otopuke and resident of Otopuke).

It must be remembered that the simple fact that an informant belonged to a group at the given date is no guarantee for his or her information pertaining to the particular group at the particular time horizon. With a view to restricting the information sought to the desired group at the desired date, interviews were conducted by focusing on the visible and concrete activities of that group to which the informants belonged at the date. This means indirect observation by which the investigator may examine indirectly to some extent the actual and concrete workings of the group through descriptive information about the actual daily behaviours and activities of the informant himself in the group and of his fellow members and neighbours. From this concrete but fragmentary information the investigator may extract relations existing between those activities. This process was of particular importance, because by interview technique there would be the danger of the informants supplying their own generalized and theorized explanations in place of information about the concrete activities from which the investigator is to deduce some relations. Actually there exists such a strong tendency which might lead the research worker to false interpretation.

In the present study a comparison is made of the relations thus observed in different Ainu groups at our time horizon and a generalized description is made of those relations which are common to all the groups. Where there is some important variation found in any group a note was added. It should be noticed that, besides the first-hand information supplied by the three informants mentioned above on the old-time Ainu groups, a considerable amount of data was obtained from at least 20 Ainu informants—two from the Shikot or Chitose valley (Hikoichi Oyamada and Shibakichi Imaizumi, both males), one from the Azuma valley (Kentaro Yoshimura, male), four from the Mukawa valley (Kashindeashi Katayama, male; Usamtarek Okawa, male; Takaro Miyamoto, male; Itakmainu Morimoto, male), six from the Saru valley (Hachiro Kurokawa, male; Dairoku Kibata, male; Monko Kawakami, female; Tokujiro Kawakami, male; Kunimatu Nitani, male; Mopi, female), three from the mid-Tokapchi (Ritu Yoshine, female; Taijiro Tamai, male; Tome Hasegawa, female), three from the Tushipet valley (Neusharumon Kiyokawa, female; Takeo Kiyokawa, male; Hachiro Sawai, male) and one from the Kusuri or Kushiro valley (Toyosaku Kurotake, an old Japanese born there and married to an Ainu woman). These latter belong to newer generations than the other three; they could only supply information about life experiences and observations made at periods later than or immediately following the date under survey and about hearsay from the older generations. To these occasional reference is made in the study. Descriptions with special reference to place-names other than the upper Tokapchi, Otopuke and Azuma are based on these latter data, whereas those referring to either one or the other of the three areas or to no areas at all, that is, descriptions common to all the three valleys, are based on data concerning the anterior Ainu groups obtained through the afore-mentioned procedure.

Acknowledgements.

My thoughts incorporated in this study have not matured in isolation. Among many persons who influenced them I may name Professor Kotondo Hasebe, formerly of University of Tokyo, who was the first to draw my attention to the importance of viewing man as a functioning organism and man's life as part of his function, and Professor Daryll Forde, of University College, London, who led me to a realization of the significance and necessity of ecological analysis in the study of human groups, through his treatise

(1947) and his suggestions personally given me in the course of my study at the Department of Anthropology, University College, London, as well as through implications revealed in his lectures and seminar. Without their influence and encouragement this study would never have been written. I should acknowledge this with gratitude.

Five major field surveys in 1951, 1952, 1953 and 1954 were carried out by me as a member of the Joint Research Committee on the Ainu and were financed by the Scientific Research Grant from the Ministry of Education, Japan. I gratefully acknowledge also my indebtedness to the Ministry of Education and the members of the Committee, particulary to Professor Masao Oka, Chairman of the Committee. Two other field trips were partly financed by Mr. Hiroshi Misumi, to whom I make grateful acknowledgement.

While at the University College, London, I received valuable help from many other persons. Of these special thanks are due to Drs. Phyllis Kaberry, M. Mary Douglas and D. J. Stenning, all of whom influenced greatly my way of thinking, to Dr. Farnham, M. Rehfisch, Miss Katherine E. A. Attwood and Miss Jean Baker for each kindly reading through part of the manuscripts which formed the basis of the present study, for their valuable suggestions and for their kind help in improving the English text. I owe my sincere thanks to Dr. M. Douglas who read through the whole manuscript and gave me very constructive advice.

I wish to express my thanks to many persons for their kind help in the preparation of this study, especially to Professor Tetsuo Inukai, of University of Hokkaido, Professor Akiyoshi Suda and Dr. Sugao Yamanouchi, of the Anthropological Institute, University of Tokyo, Dr. Seizo Sano and Mr. Kohichiro Shibata, of the Hokkaido Salmon Hatchery, and Dr. Shizuo Yoshino and Mr. Eiji Iwai, of Faculty of Agriculture, University of Tokyo, who brought to my attention some of the important literature and gave various facilities to utilize them along with much valuable information.

I am grateful to Professor Hisashi Suzuki, Chairman of the Anthropological Institute, Faculty of Science, University of Tokyo, and other members of the staff, and the late Professor Kenichi Sugiura, formerly of the Institute, for their interest shown in my work and their generous backing.

I thank also my Ainu informants, particularly the late Ushintasan, Ushino and Kazari, for their devoted cooperation in the field work.

Finally, I should note that those persons mentioned above have no responsibility for any statements made and views expressed in this study.

GROUP STRUCTURE

The Household.

The basic unit of Ainu social life was the simple family consisting of a father, a mother and their unmarried children. The post-marital residence was usually virilocal; namely a son, when he got married, built a new house of his own near his parents'. But there was no rigid rule of virilocal residence. Thus a man sometimes went to live with his wife's father's territorial group (pp. 13 and 17).

The Ainu dwelling house, *chise*, was built for permanent use, wooden-framed, rectangular in plan and single-roomed. All the occupants of each house constituted one household, sleeping, cooking and eating together around

Table *1*.

Names of Local Groups (ca. 1880–1885)		Local Groups in Upper Tokapchi						Local Groups in Satnai			Total
		Kuttarashi	Nitmap	Pipaushi	Kumaushi	Sanenkoro	Moseushi	Nupokomap	Munhunki	Urekarip	
Total Number of Member Houses Identified		8	7	6	8	4	11	9	3	3	59
Composition of Occupants of Each House	Simple family	7	5	4	5	4	9	8	3	3	48
	A widow plus her eldest son's family	1			1						2
	A widow plus her unmarried children		1	1							2
	A widow (? plus her unmarried children)						1	1			2
	A widower plus his eldest son's family						1				1
	A widower (? plus his unmarried children)					1					1
	An unmarried woman	1									1
	An unmarried man				1						1
	Unmarried siblings			1							1

a fireplace at the centre of the room. The occupants, i. e. the household,
usually consisted of the simple family, the composition varying to some extent
as shown in Table 1.

So far as was verified in the upper Tokapchi and Otopuke, the habitation
of each household consisted of a dwelling house, *chise;* associated structures
such as a store house for tools and crafts, *iochise;* a small outdoor cage for
the bear cub, *hepere se;* an outdoor altar, *nusa san;* open-air drying frames
for meat and fish, *kam kuma* and *chep kuma;* and other associated sites
such as one for drawing water, *wakkata ushi;* a skinning spot, *iri an
ushi;* a site for the preparation of fish, *chep karu ushi,* a bone dump, *pone
kuta ushi:* and a fur dump, *rushi nomi ushi* (p. 10). These sites were all
sacred and *inau* offering-sticks were set in them. These buildings, structures
and sites were arranged in a systematic way within an area of ca. 30-50 m.
by 50-100 m (Note 61). The fundamental pattern of arrangement was based
mainly on Ainu cosmological principles. Houses were built so that the sacred
window, *rorun puyaru,* which had important significance for the Ainu, faced
upstream (Fig. 1; Notes 59-60). The significance will be explained later in
Chapter VI.

Table *2.* Territorial Groups at ca. 1880-85.
Upper Tokapchi Valley.

			Settlement Group	Number of Houses
Part of R. G.	S. I. G.	L. G.	Kuttarashi Pennai	6 2
		L. G.	Nitmap	7
		L. G.	Pipaushi	6
		L. G.	Kumaushi	8
		L. G.	Sanenkoro	4
		L. G.	Moseushi Nyashikeshi Fulka Sarunnai	6 3 1 1
		L. G.	Penke-Pipaushi	?2 or 3

Otopuke Valley.

R. G.	S. I. G.		Settlement Group	Numbe of Houses
		L. G.	Naitai	2
			Meto	1
			Rucha	1
			Wop	3
			Ichampet	2
			Kamaune	1
		L. G.	Nipushipet	3
			Mokenashi	1
			Ochirushi	2
			Shikaripetputu	2

Satnai Valley.

R. G.	S. I. G.		Settlement Group	Number of Houses
		L. G.	Nupokomap	9
		L. G.	Munhunki	3
		L. G.	Urekarip	3

R. G.   River Group
S. I. G.   *Shine Itokpa* Group
L. G.   Local Group

The Settlement.

Families settled together and formed a *kotan*, the Ainu settlement. In the Otopuke valley several *kotans* consisted each of only one family. The number of houses or households constituting a *kotan* varied from one to more than ten, usually less than ten. This was also the case with the Ainu settlement even in 1857-58[10].

The material aspect. The *kotan* was usually named after the stream near which it was situated. Sites for *kotans* were chosen with a view to proximity to sources of drinking water and fishing and hunting grounds. The most important factor was usually the spawning beds of dog salmon. The spawning beds were well developed and aggregated into concentrations in the main stream near the junctions of tributary streams and the *kotan* itself was usually situated on the terrace of the river near the spawning ground. The distance between two adjacent *kotans* would vary from about 2 to more than 8 kms., the average being 4-8 kms. The families of a *kotan* were not concentrated in a cluster of houses but rather were scattered and often semi-isolated. The distance between dwelling houses next to each other varied from ca. 100 m. to 500 and some might be even farther away.

The social aspect. Each *kotan* group was called by the name of the *kotan*,

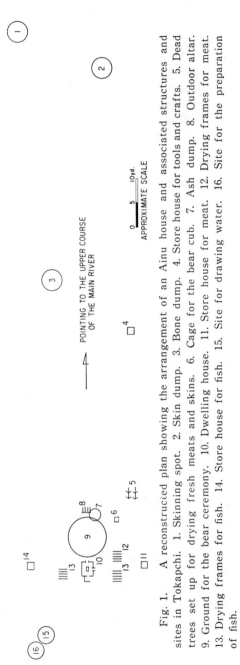

Fig. 1.   A reconstructed plan showing the arrangement of an Ainu house and associated structures and sites in Tokapchi. 1. Skinning spot. 2. Skin dump. 3. Bone dump. 4. Store house for tools and crafts. 5. Dead trees set up for drying fresh meats and skins. 6. Cage for the bear cub. 7. Ash dump. 8. Outdoor altar. 9. Ground for the bear ceremony. 10. Dwelling house. 11. Store house for meat. 12. Drying frames for meat. 13. Drying frames for fish. 14. Store house for fish. 15. Site for drawing water. 16. Site for the preparation of fish.

POINTING TO THE UPPER COURSE OF THE MAIN RIVER

0   5   10yd.
APPROXIMATE SCALE

for instance, Naitai plus *un* (*of or to be at*) *utaru* (*people*). The people of a *kotan* constituted a single group whose members used a concentration or concentrations of spawning beds (a spawning or spawning grounds) of dog salmon in common (pp. 60–62). The *kotan* is classified into two types according to size and cooperative function. Settlement Type 1 is composed of three households or less forming a single cooperative unit for some fishing and hunting activities. Settlement Type 2 is composed of more than three households not forming a single cooperative unit for any gathering activities. So far as the actual examples from Azuma, Tokapchi and Otopuke valleys are concerned, the maximum size of a cooperative gathering unit is three households. Moreover the cooperative unit is usually or almost always composed of households from the same settlement (p. 43).

The Local Group.

The *kotan* group did not always constitute a socio-politically integrated territorial unit, that is, a local group. The presence of the two categories labelled by the present writer as 'settlement group' and 'local group' has already been noticed in some works, although those were not clearly defined[11]. The local group as a politically autonomous group could either consist of several *kotan* groups or of only a single *kotan* group. The unity and integrity of the local group were manifested in the presence of a common headman, collective ownership of the named concentrations of the spawning beds of dog salmon (pp. 60–62), group participation in certain rituals such as the salmon ceremony (pp. 72–73), and cooperation in house-building. The local group as such was called by the name of the settlement, *kotan*, in which the headman lived plus *un* (*of or to be at*) *kuru* (*a man*) *koru* (*to possess*) *utaru* (*people*). It means the people of such and such a headman.

The Ainu local group is classified into two types: Type A, the single-settlement local group and Type B, the multi-settlement local group. Type A is further classified into two subtypes: Subtype 'a' with Settlement Type 1 and Subtype 'b' with Settlement Type 2. Type B is also classified into two subtypes: Subtype 'a' with Settlement Type 1 and Subtype 'b' with Settlement Types 1 and 2 mixed. The local group of Type B with Settlement Type 2 only has never been encountered by the present writer. So far as the local groups at ca. 1880–85 as identified by the present writer are concerned, the actual situation is shown in Table 2. The size of the local group varied: the smallest was of Aa type with 3 households and the largest of Bb type with 11 households, the usual size being 5 to 10. Of 7 local groups identified in the upper Tokapchi valley, 4 were of Ab type, 1 was of Type A but not ascertainable whether Aa or Ab, and 2 were of Bb type. In the Satnai valley, 2 of 3 local groups in total were Aa type and the third was Ab. In the Otopuke valley, however, both of 2 local groups in total were of Ba: the one consisted of 6 *kotans* with 10 households and the other of 4 *kotans* with 8 households.

As has already been described, there were two types of Ainu local groups, a concentrated- or mono-settlement type and a dispersed- or multi-settlement type. The proportions in which the two occurred in different river groups did not vary much but, as far as the present writer has investigated, either one or the other seems to have been predominant. On the Azuma in the 1880's for instance, all the local groups (three in total) belonged to the mono-settlement type with Settlement Type 2. On the Shikot a case is found of an overwhelming number of local groups of mono-settlement type mingling with a few of multi-settlement type. The data for the last-named, however, are of a later period than those for the other rivers.

A settlement of the mono-settlement local group contained no less than 3 households, usually 5 to 10. In a settlement of multi-settlement local group, though nothing definite can be said except for the Otopuke and the upper Tokapchi, the number was much smaller; 1 to 2 as a rule, 6 at very most. According to the records on Ainu settlements, in Hokkaido, contained in MATSUURA's expeditionary diaries written in the 1850's, a settlement with 10 households on any river course, excepting the Saru, was classified as large. The Teshio and the Tokapchi were particularly remarkable for the predominance of 1 to 2 house settlements. Special attention should be drawn to the fact that the size and distribution in the 1850's of the pre-agricultural, as it seems, Teshio settlements and of the Tokapchi settlements with no cultivated plots as yet except near the sea coast, bore a striking resemblance to those of the tiny scattered settlements of the Otopuke Ainu who practiced no plant cultivation at all even at the period under the writer's investigation (Note 10, tabulated data from MATSUURA's diaries in MASAMUNE, ed., 1937).

Occasions for collective activities of the local group seem to have been rare: the only two which could be ascertained are the salmon ceremony and house-building. The salmon ceremony (p. 72), was organized and directed by the headman, and the male household heads of his local group participated in it. In house building the Ainu first constructed the roof part on the ground and then put it on top of the posts set in the ground. It was the lifting up of the roof which required a number of hands at one time. In this work all male househeads and even housewives of the local group came to help the family concerned. Cooperation in gathering of the local group as a whole could take place when it was of Aa type (p. 43).

For all economic purposes the local group was self-sufficient. Ainu technology did not require the cooperation of a unit larger than the local group. In fact the family was often self-sufficient in this respect although members of a few families sometimes joined together for certain activities (p. 43). Social intercourse beyond the local group seems to have been rare, although there had been a degree of intermarriage. The principal occasions for Ainus to meet members of other local groups were at the bear ceremony in winter (pp. 73–76).

The Headman.

The headman was called by various titles: *kotan koru kuru*, man who possesses the *kotan*, was used by outsiders; the name of the *kotan* in which the headman lived plus *un kuru*, man who is in such and such a *kotan*; *aneram ushinnu kuru*, man by whom we are relieved; *kotan shikamak kuru*; *kotan* (*or utaru*) *spahane kuru*, headman of the *kotan* or people; *utaru koru kuru*, people-owning man. He was head of a local group and leader of a kin group which constituted the core of the local group. He was expected to be the man to lead and to look after his people on behalf of their parents. He was also regarded as the man who knew everything, especially ancestral traditions. He was not only an official in charge of the political regulation of his group but also a chief adviser to individuals in the group. Collective enterprises organized and directed by the headman would seem to have been restricted to narrow sphere of activities such as religious rites. The only ritual known to have been organized and directed by the headman and whose details my informants remembered clearly, was the dog salmon ceremony; there is, however, a possibility of other rituals belonging to this category. His main function seems to have been religious-ritual regulation over his group. His main tasks were the following: 1) external affairs; a) observance of rituals for affiliation of a newcomer to his group (pp. 14-15), b) ritual sanction of a trespasser, c) ritual permission to non-members to exploit resources (pp. 77-78), d) negotiation of inter-local-group affairs; 2) domestic affairs: a) leadership in observance of the dog salmon ceremony (pp. 72-73), b) being kept informed of the areas where hunting with spring bows and poisoned arrows was taking place and of the people engaged in it (p. 67), c) supervision of the proper observance of rituals and taboos by individuals of his group, d) protection of an individual family short of food, e) giving advice to individuals of his group in practical and moral difficulties which varied from production technique to medicine.

He did manual work himself, but from the above point of view he was respected and was always given an honoured position on such an occasion as the bear ceremony.

Kinship Organization of the Local Group.

This is one of the most obscure aspects of the Ainu life. Published data on the subject are scanty and fragmentary[12]. The description below is based on the data from Tokapchi and Otopuke. This aspect among the Azuma Ainu could not be ascertained; Ushintasan, the chief and competent informant from the area, died before giving sufficient information concerning the subject.

Each local group had its core which was held to be a group of male patrilineal kinsmen descended from a common male ancestor and from which the headman was usually drawn. The kin group was known as *shine ekashi ikiru*, one and the same male-ancestor descent. The overt expressions of membership of this group were the possession of a common male-ancestor mark, *ekashi itokpa*[13] (Note 15), to be engraved on *kamuinomi inau*, the offering-stick for *kamui*-deities, and the observance of common rituals for these deities. The right to perform the ritual belonged to males exclusively. An *ekashi ikiru* might be and was usually divided, each section belonging to a different local group in the same river valley as distinguished by the Ainu.

The local group often included a few males semi-adopted to the core *ekashi ikiru* group. Virilocal marriage was preferred but was not a strict rule. A man of a different *ekashi ikiru* might take up uxorilocal residence and was thus affiliated with the local group. If a male of a different *ekashi ikiru* wanted to come to live with the local group as one of its regular members, he had to marry a patrilocally residing daughter of a male of the core *ekashi ikiru* so that he could obtain the right to perform the *kamuinomi* ritual associated with the ancestor mark, *ekashi itokpa*, of the core *ekashi ikiru* and he had to observe these rituals when it was necessary[14].

The transmission of *ekashi itokpa* and the associated ritual had to be performed by the headman of the daughter's father's local group. The *ekashi itokpa* newly obtained was called *matchama itokpa*, the *itokpa* of woman's side. It was the duty of the newcomer to observe the ritual for deities of his wife's father's *ekashi ikiru* with the offering-sticks, *kamuinomi inau*, bearing the *matchama itokpa* on some necessary occasions. The bear ceremony was certainly one but what others were could not be identified. The new comer was thus affiliated with the local group of his wife's father but he continued to hold his own *itokpa* inherited from his father and to observe the ritual associated therewith[15]. It means that he was not fully adopted to the core *ekashi ikiru* but was semi-adopted. But with his sons it was not so. The first son was affiliated with his father's *ekashi ikiru* and not with that of his mother's father; he was expected to go back to live with the local group to the core of which his father or his patrilineal male ancestor belonged. All sons except the first were expected to live with the local group in which they were born; however, they might be affiliated with either their father's *ekashi ikiru* or their mother's father's, i. e. the core *ekashi ikiru*. Which of the above *ekashi ikiru* they were to be affiliated with was determined under the direction of their headman. In case of affiliation with their father's *ekashi ikiru* they had to inherit the *itokpa* and the associated ritual of their father as their own to "follow the ancestors of their father's side". But to live there as the regular members of the group they had also to obtain the *itokpa* of their mother's father's *ekashi ikiru* besides their own and to participate in the ritual of the group on some necessary occasions. In case of adoption into their mother's father's *ekashi ikiru*, i. e. the core *ekashi ikiru*, they inherited the *itokpa* and the associated ritual of their mother's father to "follow the ancestors of their mother's father's side", and lived with them. The senior son could also remain to live among the local group in which he was born by going through the same procedure as his father had gone through when he came to live there.

All the procedures stated above had to be followed under the direction of the headman of their local group and the transmission of the *itokpa* and the associated ritual had to be observed by him.

In some Ainu local groups there were found, besides regular members, a certain number of persons in the category of *anun utari*,* foreign people. The word was prefixed with the name of the river where they stayed, e. g. *Oto-puke anun (utari)* and so forth. By *anun utari* is meant observers of *anun kamuinomi* or non-local *kamuinomi* rituals. They fall under two classes.

* *Utari* is a variant of *utaru*.

To one class belonged those from other places who, relying on some affinal relationship or kinship with a local member, had come to stay as a sort of guest by his or her side. With the aid from the member and the headman, they were to remain for a year or two, or even four or five, enjoying hunting and fishing with regular members and then to go home again to their native area. They were usually married and were with their families. To the other class belonged those who had no relations among the local group members but, pressed by narrow circumstances, had come for aid from them. After passing certain questionings by some one headman they were taken in and then, whether married or single, male or female, were temporarily housed for the first year or two by the side of the headman's house, e. g. under the floor of his elevated storehouse built on piles. Provided also by him with food and clothing, they were to live by helping in manual work for the headman and his people, all under his directions and supervision. They were called *ussiu*. Eventually, as their character and personal cirumstances became known, the headman, if convinced of their good intention, real need and absence of selfish conduct, gave permission for them to build and to live in a house of their own somewhere in the area according to his directions. Nevertheless, they remained *anun utari* just as before ; at all times in hunting and fishing they were under watchful supervision in case they should behave wrongly or thoughtlessly and ignore the nature-spirits venerated by the local members. If they were single, the headman usually arranged marriages for them with some local women with whom to make a home in the area. No longer *anun utari*, they were then counted as regular members. The marriage procedures and the resultant new status seem to have been all similar to those previously described for affiliates with the local group. Though in point of fact not much is known of their concrete activities and status, some evidence will bear out their existence[16].

Shine Itokpa Group.

Neighbouring local groups were aggregated into larger territorial groups[17]. The larger group was called as *shine itokpa uko koru utaru*, one and the same *itokpa* jointly possessing people, or in abbreviation *shine utaru*, one and the same people. The present writer calls it *shine itokpa* group. The group usually consisted of several local groups next to each other along a river as distinguished by the Ainu. In Azuma, however, one of the two *shine itokpa* groups nearer to the coast consisted of a mono-settlement local group called *pishun kotan* or *pishun utaru* (Note 43). The cores of the member local groups were held to be a group of patrilineal kinsmen, *shine ekashi ikiru*, descended from an ancient common male ancestor of local origin. It was the *itokpa* of this ancestor which was possessed by every member of the *shine itokpa* group whether obtained by adoption or by birth. In either of the Otopuke and Satnai valleys all the local groups formed a single *shine itokpa* group. But the local groups who lived in the Tokapchi valley were divided into several *shine itokpa* groups: the one in the upstream area consisted of seven local groups of Kuttarashi, Nitmap, Pipaushi, Kumaushi, Sanenkoro, Moseushi and Penke Pipaushi, another group on the middle course consisted possibly of five local groups of Kene, Memroputu, Pipairu, Fushiko and Shupusara, and perhaps one or two more *shine itokpa* groups further downstream which could not be identified.

The group had neither single authority nor common territory. The only collective action of the *shine itokpa* group, so far as identified by the present writer, was the bear ceremony (pp. 74-77). It provided the only occasion for meeting many of their relatives and friends who resided outside the local group. In normal times no group larger than the local group took part in any collective enterprise, though on rare occasions two related families from different local groups within a *shine itokpa* group might and actually did privately join to cooperate in hunting or fishing. Formal relations between local groups were rarely established, but through intermarriage (p. 17) there might have been many individual contacts between kin and affines in different local groups.

The River Group.

The river group is an aggregation of all the local groups which lived along a river as distinguished by the Ainu[18]. It was called by the name of the river plus *un utaru*, the people in such and such a river. The river group might consist of a single *shine itokpa* group as in each of the Otopuke and Satnai valleys or consist of several *shine itokpa* groups as in the Tokapchi valley. They regarded the river basin as their own territory, claiming exclusive rights to exploit all its resources, which they defended against the trespass of outsiders (pp. 56-57; 67-68; 77-78). Hence they were also called *shine iworu ukokoru utaru*, the people jointly possessing one and the same *iworu* of the river valley as distinguished by the Ainu. However, at least in normal times, there was no single authority controlling the group as a whole. The main bond which linked the people of a river together not only seems to have been economic interests but a deeply rooted cosmological background. There is evidence that each river as distinguished by the Ainu was associated with one or several particular *ekashi itokpa*. It was the *shine itokpa* group which had one of these aboriginal *itokpa*. Only the people having the aboriginal *itokpa* associated with the river, observing the associated ritual for local deities and living in the river valley, were regarded as the real people of the river who were entitled to be guardians of the river valley and of the deities that were believed to live there and look after them (pp. 70-71; 77-78). The river group appears to have observed collective rituals against catastrophic natural phenomena but any collective actions in normal times by the group as a whole could not be identified by the present writer.

Marriage and Intermarriage.

The most notable of the Ainu habits concerning marriage might be the avoidance of coupling of the matrilineally related. Women of common descent through female line from an ancestress were called *shine huchi ikiru*, one and the same ancestress descent, who regarded themselves as female relatives, *menoko iriwaki*, to one another. The *huchi ikiru* kinship, however, could not usually be traced at most beyond a depth of three or four generations[19]. The implication of the avoidance is that men should not marry women of the same *huchi ikiru* as their mothers[20].

It might be said that women related by *huchi ikiru* kinship constituted a kin group; however, the present writer has found no reason to regard them as a corporate kin group. They had no single authority. They did not hold any common property and never came together to carry out any collective enterprise organized on the level of a *huchi ikiru* group as a whole.

It is true that women who assisted a woman in marriage, childbirth, illness and death, were her *huchi ikiru* relatives[21]. These activities of mutual help seem to have been based on the person-to-person relation of *huchi ikiru* kinship.

To what extent intermarriage was practised is only partly known[22]. The present writer was able to identify premarital and postmarital residences of the married persons who lived in six of seven local groups which formed a *shine itokpa* group on the upper Tokapchi at ca. 1880-85 (Table 2; Genealogical Charts 1-6), and obtained the following result.

1) Marriage between the members of the same local group 15
2) Wife married to live with her husband in the local group where he was born:
    A) From one of the member local groups of the *shine itokpa* group of her husband 12
    B) From outside the *shine itokpa* group of her husband:
        a) From one of the member local groups of the same river group as her husband's 3
            (2 from Perutnai, 1 from Memroputu)
3) Husband married to live with his wife in the local group where his wife was born:
    A) From one of the member local groups of the *shine itokpa* group of his wife 3

   B) From outside the *shine itokpa* group of his wife:

      a) From one of the member local groups of the same river group as his wife's 1

         (from Memroputu)

      b) From river group other than his wife's.................... 3

         (from Asahikawa in Ishikari)

In the *shine itokpa* group in the Satnai valley at ca. 1880-85, which consisted of 3 local groups with 16 households and formed a single river group itself, the proportion of the number of wives who married in from outside the *shine itokpa* group to the number of wives who were born and married inside the group seems to have been much greater than that in the *shine itokpa* group in the Tokapchi valley which was previously stated. The details will be given in Notes 23-24 on the following genealogical charts.

Nitmap (N)[23]

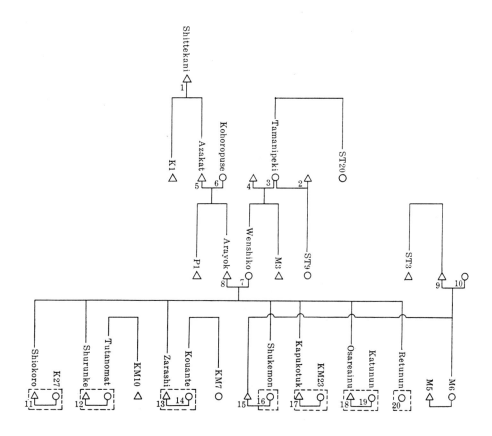

Pipaushi (P)[23]

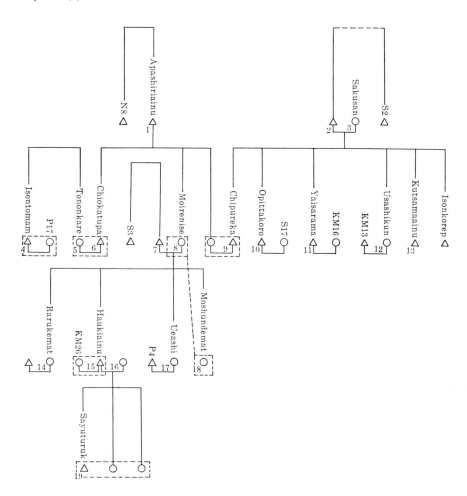

GENEALOGICAL CHART 5

Sanenkoro (S)[23]

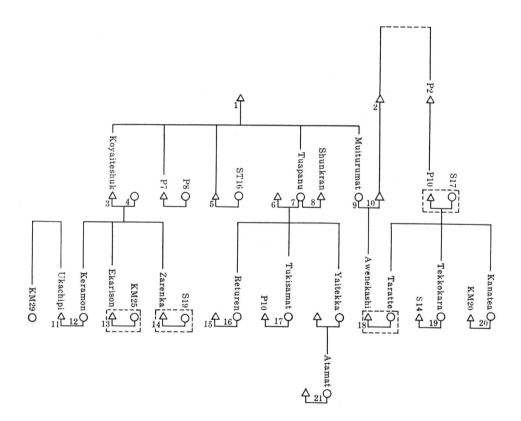

III

FOOD-GETTING ACTIVITIES

So much has been written about the gathering devices and techniques of the Ainu that it is all but impossible to enumerate individual writings on the subject. Comprehensive articles have been published in particular by HITCHCOCK (1891), MONTANDON (1937) and NATORI (1945, pp. 135-212). However, they have all followed the morphological or typological approach to the so-called 'material culture' study, devoting most of their studies to such items as the bow and arrow and the salmon spear to the exclusion of such important items as the fishing trap and the fishing net. In short, little attempt has been made to describe or analyse the Ainu system of interrelated food-getting devices, techniques and activities, the elucidation of which system forms the chief object of the present chapter. While dealing with those latter items as well, it leaves out much about their technological details. It will be seen that a greater importance is attached to the essential structure, mechanism and use of those Ainu implements in relation to their activities whereby they adapt themselves to their habitat, and to the organization of those activities.

One of the basic problems in ecology is the periodicity of community activities. In this chapter, the time of the beginning or end of each seasonal activity of the Ainu will be referred to by the Ainu month and/or the solar calendar month[25]. However, what is important in this paper is not the time itself but the degree and nature of correlation between the periodicity in Ainu activities and that in the phenomena in their habitat. To examine this, data concerning ecology and ethology of biotic species are indispensable, the most important of which are given in the notes of this chapter.

Fishing Devices.

The Fish-spear.

The fish-spear, *marek*, is a long wooden shaft, with a flexible iron prong so fixed to the end that the point may be hooked to prevent the fish caught from falling off in bringing it up (Fig. 2, a). The spear was classified into two types: those with a large hook, *shiipe koiki marek*, used for such larger fishes as dog salmon and Hucho perryi, and those with a smaller one, *ichaniu (or ichanui) koiki marek*, for such fishes as cherry salmon and dace. Both were used alike by the fisherman either standing in a dugout, on the bank or in the stream, or sitting in the peep-fishing hut, *worun chise* (Fig. 2, b). Night spearing was accompanied with a torch for illumination. Torch-light

20

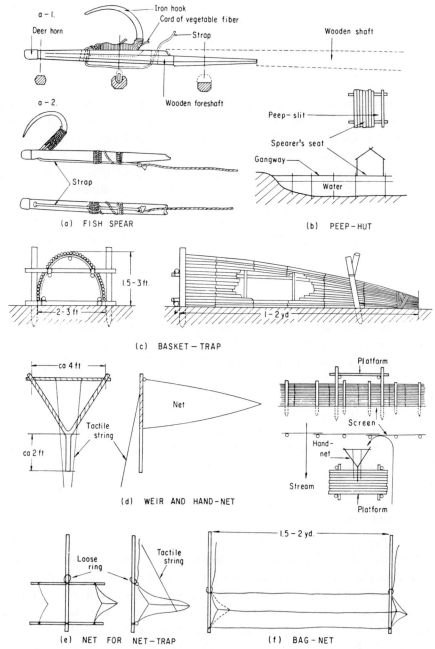

Fig. 2. Fishing gear. (a), 1-2, Tokyo University Anthropological Institute
Collection.   (b)-(f), reconstructed on the basis of the data from the Ainu informants.

spearing, *shune marek*, as described later was in active use for the capture of salmon coming together in spawning grounds. The use of the *marek* was, though not invariably, confined to men. Taboo was placed specifically on use by women at the named spawning grounds of dog salmon controlled by the male members of the local group. The *marek* was as important a fishing implement to men as the basket-trap, *urai*, was to women. What characterized the former as distinct from the latter was that with it any sort of fish could be captured: fresh-run brisk salmon still untinged for spawning, salmon ready to spawn or under spawning activities, or the fish in hiding in the daytime or in activity in the night. In the use of the spear skill played a greater part than with the *urai* and other kinds of fishing gear. It seems that as a result the amount of catch differed considerably with different persons. It is said that the catch in one night varied from 10-15 at the minimum to 40-50 at the very maximum. It was to supplement the catch with the *marek* by each family that the fish-trap, *urai*, was used.

The Torch.

The period from mid- or late November, when silvery salmon appeared in the rivers, to the middle or end of December, when the fish had finished running, was the later salmon season. During this period the Ainu manipulated the *marek* by night with the aid of torch lights, *shune*. Torch-light spearing was more effective at and about the spawning areas where the salmon came together. The torch employed for the purpose was made of a bundle of dried Miscanthus or of strips of dried birch bark. Among the Ainu on the lower course of the Tokapchi as well as those on the Azuma, the Mukawa and the Saru, torch-light fishing in a dugout was usually conducted by a team of three—the spearer, *naniun*, at the bow, the pole-operator, *umun*, at the stern, and the torch-holder, *shuneani*, standing between. When not going by dugout as on the upper Tokapchi and the Otopuke, the team would consist of the spearer and the torch-holder. The torch-holder and the pole-operator were by custom female, each team generally being formed by members of the same family.

The Peep-fishing Hut.

The peep-fishing hut, *worun chise*, was a simple construction erected on piles over the stream, linked with the bank by means of a gangway (Fig. 2, b). It was used by a single male, who sat in it and speared with the *marek*. The walls and the roofing were of butter-bur leaves or other leafy twigs, and part of the floor was cut open for the fisherman to peep through. The hut was built over the run, *pet netoba*, about the spot where ascending fish were in the habit of halting, *chep kusushi*. The same hut was used for dog salmon and cherry salmon alike. Peep-fishing was well adapted to the habit of the fish in the run, so that it was less efficient during the daytime when they usually remained inactive. It was used towards evening when the fish began to stir and again towards daybreak when they ceased to move about. It was a method most effectively employed in the earlier phase of the run, i.e. the period before the spawning of dog salmon and cherry salmon, when they continued their ascent. When the spawning time arrived, its place was taken by the more efficient method of spearing in the spawning grounds. Each family set up one hut, which was used by one of its male members, usually the house-head. Each family usually owned its own *worun chise*, which they erected anew each year on the same site, unless there was any great change in the site or surroundings. In reality the hut was open to the danger of thaw in spring and its conditions were made precarious by floods which recurred annually. At least in Mukawa those groups located near the estuary built cone-shaped dark huts, *shimpui chise*, on the frozen river and speared dace, Hucho perryi and other fishes through a hole.

The Basket-trap.

The basket-trap, *urai* or *rauomap*, made of pliable twigs and semi-conical in shape, was, like the *marek*, one of the most familar fishing devices known to the Ainu (Fig. 2, c). It was in extensive and general use for a great variety of fishes including dog salmon, cherry salmon and dace. Pointed at one end and open at the other, the trap was attached to the bottom of a V-shaped wattle-work fence or leader made of piled stones narrowing in the downstream direction. It was sometimes set to catch fish running upstream. In this case an accessory made of twigs was attached inside the mouth of the device to prevent fish from turning back outside.

When the spawning season set in, there were great runs into the glens of the cherry salmon that had been waiting in the larger and main streams. In order to catch them the basket-trap was set mostly in the glens and at their mouths. The main spawning grounds of the dog salmon lay distributed in the main streams as distinguished by the Ainu along which their settlements were located. They set the trap in the shallower and more rapid streams divided by shoals (*pet arikehe*) to trap dog salmon as they came down circling about and between the spawning areas. It played an active part as the fish began to spawn. The implement was usually made, erected and used by each family at the hands of women, although in time of a spate male members might help in driving piles and other work. As far as the salmon was concerned, the womanly device, the *urai*, played a supplementary role to the manly device, the *marek*. Thus the smaller the catch with the *marek* by a family, the greater the number of the *urai* it used. In the same local group where some families owned none, others might have three or four, the

average number being one or two. To the Ainu the *urai* was the commonest
and most essential of fishing gear second to the *marek* in importance.

The Weir.

The weir, *tesh*, was made of a wattle-work screen tied to a row of wooden
piles driven across the streams (Fig. 2, d). By this means the Ainu inter-
cepted ascending cherry salmon and, in some cases, dace. The *tesh* was the
chief fishing device indispensable in particular for catching ascending cherry
salmon. By custom one end of the weir was always left open so as not to
shut the entire passage to the fish. Close below lay one or two platforms,
on each of which stood one Ainu manipulating a small handnet, *tesh koru ya*
or *pon ya*, and caught fish turning back from the weir. The *tesh* was set in
a wadable shallow in the way of run, usually the deeper and slower of the
streams divided by shoals in the main stream, *pet netoba*. The device was
generally used by night when the fish made their way upstream intensively.
It was prepared and constructed either by two or three families working
together or by a single family. The wattle work for the screen by women
and its setting up by men were directed by some able member of the *tesh*-
group (p. 59, the chart), usually an elderly male.

The Bag-net.

The net, *yaroshiki ya*, was a rectangular bag-net with a handle attached
at each end (Fig. 2, f). Nets of the same name and similar shape were used
for both dog salmon and cherry salmon, but the meshes were coarser in that
for dog salmon than for cherry salmon. In operating the bag-net, two operators held it in position by the handle at each end with the mouth turned
upstream and caught fish as they were chased in by a driver. The device
was used in the daytime around pools, *ooi*, or deposited roots of drift-wood
near the spawning grounds, where fish concentrated by day lurking inactive.
For dog salmon it was employed in the main streams where there were
densely-distributed spawning beds. For cherry salmon it was effectively used
also in glens or side streams. Those places exploited with the bag-net were
also where the *marek*-spearer worked by day, so that the same daytime
spearer served as the driver in the bag-net fishing party.

Bag-net fishing was conducted by a single family or by cooperation of a
net-group formed by two or three families usually from one and the same
settlement (p. 59, the chart). The net was made of plant fibre. It was used
by the members of the group who had made it. When more than one family
participated, the team of three necessary for the work was drawn by custom
from the different families. When part of the member families used it, the
catch was shared by all the member families.

In practice it was usually women who operated the bag-net. But during the period from the beginning of the dog salmon season to the appearance of *meorun-chep* or silvery salmon, bag-net fishing was under taboo. So also was its use at the spawning grounds themselves that were named and controlled by the local group (pp. 60–62). A net of similar shape but smaller in size, *pon ya*, was used in catching dace and other smaller varieties.

The Net-trap.

This fish-trap, *ya urai*, was made of V-shaped wattle-work fences narrowing downstream with a kind of bag-net with one handle only, *urai koru ya* (Fig. 2, e), attached to the lower end of the fences. The device was not automatic: it was operated by a single Ainu taking his position on a platform attached to the trap and drawing up the net by the handle on feeling a catch by means of a touch-line connected with the net. The trap was set in a small tributary or one of the streams divided by shoals in the main stream, the same streamway for the basket-trap, to catch dog salmon, cherry salmon and trout all coming down-stream. It was usually operated by night when the fish were astir. The device proved also effective when the rain had swollen the river and made it too muddy for spearing by sight. The net-trap was set only by a few families from a settlement. In the upper Tokapchi area it was used in smaller tributaries chiefly for catching trout which came gathering to eat the eggs of cherry salmon and it was thought difficult to haul with other devices at their command; there is however no trace of it being used for dog-salmon as it was in the Azuma area. Those families possessing a net-trap not only used it for themselves but invited other families in the settlement to use it.

The Trawling-net.

A net similar in shape and size to the bag-net, *yash ya*, was used by some groups for trawling the varieties of salmon (Fig. 2, f). Two operators in a pair of dugouts stood at each bow with the trawling net held by each handle and dragged it along as the boats floated down to catch fish running upstream. The trawling was practised more actively during the night when the fish ran in shoals. This method of fishing required that the streams should be sufficiently wide and without many hazards to the net like drifted roots deposited in the streams, so that its practice was limited to specific areas in the main stream along which the settlements were located. The groups living upstream on the Tokapchi and all the Otopuke groups never used trawling-nets. Somehow, it was not their custom to use even dugouts for fishing purposes at ordinary times; to them the craft was chiefly for traffic. The same groups that did not practise trawling were also without the meshing-net, *chama ya*, which will be described later. On the other hand, in downstream areas where there were fewer spawning grounds of dog salmon in and around which Ainu fishing techniques were suitable, trawling was the most efficient mass technique. Fishing with the trawl-net, requiring as it did a pair of dugouts, two net-operators and two boatmen besides the net itself, was conducted by male and female members from at least two families forming a trawling group.

The Meshing-net.

This was a small-sized fixed net, stretched upright in a straight line across the stream to mesh fish striking it. Though not used by groups on the upper Tokapchi and the Otopuke, the net, *chama ya*, seems to have been in extensive use for dog salmon, cherry salmon and dace, in areas on the lower Tokapchi. Clear evidences for the use of the net were obtained from Azuma, Mukawa and Shikot. It was set in position between a deep whirling pool and the main current parallel to the latter so as to entangle ascending fish as they swept round with the whirlpool. The device played an important part in catching early and scattered runs of fishes. When spawning began and the fish ran in shoals, it gave its leading place to spearing and trawling. A dugout was required for setting the net and for going round to see and take in the haul. The net was made and used by an individual family.

The Rectangular Basket-trap.

The trap, *kutu*, consisted of three parts: a V-shaped wattle or stone fence, a leading trough of woven twigs with one end pointing downstream and put up against the top of the fence and the other submerged and pointing upstream, and a wattle-work basket fixed to that end of the trough rising above the water. Fish shooting downstream were stranded on the trough and were taken automatically in the basket. The device was in use for instance among the Ainu in Shikot and Mukawa shortly after the land allotment for the capture of dace, cherry salmon and even dog salmon, although there is no evidence for its use in Tokapchi, Otopuke and Azuma in the period under survey. It was applied most effectively to rapids where there was some head of water and where descending fish were swept down in the current with little chance of turning back. The use of the *kutu* was accordingly limited to the upper-stream groups on some particular river courses.

Fishing Activities.

Spring Fishing.

With the disappearance of the base snow from the plains, the whole Ainu population suddenly emerged from their winter inactivity. In every Ainu household there was still some store of dried fish and meat left over from

the old year. But the revival of desire for anything fresh drove them forth
to fishing as well as hunting and collecting. Nevertheless, it was not until
the coming of cherry salmon that they went into any intensive fishing activity.
Nor did the total amount of catch in this period come to so much as might
be stored away for any great length of time. The major species of fish taken
in this period were *chirai*, Hucho perryi, *supun*, Tribolodon spp., and *kabachep*,
Cottus spp.

The large Hucho which appeared first with the thaw in the rivers, were
speared with the *marek* usually in tributaries where water was clearer (p. 54).
With the coming of the season, at least in Nitmap on the upper Tokapchi,
the headman went every day to a prescribed spot on the Sahorun, a tributary
of the Tokapchi, to watch for the arrival of the first fish (Note 62).

For catching the *supun* the basket trap, *urai*, was used in the main stream
and/or tributaries, and the small bag-net was manipulated by two operators
usually in streamlets. Although the bullhead or *kabachep* could be found all
the year round, it was captured with the small bag-net only in early spring
when few other varieties were to be had. The Ainu seldom stayed out over-
night fishing these varieties. Attention should be drawn to the fact that the
Ainu, at least in Tokapchi and Otopuke, treated Hucho perryi and even Tribolodon with some ritual, as they did dog salmon and cherry salmon (Note 62).

Cherry Salmon Fishing.

The cherry salmon, *ichaniu* or *ichanui*, Oncorhynchus masou[26], was one
of the major food supplies of the Ainu. Ecology and ethology of the salmon
related to Ainu fishing habits are summarized in Note 26. With certain difference in time in different rivers and in the upper and lower courses of the
same river, the runs of the salmon began in the upper Tokapchi and the
Otopuke in *shimauta chup* or around July; in the Azuma in July or August
(p. 54). When the fish were ready to appear in the river near their own settlement, the Ainu observed a pre-fishing ritual at a prescribed spot on the
bank of the river along which their settlements were situated (Note 62). The
function was one of the major events in the whole cycle of their seasonal
activities, for it marked the opening of a new season devoted to fishing. Indeed, from then to autumn no regular hunting was undertaken. After the
observance of the ritual they immediately set up a sort of weir, *tesh*, in the
river close to the site of the ritual. The ritual and the weir fishing were
carried out by the cooperative group of families (p. 43). The weir was used
effectively during the night when the runs became active. To catch ascending shoals those groups living downstream on the deeper and broader water-
courses usually employed the trawling-net, *yash ya*, which they operated from
a pair of dugouts at night. While at weir-fishing every night, they took a

nap and rest by turns in the hut built by their weir. Every morning they returned to the settlement to take their catch home. It is the habit of the salmon to lurk inactive during the day in a pool or under a drifted tree root. Before the land was cleared and the the rivers were improved there was a great amount of drift-wood in every watercourse. The Ainu went about in search of such places by day, spearing hiding fish with the *marek*. Fish that were missed or driven out were captured by partners, usually females, using the bag-net, *yaroshiki ya*.

Around August the salmon began to run up into small tributaries or glens for spawning. In this period, the automatic basket-trap, *urai*, was set at the mouth of a glen to catch fish coming downstream after spawning, while fishing in the main stream went on.

The Ainu of the Azuma and the Otopuke valleys remained all through the season at their settlements, fishing only in the neighbouring streams. But the local groups on the upper Tokapchi migrated every August to a tributary of the Tokapchi, the Sahorun, when the salmon had already run up to its upper reaches (Map 2). The daily cycle of the fishing here was a little different from that in the main stream: in the Sahorun, no peep-fishing was practised, while the basket-trap was used to catch fish descending from a glen after spawning. They formed cooperative groups (p. 45, the chart) to stay, till the end of September, at fishing-huts set up along the tributary. Details will be given on pp. 46 and 52.

In September when the rivers swollen with melted snow receded and the water became clear, each family built a dark-hut or peep-hut, *worun chise*, in the main stream near their settlement. In this season runs became more brisk. It was the older male Ainu who speared salmon with the *marek* in the peep-hut towards evening and in early morning when there were active runs. The hut built at this time was successively used even in dog salmon fishing. The Azuma Ainu, however, did not practice the peep-hut fishing at all.

Cherry salmon fishing continued till dog salmon fishing began.

Dog Salmon Fishing.

The rivers in Hokkaido used to be, and still are ascended by dog salmon, Oncorhynchus keta, from around September till December or January, though strictly speaking, the running period of the salmon varies to some extent in different years and in different rivers and on the upper and the lower stretches in the same rivers (OYA, 1954). During the period of base snow which covers the entire island, the Ainu had to live on stored provisions consisting chiefly of dried dog salmon and venison. The amount of the salmon, which arrived immediately before their wintering season had a profound effect on the subsistence and daily life of the Ainu[27].

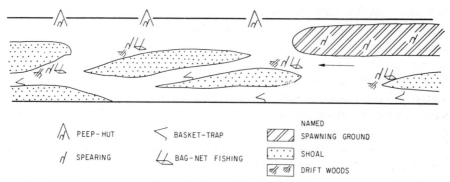

Fig. 3. Diagram representing the distribution of dog salmon fishing sites.

Dog salmon migrate and ascend rivers in large shoals in order to spawn. Various conditions restrict their spawning sites, in search of which dog sal- mon come gathering in specific areas. As a result, the relationship between the Ainu and the fish grew up and was maintained with these spawning grounds as centre. The spawning habits of the dog salmon[28], e. g. the parent salmon standing by their spawning bed while in breeding, their spawning in comparatively shallow water, and almost regular recurrence yearly of spawn- ing grounds at the same places, may be regarded as limiting factors in the group ecology of the Ainu in regard to salmon fishing.

At least on the upper Tokapchi and the Otopuke as well as on the Azuma, the Ainu fished the salmon during the period from around October to Decem- ber[29] (p. 53). Each local group began its salmon fishing with the arrival of the fish near its own settlement. The methods and the sites of fishing changed as the season wore away (Figs. 3 and 4). Observance of a ritual before the first run marked the beginning of all Ainu dog-salmon fishing (p. 72). Mean- while, there came an interval between the first run in the area about the settlement or settlements of each local group and the first spawning in the spawning grounds near their settlement. For example, about Kuttarashi and Nitmap on the uppermost Tokapchi there were scattered spawnings 3 or 4 days after the first run; near Naitai settlement on the uppermost Otopuke spawnings occurred sporadically 4 or 5 days after the first run. It is ichthyo- logically known that the spawning of the dog salmon, like that of the cherry salmon, occurs gradually from the upper down to the lower reaches in the same river course (Note 28). For instance, it usually began about 2 days later about Kumaushi settlement than at Nitmap which lies directly above it; at Sanenkoro settlement 3 or 4 days later than at Kumaushi which lies above it (Map 2 and p. 61). The result was that the lower the settlement the longer the period of runs with no spawning. During this period Ainu males speared fish with the *marek* at peep-huts set up on the running course.

Peep-fishing proved most effective at hours before sunset when the fish resumed their active ascent and again at daybreak before they became inactive
and went into hiding. In the daytime the spearers went round to spear salmon hiding in the bank-side deeps and under drift-wood. The basket-trap,
the main fishing-gear for Ainu females, did not work with any efficiency
until salmon started spawning. The use of the bag-net was tabooed till the
latter part of the dog-salmon season, i. e. *meorun chep* season (Note 30). When
spawning began in the spawning grounds near their own settlement, the Ainu
started spearing the fish at the spawning grounds at sunset and in early
morning. It will be seen from the ichthyological data in Note 28 that all the
spawning and ascending activities of the fish usually become brisk at night
between sundown and daybreak. The basket-trap, an automatic device, was
set effectively to catch fish moving up and down around the spawning grounds,
while in daytime fishing, spearing salmon in hiding was the only productive
technique. In the earliest phase of the breeding season, i. e. before heavy
spawning set in, peep-fishing in the running course still played a more important part than spearing at and around the spawning grounds. In the upper Tokapchi women were prohibited to use the spear, *marek*, in this phase.
In the Tokapchi, the Otopuke and the Azuma, heavy spawning was
interrupted by a fall in the runs with mostly spawned fish remaining in the
rivers and few fresh salmon to spawn—a period of several days. This period
of falling off, however, was again followed by another of fresh runs. The
arrival of fresh-run salmon seems to have been correlated roughly to the
appearance of snow-ice lumps, *mompe*, in the Tokapchi, the Otopuke
and the Azuma as well as the Mukawa and the Saru. These later runs, to be
regarded as 'silvery salmon' which ascend late in the Oncorhynchus keta
season in Hokkaido, were distinguished from the earlier one by the Ainu as
meorun chep or *mata chep*[30]. The *meorun chep* did not run so far upstream
as the earlier groups but spawned in the same areas. The Ainu used, besides
the same devices, torchlights and bag-nets which were prohibited for the
earlier runs. The prohibition of the use of both these devices was verified
only in Tokapchi, Otopuke and Azuma; that of torchlights alone is detectable
among the natives of Mukawa and Saru, whereas the exclusive use of torchlights for the later runs is found among the Shikot Ainu. On the arrival of
the *meorun chep* season all the Ainu began spearing salmon at night by
torchlight. The method was employed most effectively, and therefore mainly,
for fishing in spawning grounds, though it was also the one for running fish.
In the daytime women came out to take part in bag-net fishing in combination with spearing by men in hidings of the fish. During this cold season
the older males were occupied in catching running salmon mostly in peep-huts.
At the end of *meorun chep* spawning in the areas controlled by each group,

30   The Ainu Ecosystem

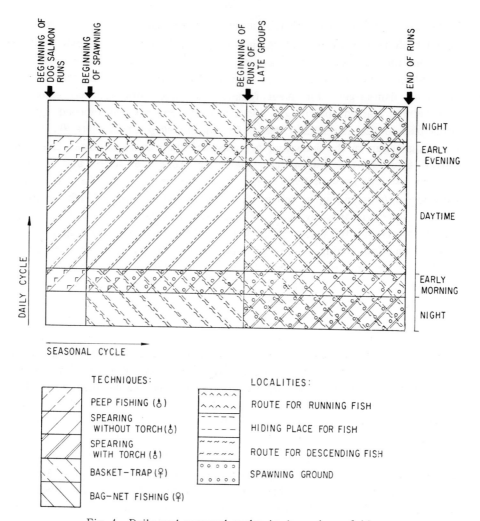

Fig. 4. Daily and seasonal cycles in dog salmon fishing.

a post-run ritual was performed to mark the close of dog-salmon fishing,
although for some time afterwards some lingering fish might be picked up.
The end of dog-salmon runs or their entire disappearance came earlier on
the upper stretches of a river than in the lower. However, all the local
groups, those on the Tokapchi, the Otopuke and the Azuma at least, ceased
to fish dog-salmon, with some variation, in December. Salmon caught in
December were made into a sort of frozen fish, *ruibe*; but these were not at
all many. The greater part of the dog-salmon needed by the natives were
fished during October and November, being sun-dried for storing.

As shown in the previous description of the fishing gear and Figures 3 and 4, the various Ainu fishing techniques, fishing localities and fishing seasons were closely adjusted to the habit and ecology of the dog salmon. Thus the Ainu activities in catching the fish were concentrated to and around its spawning grounds. Both the ichthyological data cited in Note 28 and Ainu information indicate the annual recurrence of the major spawning grounds in the same places. Each local group controlled a certain number of these spawning grounds which were distributed near its settlement or settlements, and each settlement group exploited intensively the ground or grounds nearest to them and controlled by their local group (pp. 59-60).

Hunting Devices.

   Bows and Arrows.

   The bow and arrow were the only hand weapons of Ainu hunters. Some Ainus kept spears with iron points which were obtained by means of trade, but there is no evidence that the spear was ever used in their regular hunting activities. They hunted deer and bears with the hand-bow, *chiani ku*, and the spring-bow, *amappo*, both simple bows (Fig. 5, a & b). The arrow shaft for the former is a grass stem and that for the latter wooden. Both have an arrowhead made of a kind of bamboo and are always coated with aconite poison. Only the males were to handle them.

   The spring bow was set firmly on a tree stump by the side of a trail, with a string fastened on one end to the trigger and stretched across the trail of bear and deer in such a way that the poisoned arrow shot automatically at the touch of any animal. The tip of the arrow was sheathed in a roll of bark to protect the poison from rain and dew. The arrow lacked the connecting line for holding the game shot. The chief duty of a hunting group staying at the hunting hut was to set a number of spring bows and arrows in the hunting ground, *kuari ushi*, and make their rounds inspecting continually.

   Apart from their use in association with the deer fence, the spring bows, set as they were alone in inconspicuous positions in a mountain hunting ground, could be a great danger to human beings as well. Accordingly, their use was strictly regulated by the headman as one of his important duties. In practice, they were set by each cooperative group of hunters working as a unit, centred in a specific area of one dale valley as a unit. The areas, *kuari ushi*, places for setting bows, were found either on the upper reaches of the dales which feed the river along which their *kotans* were distributed, chiefly for deer hunting, or in the dale valleys at the sources of the river for bear hunting (Fig. 8). Unless abandoned, the same area was used successively by one group over many seasons. Except when used in association with the deer fence, no setting of spring bows was allowed on the lower plain or on the lower reaches of a valley, where not only hunters but Ainus in general had occasion to go about.

Deer Fence.

The *kuteki*, a wooden fence construction for catching deer, varied in length from a few hundred metres to several kilometres. It had narrow openings at certain intervals where spring bows were set with poisoned arrows. The deer fence was usually set up near oak woods, *komni-tai*, on the level plain or near woods of mixed trees by streamlets, *nitat*, on the wide slopes of a hill, intercepting the deer tracks. It was built and used either by one independent family or by two or three families from the same settlement cooperating as a hunting group. The deer track, *yuk apiri*, remained comparatively stable, so that the same structure was repaired and used over successive seasons by the same cooperative group that built it. The deer fence was usually erected neither too far from the settlement nor too near. Usually situated within only 4 or 5 kilometres, it was easily patrolled by visitors from their homes. However, some families from Nitmap in Tokapchi built their deer fences farther away than the others; the hunters migrated every season to huts erected near the constructions (Map 2).

MATSUURA, on his official exploration of the Ainu territory in 1857-58 observed and recorded an actual example of a long deer fence constructed on a hill slope not too far from Ainu settlements (MASAMUNE, ed., 1937, Vol. 2, p. 396).

Hunters' Hut.

While hunting in the hills and mountains, the Ainu used two different kinds of hunters' huts. The distinction is made, not according to the style or construction, but to the use and location of the huts. One type, set up near the winter quarters of deer and used chiefly for deer hunting was usually known as *iramande chise*. The other type, built near the hibernation centre of bears and used mainly for bear hunting, was usually called *Kimun kashi* or *kucha ko chise*. The difference in location between these two kinds will be described later in sections dealing with deer- and bear-hunting. In either case, the hut was located in a dale valley, and the area lying upstream formed the hunting ground, i.e. *ku ari ushi*, place for setting bows, for the occupants (p. 59). The hut, rectangular in plan and measuring ca. 5×4 to 3×2 metres, was roofed with bamboo grass or bark of fir trees. Usually, it had four walls, but sometimes a mere gable served the purpose. Except in the absence of a porch and outdoor frames for drying meat and the addition of a small shed, *ku o kashi*, for storing spring bows and arrows, the fundamental

33

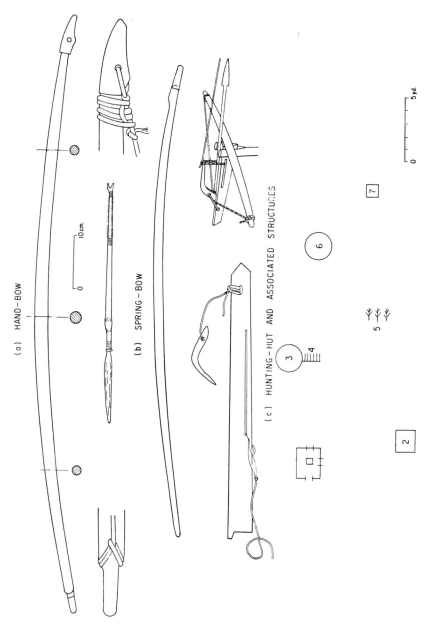

Fig. 5. Hunting devices. (a) and (b), Tokyo University Anthropological Institute Collection. (c), reconstructed plan; 1, hunting hut; 2, store-house for meat and skins; 3, ash dump; 4, outdoor altar; 5, dead trees for drying meat; 6, bone dump; 7, store-house for spring-bows and associated gear.

structure of the building itself, the kinds of the fixtures and their arrangement were similar to those at home as far as ascertained in Tokapchi and Otopuke (Fig. 1). A special window was provided facing toward the source of the river, for the purpose of taking in and out the spoils of the chase and the hunting gear (Fig. 5, c; Note 60). The hut was oriented and the fixture arranged alike to the position of the window. The structure of the Ainu hunting hut, like their home dwelling, was not merely a material shelter but also a means of maintaining social solidarity with nature.

In spring and autumn each year the hut was occupied after necessary repairs by the fixed group of hunters. The group was formed either by an individual family or by two or three families belonging to the same settlement (pp. 43 — 46). Each hunting group usually had a hut of either type to use for respective purpose (p. 45, the chart). Some groups had no bear hunting hut, in which case there was no positive activity in bear hunting. The Ainu hunters, except a few going home and back again on occasion, stayed at their hut throughout the hunting season. From this base they went round, setting spring bows and hunting with hand bows. There they dissected their spoils according to a set ritual procedure and prepared from them hides, meat and fat to be kept till the time of carrying them home. The occupants of the hut might be all males or mixed, with females doing such domestic work as cooking and so on, as was usually the case at the deer hunting hut where there were more hunters and more spoils brought in. Female helpers, however, were quite few in either case : about one at a bear hunting hut and not many more even at a deer hunting hut. They were mostly hunters' unmarried daughters or unmarried sisters, who were usually at home doing house work but were called up when spoils were more than could be skinned or carried off by the occupants themselves. The Ainu of the upper Tokapchi, Otopuke and Azuma valleys as well as those of the Mukawa valley had two huts for bear hunting, one deep in the source area of the river and another midway or comparatively near their homes, examples of which are given in the chart on p. 45. Some Ainu inform that Ainu hunters used one or the other according to the conditions of the season ; but there are also indications that they used the first for bearhunting in spring and the second in autumn.

Hunting Activities.

Deer Hunting.

The deer, Cervus nippon, was hunted in two separate seasons, spring and autumn. Autumn deer were to the Ainu as important a source of winter food as were dog salmon. In summer as well, deer roamed about in herds over hills and plains. The Ainu might have caught them, if they so wished, in any season. But summer was the time devoted to fishing and collecting; besides, summer meat and skins were not much valued because they believed that summer meat was not greasy enough, summer furs did not keep warmth well and both were more easily infested by vermin (cf. INUKAI, 1943, pp. 16-7); usually neither deer nor bear was chased in summer. As an item of food, venison was of greater importance than bear flesh. Deer skins were partly used for their own clothing and partly as articles of barter with Japanese traders; but at least in Otopuke and upper Tokapchi the stock left was dumped every summer, before or after being spoiled by vermin, with a simple ritual procedure by each household (Fig. 1). There were no ritual activities worth mentioning here in relation to deer hunting.

Autumn hunting.—Autumn hunting, *chuk iramande*, extending in reality to winter, was divided into two successive phases, the first characterized by field hunting and the second by hill hunting.

Field hunting.—This phase started in *Urepok chup* or around October when the fur of the animal began to change for the winter[31] and the meat to get greasy (p. 54). The Ainu set spring bows and poisoned arrows to the deer fence on the fields at the foot of a hill or on the gentle slope of a lower hill and frequented the fence usually from their homes in the *kotan* while being engaged in salmon fishing in the river (Map 2; Fig. 8). On the way to and from the fence they also hunted deer with hand bows and arrows. Hunting with hand bows came into full swing with the arrival of the mating time (Note 31). Mating of deer took place most frequently on and around marshy tracts, where, usually not far from the Ainu settlements, the animal was decoyed by the deer whistle, *irektep*, to be shot with hand bows and poisoned arrows. Field hunting continued until the base snow came to cover the food plants for the deer, which then retreated from the fields to their winter quarter[32]. Of the two autumn phases, the first one of field hunting was the more important, for in this period more or less sufficient quantity of venison could be secured to last the winter.

Hill hunting.—When the base snow came and all the deer tracks had disappeared from the field, the animals all gathered at their winter quarters, where they stayed till the spring (p. 53). Deer in Hokkaido pass the winter in sunny areas with less snow and with sufficient food plants such as bamboograss (Note 32). So far as the areas surveyed by the present writer are concerned, the winter quarters lay as a rule on hills which bordered the valley of the river along which Ainu settlements were distributed, that is, on slopes stretching under mountain ridges and wooded with evergreens, chiefly firs; of these the distinctive ones, which were named so-and-so *rikoruya* or *yuk ria ushi* by the Ainu, were found on hills well wooded usually with firs, chiefly *hup*, Abies sachalinensis[33]. In the second phase the scene of hunting shifted accordingly from the fields up to the hills. Hunting on the fields was usually done by hunters out from their homes in the settlement for the day, whereas for the hill hunting the hunters from most settlements migrated in parties to near the area where deer concentrated to pass the winter (Fig. 8 and Map 2). The hunters stayed at their huts in the valleys of streams down from the winter quarters, chasing their game with hounds and with hand bows and poisoned arrows. They usually returned home when the snow was too deep for them and their dogs to walk in. In both Tokapchi and Otopuke, hunting activities during this second phase were performed only by part of the hunters, and in Nitmap on the upper Tokapchi at least, by some younger, unmarried hunters. In short, those activities were more or less supplementary to field hunting. They seem to have fluctuated in proportion to the scarcity of meat in actual store.

Spring hunting.—In spring the surface of the snow on the hills thawed by day and hardened again by night. Then deer hunting was resumed by hunters back at their huts near the winter quarters (p. 54). For some time early in the season, they used their hounds to drive the animals from their quarters down into glens still filled with snow and then shot them with hand bows as they fled struggling in the hardened snow. They also hunted the game lured by fresh leaves or small twigs of trees fallen on the ground, with spring bows set around them. As the snow began to disappear and the plants pushed forth their buds, deer gradually came down in herds to the lower plain in search of food. From the winter quarters down to the fields deer passed by way of the ridges of hills. Their tracks, *yuk apiri*, were much more fixed between the winter quarter and the bottom of the ridge than on the open fields. They continued hunting by means of spring bows set along the migration tracks as well as by hand bows till the base snow disappeared from the fields and the downward migration was completed. Each hunting party constituting a hut group (pp. 43-46) practised the spring bow hunting in their own hunting territory, that is, the dale valley in which their hut was located (p. 31).

Besides the methods mentioned above, the Ainu hunted deer down with dogs, caught them by the horn or neck with ropes and killed them with clubs as they fled struggling in the snow or crossed the rivers[34]. This method was widely practised among the Ainu; however, it seems to have been only supplementary to the others. It was also the only method of deer hunting by women and children.

Bear Hunting.
The Hokkaido species of bear belongs to Ursus arctos, a kind of brown

bear[35]. It grows to a large size and is of ferocious nature. The Ainu hunted for it and killed it in an active way with spring bows and arrows tipped with poison prepared from the wolf's bane, Aconitum, and even with hand bows. The Ainu were most probably the only known people to use bows and arrows as chief implements for hunting the brown bear (WATANABE, 1953). Moreover, it seems that no people in the neighbouring areas ever hunted the bear with such degree of active, organized effort as the Ainu. The Ainu habits of capturing and rearing young cubs and of their ritual killing were quite remarkable (p. 75), as was their well developed method of bear hunting. Furs of the animal were the most important item of barter with the Japanese. Seen from the food economy of the Ainu the bear was not so important as deer or salmon. Throughout the areas investigated by the present writer, rather few Ainu hunters could bring down or capture as many as eight bears, including cubs, in a year.

The bear has a hibernating habit. In early spring in Hokkaido the bear gradually came out of its den and, tracing chiefly the ridge where the snow melts earlier, came down to the lower hills and the level plain where food could be found early. In autumn the bear went about in search of nuts and berries growing in plenty by the mountain streams. It grows very fat during the autumn. When snow came, the animal began to retreat upstream to the depth of the mountains, where it went again into hibernation in its den. Zoological data on those habits of the brown bear in Hokkaido have been given by HATTA (1911) and INUKAI (1933)[36].

In Hokkaido, hibernation dens of bears were found in comparative abundance in those rugged mountain districts where rivers have their sources[37]. The hibernation centres as known to the Ainu were distinct from the winter quarters of the deer even in the same river valley. These latter developed on the strip of lower hills mostly wooded with firs and lying on each side of a river valley (Notes 3, 4 and 33). The tracks for the seasonal and local migration of the animal, known by the Ainu as *noru* or *chikushiru*, were more concentrated, mingled and permanent on the ridges and in the small glens nearer to the hibernation centres. Farther away or downstream, they were more scattered and less stable. Moreover, the bear is non-gregarious; its tracks were narrower and less distinct than those of the deer which is gregarious.

With full knowledge of their game, the Ainu selected bear hunting grounds in those source areas of rivers where there were hibernation centres (Note 37) and in each ground a hut was built for hunters to pass each season. These hunting grounds lay farther from the settlements and more interior than the deer hunting grounds (Fig. 8 and Map 2). Though much fewer, bears could be found outside the source areas; if found, they might be caught by hunters in chase of deer. Such an act, however, must be distinguished from the regular and organized bear-hunting under consideration. Bear hunting was practised in two separate seasons, spring and autumn. No regular bear hunting was practised in the time when their furs were summer ones (Note 36, a and b). In each season bear hunters formed a party and went to stay at the hut away from their homes. The spring hunting, *paikaru iramande*, began at about the time when the mountain snow became hard enough to walk on and bear cubs had been given birth in the dens (Note 36, c). Earlier in spring before hunting with spring-bow began, they carried out raids on the dens while the inmates still lay in hibernation. After building up a wooden palisade to blockade the entrance of the den, they stirred up the adult animal in the den to come out and shot it with hand bows and poisoned arrows. After killing the parent bear they captured the young cubs left, which they took home to bring them up. As the mountain snow began to melt, the hunters started hunting bears coming out of their dens by means of spring bows set on their tracks mainly on the ridges where the snow melts earlier. The season came to its end at about the time when most bears had left their dens (Note 36, a). So far as hunters from the upper Tokapchi are concerned, most of them returned home once after their raids on bears' dens, stayed there until about the time when bears began to come out of their dens and then went back again to the mountain huts to hunt with spring bows. The season of autumn bear-hunting, *chuk iramande*, covered a period between the time when bears began to retreat to their dens and the time when almost all the bears had finished retreating (Note 36, b). In this season spring bows were set on the tracks usually along the small glens where foods for the bear, such as nuts and berries, were plenty. They hunted the animal with hand bows as well and some hunters chased bears even to their dens. The date of the retreat is delicately influenced by the conditions of snow-falls of the season, so the hunters used to enter mountains at a much earlier date than expected.

Collecting of Plants.

Major items of plants collected by the Ainu were the following. After the Ainu and scientific names the place of occurrence and the parts used by the Ainu are given[38].

Food plants:

Ainu Name	Scientific Name	Habitat	Parts Used
1. Eha	Falcata japonica	Roadside and grassy meadows	Legumina under the ground
2. Mukl	Codonopsis ussuriensis	Woods and grassy meadows	Roots

Ainu Names	Scientific Names	Habitat	Parts Used
3. Pukusa	Allium victorialis	Shady woods	Young leaves
4. Korokoni	Petasites japonicus	Common	Young stalks
5. Soroma	Osmunda cinnamonea	Wet places	Folded leaves
6. Shikerepekina	Spathyema foetida	Wet places	Young leaves
7. Pukusakina	Anemone flaccida	Half-shaded woods	Young leaves
8. Tuwa	Pteridium aquilinum	Open or half-shaded places	Folded leaves
9. Ukurukina	Hosta japonica	Open or half-shaded, somewhat wet places	Young stalks
10. Trep	Cardiocrinum glehni	Shady woods	Bulbs
11. Pui	Caltha barthei	Open stream-side	Young leaves and stalks
12. Ninum or niseu	Juglans manshurica	Terrace along streams	Nuts
13. Shikerupeni	Phellodendron amurense	Deciduous woods	Fruit
14. Hat	Vitis coignetiae	Woods	Berries
15. Kutchi	Actinida arguta	Woods	Berries
16. Setara	Malus baccata	Sunny places	Fruit
17. Shiuri	Prunus ssiori	Woods	Fruit
18. Komni	Quercus dentata	Hills and plains in coastal regions	Nuts
19. Peroni	Quercus crispula	Hills and mountains	Nuts

Plants for raw materials:

Ainu Names	Scientific Names	Habitat	Parts Used
20. Sariki	Phragmites communis		Stalks for roofing, walls and receptacles (*rusa*)
21. Shiki or ki	Miscanthus sacchariflorus		Stalks for matting (*aputuki*) and torch for salmon fishing
22. Shikina	Typha latifolia		Stalks for matting (*toma*)
23. At-ni	Ulmus laciniata		Bast fibres for clothing (*attush*)
24. Tat-ni	Betula spp.		Bark for receptacles (*yaru*), torch and spills
25. Suruku	Aconitum		Roots for arrow poison
26. Kap-hai	Laportea bulbifera		Bast fibres for thread
27. Hu-hai	Celastrus orbiculatus		Bast fibres for fishing-nets

In spring when the snow had disappeared from the plains, the Ainu set to work collecting wild plants. Their work continued incessantly and with persistence till it was autumn when dog salmon began ascending the rivers. Of the species listed in the chart, Nos. 6, 9 and 19 were especially important as food for bear cubs kept in their homes. Most of the plants collected were dried and stored away in sufficient quantities to last the winter. During spring and summer all varieties with edible leaves, stalks, or roots which the Ainu needed were taken in. In summer *trep* roots were chiefly collected. Those groups that did no farming as in Otopuke gathered these roots with hardly a day's rest during the season. The roots were made into starch for storage. On the other hand, those groups that did some farming (p. 41) seem to have gathered roots with less frequency and in smaller quantity.

In autumn, fishing and hunting activities of the Ainu reached their climax in preparation for the approaching winter. But even at this season certain kinds of edible plants such as nuts, fruits and berries, were collected, though not in such quantities as would last any great length of time. A few varieties of nuts, for instance, acorn and walnut, were exceptions.

The greater part of plants for raw materials were also gathered during autumn, a task in which women again played a major role. In this manner, when base snow covered the ground, the Ainu had completed all their collecting activities. All these activities were arranged in season, so that they were adapted to the ecology of plant life. On the basis of vegetation the Ainu classified the different parts of their land into the following types as forming their main collecting grounds.

Types of Land	Ainu Term	Plants Mainly Collected
Woodland on river bank	*kenashi*	3, 5, 7, 9, 10, 12, 14
Woodless field on either river bank or river terrace	*nup*	1, 2
Oak wood on river terrace	*komni tai*	1, 2, 3, 8, 13, 18
Woodland by the side of streamlets on river terrace	*nitat*	6, 9, 10, 11, 12, 13, 14

Numbers correspond to those associated with the plant names cited in the list.

The terrace on which the *kotan* stood and its adjoining river bank provided the collecting grounds for their food plants (Fig. 8). Here also were found flora for raw materials, fire-wood, and almost all other plants, excepting a few special items like Ulmus laciniata for clothing or Aconitum for arrow poison. The former species were usually found distributed in plenty and collected in the mountains in the upper reaches of a river (p. 66). Aconite of the kind which was believed to be best for arrow poison was localized in its occurrence (p. 66). The four types of land cited above were invariably distributed along any river, so that almost all necessary collecting was usually done within a short radius of the *kotan*, or within a day's trip and back at the most. In the case of those particular species that were necessaries and that could only be found a long way from their homes, expeditions were sent out. The task of getting almost all edible plants, as well as varieties for raw materials, was undertaken by women and children.

Cultivation of Plants.

Before the land-allotment to the Ainu by the Japanese Government (Notes 9 and 10), the Ainu in the Otopuke valley and a half of the member households of the local group in Kuttarashi who lived furthest upstream on the Tokapchi and at least a household in Pipaushi further downstream, had done no farming, but other Ainus in the Tokapchi valley as well as, for instance, those in the Azuma valley, had done some small-scale farming[39]. The old techniques were simpler and the farm work was usually performed by women. The main crops were a variety of Panicum crusgalli, *piyapa* or *ayushi amam*, and a variety of millet, *amam* or *toita amam* or *munjiro*. Preparation of field and sowing were done in July after storing of chief varieties of edible leaves was finished. Suitable plots on the river bank near their settlement were cleared and levelled with small wooden picks, *shittap*, which were also used for digging up roots and plants. Some families on the Tokapchi used a kind of sickle besides the above-mentioned implement. After the plots were prepared, sowing followed without making any ridges. Weeding was done only once or twice between the time of sowing and the harvest. The crops were harvested by picking ears with an implement made of a mollusc shell collected in the river, dried and stored. These jobs were done during the period between the last part of September and the middle or last part of October. The area cultivated by an average household in Azuma, Saru, Mukawa and Shikot is estimated by the present writer to have been between ca. 1000 and 2000 square metres. When the soil was exhausted the plot was abandoned and a new one prepared. In any valley there seems to have been no shortage of land for cultivation in those days. The cycle of shifting cultivation appears to have varied from area to area.

Food-getting Activities.

Every individual of every species of animals must get its food in order to sustain itself, and food-getting activities may claim to be of basic importance in its existence. Up to comparatively recent times, before the introduction of agriculture in its rudest form, the Ainu had lived by hunting and fishing and by gathering wild plants. Their animal food supplies came chiefly from deer and species of salmon, while other animals or fish except bear were rarely sought with as much industry. The plant food, though more varied in kind, played rather a subsidiary part in Ainu diet.

The devices used by the Ainu for getting their food were both simple and limited in variety, whereas the methods of their employment reveal manifold variations. The Ainu manipulated those implements, singly and in combination, in accordance with different seasons and different places. At the same time they developed multiple ways of using their devices to adjust to particular circumstances under which they obtained their food. In the exploitation of their habitat the Ainu attained a high degree of efficiency by virtue of close adaptation to natural environment coupled with mechanical principles of techniques and skills employed. In order to exploit efficiently their limited resources they developed a multiplicity of ways to suit the biotic communities in their daily and seasonal changes. And by further applying such automatic devices as the spring bow and the fish trap, they succeeded in overcoming restrictions met with in space and time. Thus they adapted themselves to their habitat through a system of interrelated devices and techniques on the one hand and a system of organized activities in manipulating those devices on the other. By means of exploiting their habitat in such manifold ways and laying up stores for the scarcity season of winter, they had always remained a gathering people without ever turning to nomadic life[40].

IV

COOPERATION AND DIVISION OF LABOUR

The gathering techniques of the Ainu were adapted to the seasonal cycles of activities of biotic species, while the seasonal changes of those biotic species took place almost synchronically in different places. The Ainu, omnivorously dependent upon various food supplies of such character, had to carry out their activities of various kinds at different places at the same time. They solved this problem by means of intrafamily division of labour and intrafamily or interfamily cooperation as well as by some automatic devices.

Cooperation.

The Ainu techniques of gathering did not require any large-scale cooperation, for some important techniques required a single person only, while most of the other techniques needed no more than a few to carry them out. Not a few families were industrially self-contained units, gathering independently all the materials of living, whether the family lived together with other families in a single *kotan* or lived singly forming a *kotan* by itself. But other families obtained part of their living through cooperation with other families, although this interfamily cooperation was of a limited scale: usually no more than three families cooperated in any kind of food-gathering activities.

Cooperation was usually between families in the same *kotan*, whether the local group consisted of only one *kotan* or several. Cooperative gathering activities clearly identified are bear hunting, deer hunting, weir fishing, and bag-net fishing. The general Ainu term for this kind of cooperative group is unknown, though particular groups were severally called, according to the kind of the activities, as *something ukashui utari*, meaning such and such work partners, *uko iramande utari*, meaning collective hunting partners, or simply hut fellows in hunting as well as in fishing. The members of the bear hunting group were patrilineal close kinsmen usually within the category of male siblings and their sons, but cooperative groups in other types of gathering tasks sometimes comprised even men of different *ekashi ikiru* (p. 13) and/or their families. These cooperative groups acted under the leadership of the most capable person in the given group.

A small settlement group of three families or less usually formed a single cooperative group, while a larger settlement group got split into more than one cooperative unit, each usually formed by three or less than three families.

There could not be any cooperative gathering work of the local group as a whole except when it consisted of a very few families and formed a single *kotan*. In the Otopuke valley the local group split themselves into several *kotan*, the upstream one with 10 families into 6 *kotan*, the downstream one with 8 families into 4 *kotan*, each of which was a single cooperative unit consisting of 1-3 families. In the Tokapchi valley the *kotan* were larger on an average than those in the Otopuke valley in terms of the number of member families; of the two *kotan* analysed, Nitmap with 7 households and Pipaushi with 6 households had been divided into several cooperative units. This was also the case with the single-settlement local group with ca. 10 households in Tonika of the Azuma valley in the 1880's. For example, Nitmap group, a single-settlement local group with 7 households, was divided into 4 units for either cooperative deer hunting or bear hunting and into 3-4 units in various kinds of cooperative fishing activities. Here attention must be drawn to the fact that the membership of the cooperative group might have been almost the same in the same type of cooperative work but varied to some extent in the different types of work. Factors responsible for the formation or fission of the cooperative group could not be analysed though some of them might be vaguely suggested in a few actual cases in Notes 41 and 42.

So far as gathering activities are concerned, no cooperative unit consisting of the members of more than one settlement has been known among the Ainu, though there were rare cases as, for instance, of an individual joining a cooperative group outside his settlement to which his relative belonged, to take part in such single work as bear hunting or bag-net fishing. One of the actual examples is given in Note 42. In activities other than gathering, cooperation on the largest scale was made in the setting up of the roof of a house in house-building, which required a number of hands at one time. But even in this work, cooperation remained within one local group (p. 12).

In hunting, men played the leading part doing decisive work. It is true that women occasionally hunted deer with a rope or club, helped by hunting dogs, but it was taboo for Ainu women to use bow and arrow which constituted the major weapon of the people. In spring and autumn, men of each cooperative hunting group were divided into two parties, the bear hunting party consisting of younger and more active hunters and the deer hunting party of older and less able men. The autumn bear-party was generally smaller in size than the spring one, for in that season deer hunting and dog salmon fishing were of special importance for securing winter foods. It is to be noted that at times even the deer party hunted bears if they found any, but their hunting fields were more suited to deer hunts, bears living more sparsely there (Fig. 8). And even the party that had gone after bears, if

45

Cooperative Groups in Nitmap at ca. 1885   (see Note 41 and Fig. 6, p. 48)

House Number	Household Members	Bear Hunting Group	Location of Hut	Deer-Fence Hunting Group	Location of Deer-Fence	Hunting in Winter Quarter Group	Location of Hut	Weir Fishing Main Stream Group	Location of Weir	Tributary Group	Location of Hut	Bag-Net Fishing Group
No. 1	Shiokoro (H), Shudea (W), 4 Sons, 2 Daughters	(A) / A	Nipesho Iwotonraushi	a	On the way from Nitmap to Shintoku	Groups unidentifiable:		I	Susutaiful: Upstream	1	On the Sahorun, between Shintoko and Otash	—
No. 2	Shurunke (H), Tutanomat (W), 4 Sons, 3 Daughters	(B)	Tonukariushpet Pishikachinai	b	On the way from Nitmap to Pekerepet	Half of the hunters went to the upper courses of the Panke- and Penke-kinaushi glens, the rest		II	Susutaiful: Downstream	2	On the Sahorun, between Shintoko and Otash	X
No. 3	Zarashi (H), Kouante (W), 4 Sons, 5 Daughters	C / C	Pannaksahoro Shinomansahoro	c	Penkechin	to the upper courses of the Shintoko and Otash glens.		III	Susutaiful: Midstream	3	On the Sahorun, between Shintoko and Otash	Y
No. 4	Shukemon (Ww), Aniainu (S), Ukae (S), 4 Daughters	B / A		d / d				II		2	(Later an independent group; see Note 41)	X
No. 5	Kapkotuk (H), Sakaramat (W), 1 Son	(D) / B		d / d	Penkechin			II		4	On the Sahorun, between Shintoko and Otash	Z
No. 6	Osareainu (H), Katunun (W), Tuishiruk (S), Ikintean (S), Katutaro (S), 1 Daughter	D / D / D / —	Yukktorashi, Certain area up the Sorapchi	d / d / d / ?				II		2		X
No. 7	Retunun (Uw)							III		4		Z

H: Husband, W: Wife, Ww: Widow, Uw: Unmarried Woman, Um: Unmarried Man,
S: Son, (A): Formerly Group A but no longer hunting.

Cooperative Groups in Pipaushi at ca. 1885[42].

House Number	Household Members	Bear Hunting		Weir Fishing	
		Group	Location of Hut	Tributary	
				Group	Location of Hut
No. 1	Chiokatupa (H) Tononkare (W) Uturusote (S) 1 Daughter	(A) A	Kutteki-un-pet farther up the Ochiai	1	On the Sahorun a little below Shimizu.
No. 2	Haukiainu (H) Katesan (W) Pepenouk (S) 1 Daughter	A		2	At the junction of the Pekerepet on the Sahorun.
No. 3	Sayuturuk (Um) 2 Sisters (Uw)	A		?	
No. 4	Moirenise (Ww) 1 Daughter (Uw)			2	
No. 5	Isontomam (H) Ueash (W) Children	B	Sohshipet up the Saru river.	1	
No. 6	Chipreka (H) Wife (name unknown) 1 Son (Daughters not identified)	C	Unidentifiable	3	At the junction of the Pekerepet on the Sahorun

(Legend: See the chart for Nitmap)

unfavourably circumstanced, would return to their *kotan* to engage in deer hunting and salmon fishing. The leader, *shie sapane kuru*, of each party was generally its oldest member, and was responsible for all technical practices on the hunting sites, for guidance and supervision in ritual observances, and for the disposal and distribution of the game and catch.

In fishing, both men and women had an important part to play, but the chief techniques of men differed from those of women. Generally, men took to spearing and women to trapping. Among the major fishing gear, which were fish-spear, basket trap, bagnet and weir, the first two were made and used by each family, while the other two were constructed and manipulated by cooperative groups. The local groups on the upper Tokapchi made a seasonal trip annually to fixed fishing sites in smaller streams to catch cherry salmon, where it was the custom for each cooperative group to form a unit and live in one hut to cooperate in weir and bagnet fishing (p. 45; Map 2). The construction and manipulation of those bagnets and weir were placed under the scheme and guidance of one wise man among the members of the group, usually the oldest man. Cooperation was made also in other work than these. Women and children of families less favoured with catches helped the more fortunate families in transportation and processing, that is, carrying, cutting and drying of the fish, to be rewarded with a certain share of the products.

In collecting edible plants, no cooperation between families was made. Neighbouring women of the same settlement would invite one another and go in one group gathering edible plants, but usually each collected for her own family. Their habit of collecting plants together was based on mere companionship. However, such a party when going far, was always under the leadership of a senior woman who gave necessary advice in the matter of gathering. On long expeditions, especially when there was any danger of the brown bear, they were escorted by some male member of their families.

There were some families who were habitually not very keen on bear hunting. They were not so earnest as to migrate to the hybernation centres of bears in the depth of the mountains; instead they made more efforts in fishing. It appears that such families were more frequently found among the downstream local groups than among the upstream ones. Especially among those coastal groups, *pishun utaru*, that lived in settlements near the estuaries, called *pishun kotan* or coastal settlements[43], the number of hunters specializing in bear hunting, with huts and grounds mainly for that purpose, was probably null or very small in proportion to that among the interior groups, *kimun utaru*, of interior or inland settlement, *kimun kotan* (p. 76). According to all my informants from the inland groups, it is more than probable that in the days of traditional life which they themselves experienced the coastal groups had the habit of fishing on the sea as well as on the rivers, while the inland group never fished on the sea (Note 53). Such occupational differentiation, though small, existed between the inland groups and the coastal groups, accompanied more or less by interchange of food-stuffs, usually based on kinship and affinity, and sea fish, meat and salmon were bartered or exchanged as gifts between related families, though it is not ascertained whether it was an act of bartering or of gift. This kind of interchange took place not only within the reaches of the same river but also between the reaches of adjacent river groups. There was also a certain degree of occupational differentiation among the families of the same settlement, which led to the practice of interchange of certain kinds of provisions. For instance, the female members of one family devoted themselves to collecting edible plants, some of which were given to a neighbouring family in return for some meat or fish. Another family endeavoured to catch fish, part of which procured in return some meat from a different family. It appears that this practice was partly connected with individual differences, which seem to have been practically rather great, in the skill of handling fishing spear and bow and arrow,

48

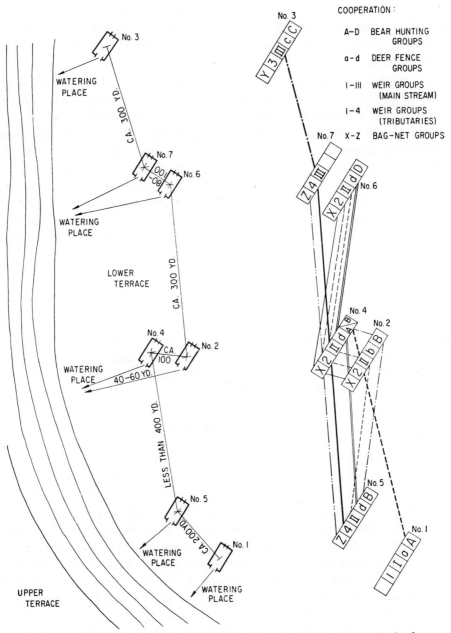

Fig. 6. Spatial arrangement of Ainu dwelling houses in Nitmap in the former half of the 1880's and cooperation between the households. The house numbers correspond to those given in the chart on cooperative groups in Nitmap in Chapter IV. The numbers are given in order of birth among the household heads who are full siblings.

which were the main personal weapons of the Ainu males for gathering food.

Sex Division of Labour.

Construction and Manufacture of Gathering Devices.

Bow and arrow	Male
Deer-fence	Male and female
Associated hunting gear	Male
Feeding of hunting dogs	Male and female
Fish-spear	Male
Net	Male
Basket-trap	Female (if the stream is too big, assisted by male)
Weir:	
Making screen	Female
Making and driving pegs	Male
Building platforms	Male
Net-trap	Male
Wooden pick for gathering roots and cultivation	Female
Knife (sheath)	Male

Operation of the Devices.

Hunting:	
Hand-bow and arrow	Male
Spring-bow and arrow	Male
Ropes and wooden clubs	Female or male
Dogs	Male or female
Fishing:	
Spear	Male (occasionally by female)
Basket-trap	Female
Bag-net	Female and/or male
Weir	Male and/or female
Net-trap	Male
Collecting:	
Felling trees	Male
Materials for mats, baskets, firewoods, nets, threads, basket traps and weir screens	Female
Roots and leaves	Female
Nuts	Female (climbing tree, male)
Bark for cloth	
Climbing and cutting trees	Male

Scraping bark	Female
Aconite plants	Male

Processing of Gathered Materials.

Bear and deer:	
Skinning:	
First cutting	Male
Other skinning work	Male and/or female
Abstracting fat	Male and/or female
Scraping skin	Male and/or female

Feeding bear-cub	Female

Fish:	
First cutting of first dog salmon	Male
Other cutting and processing work including roasting and sun-drying	Female or male

House building:	
Constructing frame	Male
Thatching and walling	Female
Lifting up the roof	Male and female
Building dugout	Male
Boiling, drying and storing edible plants	Female
Manufacturing wooden utensils and furniture	Male
Weaving, knitting and sewing	Female
Making threads	Female

Cycles of Gathering Activities, Sex Division of Labour and Changes of Activity Fields.

    The Ainu had two major cycles of gathering activities: a leisure season in winter for about two months and a work season for about ten months from spring to fall. During the work season their labour was devoted to hunting by men for about two to three months, to collecting by women for about five to six months, and to fishing, mostly salmon, by men and women for about eight to nine months.

    Spring.—When the snow season was over and thawing began, biotic communities started their lively activities, which the Ainu, as part of nature, joined by resuming their vigorous outdoor, especially gathering, activities. Their grown-up males organized bear or deer hunting parties, and migrating, the former usually to river-source mountains, the latter to lower hills along and between rivers, and living in huts, did their hunts. Female members. however, except those who went with the parties to cook for them, remained at home and busied themselves gathering edible plants, especially herbs, on the neighbouring river-banks or river-terraces, and boiling and drying them for storage. These female activities, essential to support winter life, lasted intensively until midsummer or throughout the whole summer. During the spring, the river fish were not yet plenty, but there were some runs of fish such as *chirai*, Hucho perryi, or *supun*, Triboloden spp. The deer hunters, who had migrated to their huts, returned by turns to their houses, even during the deer season, to carry home their game, and they utilized such opportunities to catch these river fish. When the hunting season was over, the hunting parties returned in the middle of spring to find little to do except this kind of fishing, until the cherry salmon appeared.

Summer.—This season was the time devoted to fishing and collecting. In early summer, all men, now living at home with their families, began catching cherry salmon that appeared in the river near their settlement. And when by and by the cherry salmon began to spawn, they moved their major fishing grounds from the river to small tributaries. At this stage, some local groups on the upper Tokapchi (p. 27) migrated regularly to the same streams at some distance from their settlement and lived in huts which served as their fishing bases, while others fished near their own settlement, living at home. Females also took some active part in fishing, and broiled and dried their catch to preserve them. Females, however, had more important work to do during this season. They had to gather certain edible roots (Cardiocrinum glehni) chiefly along the river banks, and make starch from it; besides, they had to do such domestic work as weaving bark cloth and making baskets. Therefore, when the local groups went migrating to some cherry salmon fishing sites, part of the female population, especially housewives, remained at home. Again, some members of the fishing groups in the huts at the fishing sites returned home by turns frequently, chiefly to carry home their catches.

Autumn.—It was at this season, when dog salmon ran upstream in place of cherry salmon and deer's meat grew greasy, that the Ainu prepared their main food for the winter in which it was difficult to gather any. Therefore, their food gathering activities became most intensive at this season. Most of the males remained at home with their families, catching dog salmon in the neighbouring rivers and pursuing deer in the fields on the river-terraces near the settlement. But some of the males, younger and more expert hunters, did so only in the early part of this season, and with the coming of mid-autumn, sped migrating to their huts near the hibernation centres of the bears to hunt them. The autumn bear party was generally smaller in size than the spring one, for in that season deer hunting and dog salmon fishing were of special importance for securing winter foods.

Winter.—When the base snow began accumulating, those animals concerned stopped their local migration and became inactive. Then the Ainu, whose techniques were adapted to such ecology, stopped their positive gathering activities to remain inactive until the next spring, like all other animals; neither deer hunting nor salmon-catching was their business any longer, all bear hunters home from the deep mountains. It is true that some Ainu hunters went to the winter quarters of the deer to supplement the winter provisions for their families or their neighbours in the same group, but it seems that such supplementary or secondary activities used to be all over within the earliest part of the season. And now that their stores were filled and their outdoor activities over, festivity thrived among them all; they gathered for feast and ceremony, to which relatives and friends were invited from different local groups to observe the ritual killing of the bear-cub, which had been kept and fed specifically for this occasion (Note 67).

Except active hunters who used to go to their hunting huts every spring and autumn for a period of usually about a month or more each, every one lived in his own settlement throughout the year and would be engaged in collecting, fishing, and even hunting. The food plants which they collected were found distributed all over the river-banks and river-terraces. The distribution of resources were not restricted exclusively to any particular place, but in relation to their techniques, fishing and hunting grounds were roughly localized. For the Ainu fishing techniques, a concentration of dog-salmon spawning-beds and the surroundings were the best grounds. Thus the greater part of their time and energy for gathering was spent around their *kotan* near the river. It is very likely that the dispersion or concentration of a local group was correlated closely with its ecology in relation to salmon fishing, especially its adjustment of fishing techniques to the spawning grounds. The interrelationship between cycles of gathering activities, sex division of labour and changes of activity fields are diagrammatically shown in Fig. 7.

The sequence of gathering activities and their correlations with seasonal changes in their respective habitats are practically the same in Tokapchi, Otopuke and Azuma except for minor fluctuations in individual activities and time of changes. The following phenological chart refers to Nitmap in the upper Tokapchi.

Phenology of the Activities of the Ainu

Ainu Month (cf. Note 25)	Phenomena in Ainu Habitat	Activities of the Ainu
Shunean chup	Middle part: repeating light snow falls; bears begin moving into deep mountains seeking dens for hibernation. Snow-ice lumps on rivers when it snows; first run of *meorun-chep*.	Middle or last part: bear hunting with spring-bows begins in the mountains. Torchlight fishing of dog salmon begins.
Kuekai chup	Early or middle part: most bears already in hibernation. Last part: some base snow on the fields; no more deer seen on the fields. End of salmon runs.	Early or middle part: bear hunting over; most hunters home from hunts. Last part: end of deer hunts on the fields; removing of spring-bows from deer fences. All bear hunters left behind return home. Dog salmon fishing over; post-run ceremony for the fish.
Zuurup chup	Early part: base snow deep on the fields; deer already gathering in winter quarters. Births of bear cubs during this month and the next.	Early part: deer hunting in the hills by part of hunters. Collective activities in bear ceremony between this month and the next.
Toetanne chup	Middle or last part: snow on the fields hardens.	
Haprap chup	Early part: mountain snow hardens.	Early part: bear hunters enter deep mountains, begin hunting bears and their cubs in hibernation. Middle part: deer hunters go near wintering quarters, begin hunting game by driving them out on hardened snow. Last part: most bear hunters back, the first having returned half a month earlier.
Kiuta chup	Middle part: no more base snow on the fields; deer scattered out of winter quarters. First note of Japanese bush-warbler[44]; first scattered bears out of hibernation dens. Last part: rivers swell with thaw; first appearance in the Sahorun, a tributary, of Hucho perryi.	Middle part: deer hunts in the mountains over; bear hunters go into mountains to set spring-bows; collecting of edible plants begins. Last part: beginning of river fishing with appearance of Hucho.
Shikiuta chup	Middle part: first note of Himalayan cuckoo[44]; most bears out of dens from hibernation.	Middle part: end of spring bear hunts: hunters all back home.
Momauta chup	Early part: first note of Japanese Cuckoo[44].	Early part: preparation of field and then collecting of roots (Cardiocrinum) begins.

Ainu Month (cf. Note 25)	Phenomena in Ainu Habitat	Activities of the Ainu
Shimauta chup	Early or middle part: run of cherry salmon in the main stream.	Early or middle part: cherry salmon fishing starts in the main stream; pre-fishing ritual and setting up of weirs.
Moniorap chup	Early part: flowers of *kuttara* in full bloom; cherry salmon having run to the upper water course of the Sahorun.	Early part: cherry salmon fishing in the tributary starts; part of the local group move to fishing huts for the purpose.
Shiniorap chup	Last part: end of cherry salmon run to the Sahorun; Magnolia-tree shedding leaves indicates the approach of dog salmon runs.	Last part: end of cherry salmon fishing in the tributary; fishermen return home. Repairing and preparation of deer fences. Harvesting begins.
Urepok chup	Early part of this month or late last month: first run of dog salmon. Middle part: deer's coat begins turning into winter fur, and the meat gets greasy.	Early part of this month or late last month: dog salmon fishing starts; pre-fishing and first salmon rituals of the local group. Middle part: deer hunting on the fields starts; setting of deer fences. Harvesting ends.

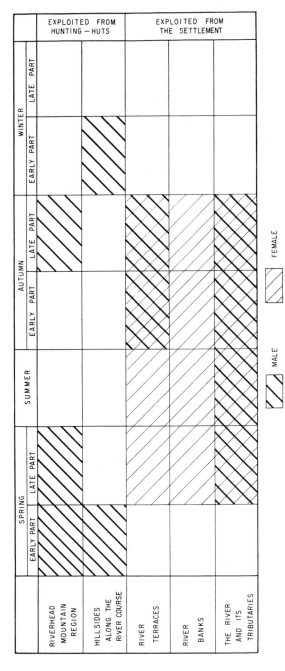

Fig. 7. Seasonal changes in the activity fields of male and female Ainus.

V

TERRITORIES AND GATHERING AREAS

A territory here is defined simply as an area defended and protected by members of a group against intruding members of other groups. Though various types of territories were held by the Ainu, all were concerned with the exploitation of natural resources found thereon. Ainu territorialism was a part of the spatial structure of their community which had a direct relevance to their adaptation to habitat. The maintenance of a territory could be an important factor in relation to the distribution and spacing of groups and to group activities (cf. BARTHOLOMEW and BIRDSELL, 1953).

Territories as held by the Ainu fall into two categories: one, the territory inhabited and utilized exclusively by a river group as a whole (p. 16), and the other, inner-territories stewarded as gathering sites by individual groups within the river group, i.e. local groups, cooperative groups and simple families.

The Territory Held by the River Group.

The territory occupied by each river group formed itself on the basis of a *pet* or a river as prescribed by the Ainu themselves and its surrounding area (p. 16). So far as the territories surveyed by the present writer are concerned, this covered an area bounded partly by mountain ridges forming watersheds for the adjoining rivers, *pet*, and partly by tributaries of the river or adjoining rivers, as seen in the case of Otopuke, Tokapchi, Tushipet, Azuma and Saru[45]. As regards the Shikot the actual line of demarcation is unknown except for that interior part which was bounded in by the crest lines forming the watersheds for the adjoining rivers. As far as the present writer has examined, the actual lines of demarcation of most of these territories, as shown on Map 2, present some difficulty in identification, especially in the lower regions, although it seems doubtful whether such ambiguity had actually existed or the memory has been lost to available informants.

Attention must be directed to the fact that a river group and its territory were not necessarily based on a geographically defined river system as a unit. Sometimes a single river group and its territory evolved around a river system, as with the Azuma; sometimes more than one river group and their territories developed around a single river system, as with the Tokapchi, each evolving around the main stream or one of the larger tributaries.

Geographically Defined River System	Component River around which a River Group Evolved	Number of River Groups & Their Territories
Azuma River	Azuma	1
Mukawa River	Mukawa	1
Ishikari River	Ishikari Shikot Others unidentified	2 (or more ?)
Saru River	Saru ?Nukapira[46]	1 (or 2?)
Tokapchi River	Tokapchi Tushipet Ashoro Otopuke Satnai	5

Each territory utilized exclusively by the residing river group can be divided according to Ainu exploitation activity into the following five ecological zones (Fig. 8):

(1) the river and its tributaries,
(2) the river banks,
(3) the river terraces,
(4) the stretch of hillsides along the river course,
(5) the high mountain region around the source of the river.

In order to supply themselves with a set of biotic species needed for subsistence, the Ainu exploited these different areas in accordance with particular ecologies of species and particular techniques for their exploitation. In this manner the territory occupied by a river group formed a nearly or completely self-sufficient unit of Ainu habitat. Sometimes, a failing supply of a needed item within its own area or discovery of better sites without, induced some members of a river group to pass across its boundary. Two of such essential items were the bear and the aconite plant for preparing arrow poison. Except for these, all river groups were self-sufficing in necessary items (p. 66). In short, the Ainu had seldom to overstep their boundaries for gathering purposes. As regards the staple items in particular, such as deer, dog salmon, cherry salmon and edible plants, every river group was at ordinary times sufficiently supplied from resources found within its own territory.

When for gathering purposes any one was to step into a river group territory other than his own, no matter for what, where and how, the person was required to obtain from some one of the headmen of the river valley concerned a formal permission accompanied with a rigid ritual procedure. And there was possibility that one could be refused by a headman who had

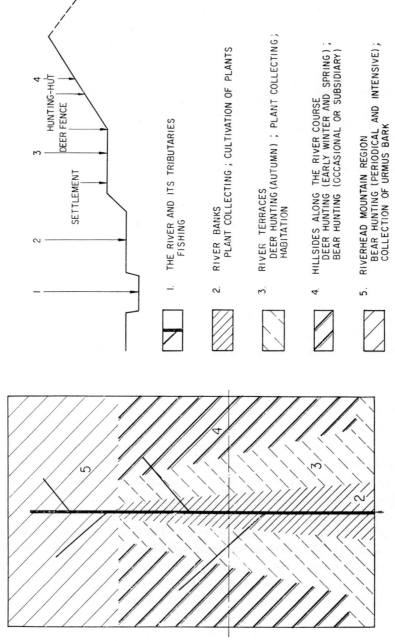

1. THE RIVER AND ITS TRIBUTARIES
   FISHING

2. RIVER BANKS
   PLANT COLLECTING ; CULTIVATION OF PLANTS

3. RIVER TERRACES
   DEER HUNTING (AUTUMN) ; PLANT COLLECTING ;
   HABITATION

4. HILLSIDES ALONG THE RIVER COURSE
   DEER HUNTING (EARLY WINTER AND SPRING) ;
   BEAR HUNTING (OCCASIONAL OR SUBSIDIARY)

5. RIVERHEAD MOUNTAIN REGION
   BEAR HUNTING (PERIODICAL AND INTENSIVE) ;
   COLLECTION OF URMUS BARK

Fig. 8. Diagram representing a river valley as the territory of a
river group and its ecological zones.

the sole power to act in the matter. On getting permission, the person was made acceptable to all other local groups within the territory through communication and introduction by the issuing headman (p. 77).

Territories Maintained by Groups Smaller than the River Group within the Territory of the River Group[47].

The following territories were maintained by individual simple families, cooperative groups and local groups forming the larger group, i. e. the river group: places for setting bows and deer-fences, named concentrations of spawning beds of dog salmon, sites for peep-fishing huts, fish-traps and weirs.

Evidence from Saru suggests that a site for digging aconite in the lower Saru was under control of the local group nearest to it (WATANABE, 1951, pp. 78-79). It is true that collecting sites for the plant of 'best' quality were localized (p. 66). The territoriality on the sites in other areas is unknown. It seems to be certain that bears' dens were owned by Ainu hunters but the category of the controlling body can not be identified clearly.

Types of Territory

Territory Maintained by the River Group as a Whole	Territories Maintained by Smaller Groups within the River Group	Controlling Body	Condition of the Place
River basin as prescribed by the Ainu	Site for peep-hut (*worun chise karu ushi*)	Individual simple family	Unstable
	Site for fish-trap (*urai karu ushi*)		
	Site for weir (*tesh karu ushi*)	Cooperative group	Stable
	Place for setting bows (*ku ari ushi*)		
	Place for deer-fence (*kuteki ushi*)		
	Named concentration of spawning beds of dog salmon (*yaicharo iki, ichan* or *ichanuni*)	Local group	Very stable

The ichthyological characters of the spawning beds and grounds of dog salmon have already been described (Note 28). It was customary with each Ainu local group to give a name to the respective spawning grounds near their settlement where spawning beds of the salmon recurred every season in a greater concentration than elsewhere and to observe annually a series of rituals for these as the controlling body of the particular fishing grounds (p. 72). Each settlement was usually situated near one of the spawning grounds of their own local group which was exploited most intensively by the settlement group. It is evident that besides these spawning grounds controlled by local groups there were many other smaller spawning grounds and scattered spawning beds which were neither named nor claimed by any group but were open to any members of the river group for exploitation without permission. Examples of spawning grounds thus named and controlled by local groups are given as follows (cf.Map 2).

Named Spawning Grounds on the Otopuke, a Tributary to the Tokapchi[48]
(in descending order of location)

Name of Spawning Ground	Approximate Length (yd.)	Group Exploiting Regularly	Controlling Body
Naitai-putu Un Ichanuni	40	Naitai settlement group	Local group of upper Otopuke*
Kamaune Un Ichanuni	200	Kamaune settlement group	,,
Wop-putu Un Ichanuni	100	Wop settlement group	,,
Nipushipet Un Ichanuni	200	Nipushipet settlement group	Local group of lower Otopuke
Ochirushi Un Ichanuni	40	Ochirushi settlement group	,,
Otopuke-putu Un Ichanuni**	300–400	Settlement groups lower than Nipushipet	,,

Named Spawning Grounds on the Upper Tokapchi[49]
(in descending order of location)

Name of Spawning Ground	Approximate Length (yd.)	Group Exploiting Regularly	Controlling Body
Kamuirokki Un Ichan	200	Kuttarashi settlement group	Kuttarashi Group as local group
Honnarakki Un Ichan	100	,,	,,
Wenshiri Un Ichan	400	,,	,,
Umshupenai Un Ichan	600 or more	,,	,,
Sustaifulsam Un Ichan	300	Nitmap settlement group	Nitmap group as local group
Nitmap Un Ichan	400	,,	,,
Parato Un Ichan	200 or more	,,	,,
Tomamapet Un Ichan	200	,,	,,
Kapotpira Un Ichan*	300	Pipaushi settlement group	Pipaushi group as local group
Ohorukot Un Ichan	200	,,	,,
Okatmapka Un Ichan (on the Sahorun, a tributary)	100	,,	,,

Name of Spawning Ground	Approximate Length (yd.)	Group Exploiting Regularly	Controlling Body
Tannepet Un Ichan	more than 400	Kumaushi settlement group	Kumaushi group as local group
Pashiushi Un Ichan	200	,,	,,
Shipenpet Un Ichan**	300–400	Sanenkoro settlement group	Sanenkoro group as local group
Enkoroomanai-putu Un Ichan (on the Sahorun)	100	,,	,,
Nupuchimip-putu Un Ichan (on the Sahorun)	200	,,	,,
Sahorun-putu Un Ichan (on the Sahorun)	200	,,	,,
Sarunnai-putu Un Ichan (on the Shikaripet, a tributary)	?	Sarunnai settlement group	Moseushi group as local group
Nyashikesh Un Ichan (on the Shikaripet)	above 200	Nyashikesh settlement group	,,
Kuttekuush Un Ichan (on the Shikaripet)	200	Moseushi settlement group	,,
Penke-pipaushi Un Ichan	?	Penke-pipaushi settlement group	(Particulars unknown)
Kene Un Ichan	600	Kene settlement group	Kene group as local group
Kiushiful Un Ichan	400	,,	,,
Reukenupuru Un Ichan	200–400	,,	,,
Chepotpiuka Un Ichan***	300	Memroputu settlement group	Memroputu group as local group
Nutap-etufu Un Ichan	above 200	,,	Probably Memroputu group as local group
Uparupenai Un Ichan	200–250	,,	,,
Kutu Un Ichan	200–250	,,	,,
Pira-chorupok Un Ichan	250	Fushikopet and Furemem settlement group	(Particulars unknown)
Memro-putu Un Ichan	100	,,	,,
Shipet-arike Un Ichan	?	,,	,,
Chep-makanpet Un Ichan	250	Ponsatnai settlement group	(Particulars unknown)

Note: Asterisks refer to explanations in Notes 48 and 49.

Named Spawning Grounds on the Satnai, a Tributary to the Tokapchi[50]
(in descending order of location)

Name of Spawning Ground	Approximate Length (yd.)	Group Exploiting Regularly	Controlling Body
Nupokomap Un Ichan	200	Nupokomap settlement group	Nupokomap group as local group
Riyoromap Un Ichan	?	,,	,,
Urekarip Un Ichan	600	Urekarip settlement group	Urekarip group as local group

The analysis of the spawning grounds on the Azuma is incomplete owing to the death of Ushintasan, the chief informant from the area. There are some data on the spawning grounds on the Saru; however, the time horizon concerned is shortly after the land allotment[51].

The nature of the hunting grounds was previously explained in relation to their hunting devices (p. 31; Notes 33 and 37). Distribution of the hunting grounds of the cooperative groups from Nitmap and Pipaushi is shown in the charts in pp. 45-46 and in Map 2.

The area of the territories maintained by a given group never extended beyond the capacity of the group for direct and efficient exploitation of them. Nor were any new grounds sought elsewhere until those hitherto utilized had fallen unproductive. If a group moved to a new locality leaving its ground in disuse, it ceased to have claim on the old territory. The number of fish-trapping sites varied to a considerable extent with different families. This means that more traps were used by families with less catch by spearing against the total amount of supply needed. How these holdings by individual simple families and cooperative groups were inherited remains to be explored.

Each territory held by simple family, cooperative group or local group served as a ground for supplying specific resources, but it was only for a period of time peculiar to the ecology of each game to be obtained. For example, the bear-hunting ground was good only in spring and autumn and the dog-salmon spawning-grounds in autumn only. As a result, territorialism held by the Ainu for their localities waxed strong in season and nearly or entirely vanished out of season. On the other hand, inter-river-group-territorialism— territorialism which a river group displayed for its own river valley—induced them to refuse a stranger or outsider to exploit any kind of its resources without permission, whether in season or out of season.

Except spawning grounds of dog salmon and colonies of aconites, these territories controlled by the smaller groups within the river group are found in every instance to be fishing or hunting grounds furnished with fixed instruments. Unless conditions for exploiting specific resources fell off, the same group enjoyed a successive use of the same site within which no outsider could bring in specific instruments or exploit specific resources. They were to 'refrain' from such acts. Spawning grounds of the dog salmon were not available even to fellow river-group-members except on permission formally obtained from the headman of the controlling local group. Such permission could be had whenever asked by anyone in the same river group (p. 77).

Except for such specified localities, the entire area within the river group territory might be utilized freely by any member belonging to the group. In this open area any person, male or female, could freely open up a new ground for set-bow hunting or trap-fishing, go hunting with hand-bow, or go about collecting plants. It appears that even the aforesaid specific localities were open to anyone in the same river group when it was not a season assigned for a particular locality.

Despite the presence of the aforesaid free-gathering areas within the river group territory, the Ainu usually were able to obtain most of their necessary supplies from the immediate surroundings of each settlement without having to go out great distances for the gathering (Map 2).

Areas Actually Covered by Ainu Gatherers (Map 2).

Fishing Areas.

Generally, the dog salmon was taken for the most part in and around the spawning grounds found near the settlement. Favourable sites for the use of fixed fishing gear and hidings of the salmon suited for daytime spearing, were all found centred around the concentrations of the spawning beds or spawning grounds which best fitted night spearing (Figs. 3 and 4). Some fishermen from each settlement went farther down their stream in early season; as the season advanced they turned upstream and then went down again in late season, for the farther downstream, the earlier the arrival of the salmon and the longer its stay and the farther upstream, the earlier the spawning (Note 26). Thus some of Otopuke and Azuma fishermen went into the area of the next settlement or even farther within the territory of their river group; but the fishermen on the upper Tokapchi seldom went to the area close to an adjacent settlement. The people of Opchapet and Ichanpet settlements in Otopuke, who had relatively few and sporadic spawning beds near their settlements, went to the spawning grounds regularly exploited by the neighbouring Kamaune settlement belonging to their local group and by permission went farther down to the spawning ground of the Nipushipet settlement which belonged to another local group. For the same reason the people of Azuma, a settlement and a local group belonging to the Azuma river group, went fishing dog-salmon up in the water area near the adjacent settlement, Tonika, another local group upstream. The people of Moseushi, a local group on the Shikaripet tributary to the Tokapchi, fished dog salmon in and around their own spawning grounds; however, as their catch there was not sufficient for all their need, some of the younger members used to go fishing in the main stream of the Tokapchi near Nitmap. Some of the young members of Moseushi local group, like Retapka and Takanru, children of Ranketuk of Moseushi, and Tunurawe, son of Kanuran, "had so many brothers that they could not get enough fish for them all in the Shikaripet but had to go fishing in the main Tokapchi as well." Every season they built temporary huts on the bank opposite the Nitmap settlement and engaged freely in spearing and basket-trap fishing in and around the small spawning grounds outside the named spawning grounds controlled by the Nitmap group. For cherry salmon fishing in the river along which Ainu settlements were distributed, the area covered by the settlement members fell in roughly with that for the dog salmon. Most members of each settlement did not usually go so far as to the area near the neighbouring settlement. Some bag-net parties from the Tonika settlement of the Azuma river group used to go down for cherry salmon fishing to the area a little beyond the next settlement, Azuma *kotan*. Cherry salmon fishing in smaller tributaries or glens, however, was not confined to around each settlement. For instance, such local groups on the upper Tokapchi as Nitmap, Pipaushi, Kumaushi and Sanenkoro, fished for cherry salmon centring on the glens of the Sahorun, one of the smaller tributaries of the Tokapchi; the four settlement groups belonging to the upper local group of Moseushi on the Shikaripet, fished for them in the glens around the Sarunnai, a small tributary to the Shikaripet.

Hunting Areas.

For deer hunting, fences set with spring bows were usually erected at the foot of hillsides near their own settlement, though some families such as the groups B and C of Nitmap (p. 45) on the upper Tokapchi built their fences farther away than the others and the hunters migrated every season to their huts erected near the constructions (p. 32; Map 2). The ground for deer hunting with the spring bow near the game's wintering quarters, usually lay on the upper reaches of some tributary near their settlement. Both fences and hunting grounds near the wintering quarters of the game for each settlement group in Tokapchi and Azuma and fences in Otopuke were usually found distributed around their settlements, although the area covered by one settlement group sometimes overlapped to some extent with that of an adjacent settlement group: such an overlapping may be seen between Nitmap and Kuttarashi groups, as shown on Map 2. There is another case like the Shikot river group, from the settlements of which hunting parties migrated each season to concentrate on one region of its territory, a favourite wintering quarter of deer on the Appenai.

Deer hunting with the hand bow was conducted also on and around the same sites near each settlement as fence-grounds and wintering quarters. It was seldom carried out in the area customarily covered by neighbouring settlement members. This meant the absence of such necessity, although any hunter with hand bow, like spearing fishermen with their movable instrument, might with justification enter an area covered by members of a nearby settlement. An exceptional case may be cited with the members of the settlement of the upper local group in Otopuke who concentrated on the area near the Wop settlement, where, alongside with local members, they chased with hand bow the deer gathering on the marshy grounds for mating.

Organized bear hunting was conducted by every river group on the uppermost reaches of the river, that is, the inmost recesses of the mountainous region where were hibernation centres of the bear. It was customary with every river group to send out their hunters in seasonal migration concentrating on the area. This does not always mean that every local group of the river group sent some bear hunter or hunters to the area. Among the Azuma river group, bear hunting parties were sent from two interior local groups, Tonika and Azuma, to the Shoruma and its surrounding area on the uppermost reaches of the river, but there is no evidence for any bear hunting party from the coastal local group, Spun, who it is said had no bear hunters. Of the Otopuke river group, the upper local group periodically sent their bear hunters to the riverhead area but the lower one did not, though some members of the latter group occasionally hunted bears while engaging in deer hunts on the neighbouring hillsides. As for the Tokapchi river group, the upper local groups, at least the uppermost *shine itokpa* group, had a number of bear hunters whose activities covered the riverhead area every season, while the local groups in the middle course had less bear hunters, who to all appearances went out in search of bears to the interior territory of the Satnai river group or that of the Otopuke river group. A few of the bear hunters from Pipaushi and Sanenkoro, both the local groups on the upper Tokapchi, went out of their river group territory into the area around the Sohshupet in the interior territory of the Saru river group, and some bear hunters from Kuttarashi, another local group on the upper Tokapchi, to an area on the upper reaches of the Sorapchi, an extention of the Tokapchi river group territory on the side of the Ishikari river. No information is available for the lower local groups on the Tokapchi. Information from Shikot, Mukawa and Saru shows that bear hunters of the generation before my informants, even those from some lower local groups, went to the areas on the uppermost reaches of their own river.

Collecting Areas.

Of plant resources needed by the Ainu some were usually unavailable from the surrounding area of each settlement: those were aconite plants for the preparation of arrow poison and Ulmus laciniata for textile material. For the purpose of collecting aconite roots, members of the Otopuke river group went out to the Shikata valley near the coast in the territory of the Tokapchi river group. The valley and its environs near the coast of the Tokapchi territory appear to have been the main source of the plants for the Ainu on the whole river system of the Tokapchi. Those of the Azuma river group went out for that purpose as far as to Zenibako in southwestern Hokkaido, an area which it is doubtful if any group claimed for its own. The Ainu of the Saru river in the days of their traditional life are said to have collected the plant from a site near Piraturu on their own river. In Otopuke and Azuma, the bark of Ulmus laciniata was collected mainly in the source areas of each river where good quality plants were plentiful. Practice among the Shikot Ainu in later times suggests that their traditional centre for collecting the bark was on the uppermost reaches of the river, i. e. in the area surrounded by Mts. Eniwa and Bibui. In the case of the Tokapchi, a river much larger than those mentioned above, its upper reaches and the surrounding areas were visited by collectors of the bark from local groups on the upper course of the river: members of the Kuttarashi group mostly went to the interior of the Sahorun or Nikoro, those of the Nitmap and Sanenkoro groups mostly to the source areas of the Sorapchi, an extention of the Tokapchi river group territory on the side of the Ishikari, some members of the Nitmap group farther up to the Tonukariushpet area, and the people of the Memro and Kene groups usually to the interior of the Pise or Sorapchi. But there is no evidence to show that local groups other than those mentioned above, i. e. local groups on its middle or lower course, came up to the area for that purpose. The Fushiko group, one of those local groups, seems to have gone out for the bark to the interior of the Satnai.

All other plants were usually gathered by most river groups around their own settlements. The Shikot group seems an exception. All their settlement or local groups had the traditional way of collecting the *pukusa*, Allium Victoralis, and other edible plants of good quality as well as the bark of Ulmus on the riverhead of their river Shikot, and the *shikina*, Typha latifolia, for matting, on the marshy grounds lying farthest downstream.

In the course of collecting such plants, it was not infrequent for members from different settlement or local groups living adjacent on the same river to come across one another on the same field. On such occasions they exchanged information as to where the plants in search grew in plenty or arranged elimination of overlapping in the sites visited.

Actions for the Maintainance of the River Group Territory.

All Ainu territories were defended and protected for the natural resources found therein. Protection of a river group territory and guarding it from trespassers, as will be seen later, comprised the following practices: reporting by any one of his or her passing or coming to a gathering site to the nearest settlement; keeping watch by each local group member over any outsider, questioning him or her about suspicious conduct and reporting it to the headman; and checking by the headman of all information brought in by his group members and keeping contact by him with other headmen in the same river area. The scheme thus functioned with cooperation of the local group members and a cooperation between headmen in the same valley. It must be noted, however, that these actions for defending the river group territory against trespassers were no specialized occupation of specific personnel but were merely side work performed by each Ainu while engaging in regular manual work. As a result, the extent of effective vigilance seems to have been confined to the area covered habitually in daily routine. It may be assumed therefore that in large but sparsely populated river valleys like the Tokapchi, especially in the mountainous regions, scattered areas occurred which were seldom or rarely visited by any Ainu at ordinary times, areas belonging to a river group but left unwatched and unprotected against trespassing.

The activities of a river group in defence of their river basin were integrated into the following customs. Every Ainu, before going on a hunt, observed a joint ritual with fellow hunters at the headman's, to whom he made known his general plans and his intended sites for setting spring bows in particular, making at the same time necessary arrangements with other hunters. If the man was going for hand-bow hunting into a mountain on his river course unfamiliar to him or not habitually covered by his fellow members, the custom was for him to call on the headman whose people knew the area well, obtain information about it and the distribution of spring-bow sites in particular, and make his plans known to him. It was also the custom for any one, when hunting in an area in the same valley covered by members of another local group, to make a salutatory report to one of the group concerned, if not to the headman. It was done by way of report or notice rather than for asking formal permission from the headman. If the hunter wished to set spring bows, he should never fail to give detailed information to the headman and get his full understanding beforehand. As regards fishing in the open area within his river group territory, it was customary for every fisherman going to a site habitually covered or exploited by another group to report to the settlement of that group either on his way there or back. Otherwise, it might cause the people of the settlement to be 'troubled and even alarmed that some stranger, that is, some member of another river group, was venturing trespass'. These procedures, instead of being formulae for asking permission, were to all appearances necessary precautions against possible intrusion from outsiders, i. e. members of other river groups. The headman was kept well informed of every development by his group members and was also in mutual contact with the headmen of neighbouring local groups of his valley. In this manner he was enabled to keep checking who were fishing or hunting in the area habitually covered by his members, where and by whom poison-arrows were being set, and whether or not rituals requisite for exploiting the given resources were conducted properly.

As has been described in this chapter, Ainu territorial actions are part of their community activities indubitably correlated with and conditioned by certain physical factors in their habitat, while they are also a result of community reactions to habitat as viewed by the Ainu themselves, i. e. the subjective or non-physical aspect of habitat, as may be seen in the next chapter.

THE SYSTEM OF SOCIAL SOLIDARITY BETWEEN
MAN AND NATURE

RADCLIFFE-BROWN, in his theory of totemism, worked out an important basic concept of the subject of relation in myth and ritual of man and nature, that is, the concept of the universe as a moral order (RADCLIFFE-BROWN, 1952, pp. 130-1). The recogniton of the concept leads to that of various processes by which the natural order is brought within the social order. The subject to be discussed here is the degree and kind of interest taken by a people in spatial orientation of natural phenomena around them, and its role in the process of bringing the natural order within the social order.

No attempts have been made to analyze the beliefs and rituals of the Ainu as integral part of the system of relationships between their group life and their habitat or, in other words, as the system of social solidarity between the people and the natural world which works as counterpart to the ecological system. Yet such analyses are thought to be essential to the understanding of the Ainu territoriality and, concurrently, of the distribution and workings of Ainu groups.

Every natural phenomenon occupies a precise place in space. Natural species, whether human or non-human, live and grow in a certain amount of space on the earth. To what extent and in what way this space factor is relevant to a people's system of social solidarity between man and nature, seems to be a problem worthy of exploration.

The Ainu personified all organisms and classified them according to religious categories[52]. But they were not content with mere personification of natural species and a mere taxonomic approach to ordering them. They brought geographical factors into their system of ordering the natural world. Every natural phenomenon has its activity and these activities are interconnected with each other in relation to time and space. Thus the earth's surface, which is seen to our eyes as the carpet of fauna and flora, was seen by the Ainu as the carpet of *kamui* groups in their temporary guises. Every topographical feature such as hill, river and sea, was seen as the field of activity of these *kamui* groups. According to the Ainu view, the whole Ainu land was divided into a number of *iworu*, fields of activities of *kamui*. Some data suggest that the sea also was spatially divided into sections or areas each associated with a particular *kamui* and closely related to the fishing ecology of the coastal Ainu[53].

River System as Seen by the Ainu.

The Ainu classified the component parts of a river system into parent
and children. In this way, for instance, the Tokapchi river system was classified into the following categories. The main river was regarded as male
parent, *zaza*, a tributary as the parent river's male child, *okkai poho*, another
as a female child, *matne poho*, and another as child whose sex is unknown to
my informants. To the geographer the whole river system is known as the
Tokapchi, but the Ainu use this term to refer only to the main river or what
the Ainu regard as the parent. The son of the Tokapchi, a tributary, is
known as Otopuke, the daughter as Satnai, and the child whose sex is unknown as Tushipet[54]. They have no term to refer to the river system as a
whole, the component streams of a river system being each regarded as a
separate unit.

They classify individual streams into *pet* and *nai*. So far as the areas
investigated by the present writer are concerned, *pet* is larger than *nai*: the
former may be called a river and the latter a glen. Any definite criteria of
the two categories, however, are not known to the present writer. Each
named stream, whether *pet* or *nai*, is the dwelling of, and is owned by, a
kamui-spirit. The *kamui* was known by the name of the river or the glen
which it possessed. For example, the river known as the Otopuke was inhabited by '*Otopuke un pet-orun kamui*' which mean the river-*kamui* living in the
Otopuke river. Another name used for the *kamui* is '*Otopuke un pet iworu
koru (or amba) kamui*'. *Iworu* means the activity field of *kamui*-spirits, and
koru or *amba* means 'to own'. The glen-owning *kamui* was called by the
name of the glen as, for instance, '*Naitai un nai koru kamui*'. The river-
owning-spirit was believed to be the chief or head of the water spirits, *nai
koru kamui*, which lived in streams flowing into the river[55].

Each river group evolved around a river, *pet*, was distinguished by the
name of the river as, for example, '*Otopuke un utaru*', the people of Otopuke.
The river basin, i.e. the area drained by the river and its tributary streams,
includes fields, hills and mountains. River basins were named by adding the
suffix '*iworu*' to the name of the river; for instance, the river basin of Otopuke would be called '*Otopuke iworu*'. In this context *iworu* refers to land.
The *iworu*, i.e. the river basin, was claimed by the river group as their territory. It was called, for instance, '*Otopuke un utaru koru iworu*', the *iworu*
which the people of Otopuke own. The relation between the river system
and the territory of the river group has already been explained in detail in
Chapter V and Note 45.

Each river group believed that the land-*iworu* of their own river was also
inhabited by a number of various *kamui* or nature-spirits and the chiefs among
them as well as the chief water-spirit, resided in the upper reaches of the

river as explained below. Each river has its own head which was thought to be especially important to the river group evolved around it and which was called by a special name. Most important of these names is the affix 'shi' meaning true, grand and parental, which is attached to the name of the river[56]. For example, one of the head streams of Otopuke is known as Shi-Otopuke. What the Ainu call Shi-Otopuke, is what they believe to be the source. The river head area was known as kimun iworu, iworu deep in mountains. Its boundary usually corresponds to the limit of dog salmon run; however, the present writer could not verify what this fact means. The top of a particular mountain at the source of Shi-stream, i. e. the source stream as recognized by the Ainu, of the river, was called iworu tapka, the top of iworu, where it was believed the chief bear-spirit lived. There also is some evidence that the chiefs of some other categories of nature spirits were believed to reside there[57]. Kimun iworu was the area which was actually visited only by Ainu bear hunters and bark collectors. The iworu tapka was believed by the Ainu to be the place never accessible to them. Ainu settlements were along the river below kimun iworu.

The tributary streams giving into each river were called children, poho, or branched people, tekehe utari, of the river and had their own names. Each of these streams or glens named by the Ainu, was inhabited and owned by a water-spirit, nai koru kamui, the glen-owning kamui who was subordinate to the river-owning kamui[58]. Ainu settlements were usually situated near the junction of those streams and the river distinguished by the Ainu as a unit, for instance, as Otopuke.

Ainu settlements were thus associated with the terrestrial homes of nature spirits, kamui. The houses of all Ainu settlements had a special type of window which was oriented towards the river-head[59]. The sacred window had a function specialized for communication between the fire spirit in the house and other kamui outside[60]. This had influenced the spatial arrangement of the habitation of the Ainu family and the pattern of the Ainu settlements (Figs. 1 and 6)[61]. In the past, settlements usually consisted of a single row of houses, which seldom lined up face to face on both sides of a road. Now that the cosmological ideas of most Ainus have changed, the traditional pattern has also altered in most settlements, which are usually seen today with a plurality of house rows.

Dog Salmon as Viewed by the Ainu.

The Ainu view of the nature of the dog salmon, especially of its seasonal run to specific rivers and its habit of spawning in specific grounds, may be summarized as follows.

a) The salmon takes the form of a fish but it is not a fish of common nature; it is the food forwarded to the Ainu by the *kamui* who lives in the sea and sends it to the Ainu. The *kamui* is referred to by different informants as either *chepatte kamui .or atui koru kamui* (Note 53), of which the former seems to be correct. The Ainu called dog salmon *kamui chep*, divine fish, or *shiipe kamui chep*, grand food divine fish.

b) The salmon is the subordinate of the *kamui* who lives in a house similar to that of the Ainu somewhere in the sea, and has a human form like the Ainu.

c) There are a number of leaders, *utaru pake kuru* (headman), among salmon spirits who run up different rivers to visit the Ainu, leading their own group of salmon spirits, *ichan kara kamui* (spawning-bed making *kamui*), under the direction of the *chepatte kamui* (or *atui koru kamui*).

d) When visiting the Ainu, they bring with them meals of salmon meat for the Ainu.

e) After giving this meat to the Ainu and being entertained by them, each spirit of the salmon assumes a human form and goes back by boat to its home in the sea. On the way back, they take with them such souvenirs given by the Ainu as *inau*-sticks.

f) Which river they run up depends upon the direction of the *kamui* in the sea. He will forward plenty of salmon to the river along which live the Ainu who respect and welcome them in proper way.

g) The fire-spirit, *apehuchi kamui*, tells the river-owning spirit, *petorun kamui*, how the salmon caught were treated by their capturers, the Ainu. The river-owning spirit communicates this to the *kamui* in the sea.

h) Salmon when caught should be treated in certain prescribed ways; otherwise, they will never come back again.

Group Activities as Their Ritual Reaction to Dog Salmon[62].

Towards the termination of cherry salmon runs, dog salmon started running. Before the arrival of salmon, each local group observed a pre-fishing ritual, *petorun kamuinomi*, to ensure their coming up. The male household heads of the local group participated in the ritual organized and directed by the headman. Prayers and offering-sticks, *inau*, were given to the fire-spirit and the river-owning spirit. The *inau* bore the ancestor mark, *ekashi itokpa*, of the headman, that is, of the patrilineal male-kin group which constituted the core of the local group. After the collective ritual at the headman's house, each household head made *inau*-offerings, *pet oren asange inau*, and went to set them up at the prescribed spot, *inau aroshiki ushi*, near the spawning ground habitually exploited by his own settlement group and controlled by his own local group as a whole.

As previously mentioned in connection with dog-salmon fishing, shoals running earliest in season have to ascend farthest upstream before they can spawn. The earliest group which run up the main stream of the river around which each river group evolved, were regarded as *kamui oren oman chep*, fish which run up to *kamui,* though the *kamui* could not be named definitely. The terminus recognized by the Ainu of dog salmon run in the main stream of each river, either the Tokapchi, the Otopuke or the Azuma, corresponds with the lowermost limit of the deep mountain *iworu, kimun iworu.*

The member of each settlement who caught the first salmon, *ashiri chep, hoshino shirepa chep* or *ashino tanepo chep,* sent it to his headman. Every food gift among the Ainu, whether to the headman or to anyone else, was regarded as an offering, *akopuni,* to the fire-spirit. Besides this gift the first fisher of each settlement invited the people to eat together from his first catch, which was cooked in his house for the first time in the season. The first dog salmon to be eaten for the first time in each house, either in the first fisher's house or in any other's, must be offered to the fire-spirit of each household and the ritual cutting must be performed by a male with his man's knife, *inauke makiri,* the *inau*-scraping knife. The mandible *paetu,* of the salmon, eaten for the first time in each household was reserved for tying to a new *inau*-stick which was to be thrown into the river at the end of the season.

When the spawning of salmon ended at the spawning grounds of each local group, each headman called together all the male household heads to his house and observed a post-run or post-fishing ritual, *petorun kamuinomi,* ritual for the river spirit, ' to see off salmon-spirits ' and to pray for a plentiful next run. The ritual procedure seems to have been much the same as that for the pre-run ritual, except that on return from the headman's house, each household head threw special *inau*-sticks, *chip inau,* or dug-out *inau,* attached with all the mandibles of the dog salmon eaten in his house during the year, into the river at a prescribed spot near the spawning ground most frequented by the people of his settlement.

Taboos concerning dog salmon fishing were much more severe with female than with male members and much more stringent for spawning grounds than for other sites.

Brown Bear as Viewed by the Ainu.

a) Like all plants and animals, the bear when in its own land is in human form and lives in a house similar to that of an Ainu. The house, *kamui chise,* appears to the eyes of the Ainu as a den.

b) The bear-spirit, *kimun kamui, kamui* residing deep in the mountains, has its kinsmen, *utari,* and its headman, *utari shikamakkuru,* the man to look after his kinsmen[63]. The chief of the bears, *metotush kamui, kamui* in the

heart of the mountains, or *nupuri noshiki koru kamui, kamui* who owns the
centre of the mountains, is believed to be the big bear that lives in a large
house on the lofty mountain top at the riverhead[64]. In Tokapchi, the abode
was believed to be on the summit of *Optateshke nupri*, Optateshke mountain,
in Otopuke on the top of *Otopuke nupuri*, and in Azuma on that of Mt.
Yubari.

c) The headman is never known to move outside of its abode to be seen
by the Ainu; but in spring, on its orders, its people put on the bear's form
ready for their visits to the Ainu.

d) When they go, they take with them bear meat to give to the Ainu
for meals. When they set out of their land, the headman gives notice to the
fire-spirit, *apehuchi kamui*, who resides in each Ainu house.

e) The messenger of the fire-spirit is the bear hound, *riep kamui*, creep-
ing *kamui*, or *iso itak kamui, kamui* who calls the bear-spirit, who conducts
the Ainu to meet the visitor. The bear, then, is not hunted by the Ainu; it
comes to visit them.

f) When the ursine visitor arrives, it enters the hunter's house by the
sacred window, *rorun puyaru*, presenting its host with the bearskin and the
bear meat it brings. In return it receives all the due hospitality for an
honoured guest. After accepting the treasured *inau*, shaved wooden stick,
the visitor, again in human form, goes back to the riverhead to his headman[65].

g) On its return home the spirit of the bear is received by the headman
and its fellow people, who all share with it the gift brought back from the
Ainu.

h) If the bear has been treated with due attention, the headman will be
pleased to send more of its people to visit the same host again next year.

Group Activities as Their Ritual Reaction to the Brown Bear.

Mention has already been made in Chapters III and IV that in Hokkaido the hibernation centres of bears as recognized by the Ainu lay chiefly
distributed in the mountains at the source areas of the rivers and that local
groups more upstream and nearer to the hibernation centres showed greater
enthusiasm in organized bear hunting than those farther away (pp. 37 and
47). It follows that more cubs were captured annually by those living more
upstream and maintaining more bear hunters, while some of those groups more
downstream and with less bear hunters seem to have found themselves occasionally short of cubs to bring up for ritual killing.

When cubs taken were brought in by each hunting party, they were
either allotted for rearing among the member families, as in the case of
Tokapchi, Kushiro, Saru and Azuma areas, or taken on in one lot by the
leader's family, all the others contributing necessary feed, as in   Otopuke.

Rearing of a cub usually took nearly a year, from March or April till January or February next year, or in some cases two years, at the end of which period the animal was killed with ritual. A large quantity of feed was necessary which was practically the same kind as food for the Ainu themselves. Indeed, the amount consumed by an average cub in one day from the first autumn on, is said to have been equal to that for several grown-up Ainus. Surplus stores of salmon and wild nuts gathered in autumn went to this purpose, as well as wild vegetables collected during spring and summer.

The ritual killing of the cub, *kamui iomante*, sending off the bear-spirit, took place in January or at latest in February, before the spring bear hunting set in once again[66]. The ritual was observed as a collective enterprise of the whole *shine itokpa* group. This group represents the patrilineal grouping of the male members who formed the core sections of the neighbouring local groups in the same river valley (p. 15). As far as the present writer has examined, the ritual killing of the cub was the only peacetime collective activity participated in with regularity by the *shine itokpa* group as a whole. The observance of the so-called bear ceremony has been widely but very vaguely known as the greatest of Ainu peacetime collective actions, but little has been made known about its social aspect[67].

Prior to the ceremony the headmen of the member local groups of the *shine itokpa* group held a meeting, *ukosanio*, at the house of one who by custom came first in order among them, to fix dates for the ceremonies at their respective settlements. The ceremonies came in a customary order. To take an example from one of the *shine itokpa* groups in Tokapchi, it was customary for the local groups forming the member sections to observe their cub-killing rites in the order of Nitmap, Kuttarashi, Moseushi, Sanenkoro, Kumaushi, Pipaushi and Penkepipaushi. In the *shine itokpa* group in Otopuke, which consisted of two local groups, the upper local group came first. In the local group on turn, each of the cubs kept by the headman and other families was killed with due rituals at the hands of its keeper, *hepere koru kuru*, and his family. Whether they were killed individually at the keeper's house, as was the case at Tokapchi and Otopuke, or collectively at the headman's where they were all brought together, as at Nukapira and Saru, the rituals were performed in a fixed order of households in each local group. First came the headman's. He had exercised a custodianship over all the cubs kept within the group. It was not until the initial killing had been performed by the headman on his own cub that other cubs in the same group were killed ritually by other keepers. The rule of the order for the latter is not known; however, in the local group at Nitmap the core of which consisted of male siblings, the headman was followed by others in the order of seniority. At Nukipet, it is informed, the order was in the nearness of kin to the head-man. The ritual killing at each keeper's house in a local group, whether it had one cub or two, was finished in a day, and it went round among all the keepers' houses in the group, one each day or every two days, until all finished. Generally a couple of days were left between the last day in one local group and the first in the next. Thus, for instance, the entire period required by the whole *shine itokpa* group, beginning with Nitmap and ending up with Penkepipaushi, extended well over a month.

The ritual in each keeper's house was also participated in by the head-men and others; however, the leading part was played by the keeper. In the ritual he offered to his bear-cub the *inau*-sticks marked with his own ancestor mark, *ekashi itokpa* (cf. Note 66). But, in Tokapchi and Otopuke at least, if he was a man of a different *ekashi ikiru* semi-adopted through mar-riage as a member of the core *ekashi ikiru* of the local group, he had to offer the *inau* bearing his wife's father's ancestor mark, *matchama itopka*. The details have already been given on p. 14 in relation to the kinship organiza-tion of the local group and the actual case is shown at the end of Note 15. Attendants of the ritual seem to have been mostly or almost exclusively members of the *shine itokpa* group. Persons married out of the member local group of the *shine itokpa* group, mostly women, were expected to attend if possible. As a matter of fact, they found themselves too busy with similar activities in their own groups. A very few who could attend came accom-panied by their husbands. Attendants at rituals in other settlements or local groups were mostly adults. At the bear festival season people often stayed away from home for more than ten days attending one ceremony after another in the member settlements of their *shine itokpa* group. Some of the seniors, it seems, were away even for a whole month.

Bear cubs were captured almost regularly each year by the interior set-tlements of the upper Otopuke local group, such as Naitai, Meto, Rucha and Wop, while with the lower settlements there were years when no cubs were taken. This seems especially to have been the case with the coastal settle-ments, *pishun kotan* (p. 47). Of the local groups on the upper Tokapchi, it is informed, three families at Nitmap, i. e. the Shurunke's, the Zarashi's and the Osareainu's, three at Moseushi, i. e. the Ritenkouk's, the Ranketuk's, and the Rarauk's, two at Kumaushi, three or four at Kuttarashi and two or three at Sanenkoro, almost always kept two cubs each; there were other houses which kept one. In case a headman failed to secure any cub for his rearing, as was said to have happened occasionally among some local groups, he was entrusted with one, if any, captured by some other member in his group. As for groups with no cubs of their own, the members, instead of having their own ceremonies, only took part in those of the other sections of the *shine itokpa* group[68].

Territoriality and the System of Social Solidarity between the Ainu and their Habitat.

The Ainu used to believe that the *kamui*-spirits which lived in the *iworu* of the neighbouring river looked after them. The inhabitants of a river, i. e. the river group, claimed exclusive rights to exploit the resources in the river basin which consisted of land- and river-*iworu*. Outsiders were allowed no access to those resources except by permission. The permission was obtainable from the headman of any local group in the river valley by going through a certain ritual procedure for the local *kamui*-spirits. Their claim to resources on land was activated not only by their economic interest but also by their cosmological system as such.

If some one wanted to fish at the spawning grounds owned by another local group, he had to ask for permission of the headman of that group. Under the direction of the headman, the applicant observed a proper ritual for the fire-spirit and the river-owning spirit and offered *inau*-sticks made by him to the spawning ground where he wanted to fish. After fishing, he would give part of his catch to the headman and the people who lived near the spawning ground and customarily fished there. The proportion of the amount of the 'gift to the fire-spirit' to his catch seems not to have been prescribed. Among the member local groups of the same river group, permission was usually given without fail.

Fishing in areas of a river outside of those named spawning grounds and private sites was freely done as occasion demanded by the people of the same river, that is, by the members of the river group. There was, however, a custom that in order to prevent any fishing by outsiders without permission, every fisherman gave information of his coming to the people of the nearby settlement. Sometimes he might inform on his way home. Also in this case, part of his catch was usually given to them as a gift to the fire-spirit.

In the case of gathering, either fishing, hunting or collecting, in the territory of a different river group, one had to get permission from any one of the headmen in the river valley, regardless of the method of one's fishing or hunting. Such permission was given on the performance of a ritual for local *kamui*-spirits concerned, but not always, because assurance was required that the fisherman or hunter be faithful to the local *kamui*-spirits. The discoverer of any trespasser must bring him to his headman or some headman available at hand in the river valley, to make him apologize as soon as possible to the local *kamui*-spirits of the river concerned[69]. Also the discovery of such evidence of trespass as salmon bones thrown in the mountains of the river was a cause for serious issue, for it meant a grave offense to the *kamui*-spirits of the river from which the people of the river or the river group received exclusive favour and which they guarded with greatest caution. The Ainu expressed the maintaining of their territory, that is, the territory of the river group, by the words 'the guard of our *iworu* owning *kamui*-spirits'. Their territoriality was actually activated not only by economic interest but by their system of social solidarity with nature as such.

The Ainu world was full of divine visitors: all the natural resources exploited by them were *kamui*-spirits in temporary guises. In consequence all their gathering activities implied social intercourse with *kamui*. Moreover, each *kamui* had its own function in relation to the economic and social activities of the Ainu. Thus there was a close interdependence between Ainu and *kamui*, and their rituals and taboos were an expression of this relationship. The relationship, that is, the social solidarity between Ainu and *kamui* was established on the principle of coresidence or local contiguity[70]. Ainu cosmology emphasized its component of spatial orientation; nature, i. e. *kamui*, were ordered on local basis. The effective ritual relationship between those spatially oriented *kamui* and the Ainu was in the hands of the patrilineal kin group of males which formed the basis of the Ainu local organization.

SUMMARY AND CONCLUSIONS

1. The Ainu territorial grouping is as follows:

Household: Usually consisting of a simple family living in a permanent house.

Settlement: Usually consisting of 1-10 households.

Located near a named spawning ground of dog salmon, being a unit group exploiting a spawning ground or grounds in common. Periodical change in population size and sex composition: men migrate to mountain-huts in hunting seasons.

Type 1: Consisting of 3 households or less, forming a single unit in any kind of cooperative work in gathering. Male household-heads not always unilineally related.

Type 2: Consisting of more than 3 households, splitting into more than one unit in any kind of cooperative work in gathering. Male heads of the households constituting each cooperative group not always unilineally related.

Local group: Usually consisting of 5-10 households, the minimum size being 3.

Type A: Single-settlement local group.

a. With settlement type 1, a single cooperative unit in gathering.

b. With settlement type 2, not so.

Type B: Multi-settlement local group.

Mostly with settlement type 1. Local group with only settlement type 2 never encountered.

Common type being A. The principal corporate group characterized by a common headman, collective ownership of spawning grounds of dog salmon, cooperation in house-building, and a collective ritual, i. e. the dog salmon ceremony. The core consisting of a patrilineal descent group: male household-heads patrilineally related, sometimes including a few males semi-adopted through marriage.

Shine itokpa group. Usually consisting of several adjacent local groups next to each other; the cores forming sections of the patrilineal kin group of males possessing a common male ancestor mark and associated cult. Collective activities in the bear ceremony but without any chief or common property of the group as a whole.

River group. Aggregation of all the local groups inhabiting a river valley as distinguished by the Ainu, consisting of one to three or a few more (at most) *shine itokpa* groups. Presence of strong group-consciousness

backed by cosmology. Claim to the river valley as their territory; the
members free to exploit without permission any resources in the valley
except subterritories (hunting and fishing sites) maintained by various
groups of lower order. Members potential collaborators in case of defence of their territory and a single unit in case of collective ritual
against a catastrophic natural phenomenon.

2. The Ainu exploited their habitat by means of a set of techniques. Each
of their gathering techniques, operated by an individual or in cooperation,
was applied to each specific resource in specific places at specific times;
gathering techniques were linked in an order in terms of their spatial and
temporal arrangement. Through the arrangement of technical devices and
activities the Ainu ecological system was structured spatially and temporally.
The spatio-temporal structure was closely connected with the cyclical changes
in the habits of the biotic species exploited by them.

3. The periodic changes of those biotic species to which their ecological
system was closely related took place approximately synchronically in different places. Accordingly the Ainu, omnivorously dependent upon various
food supplies of such a character, had to exploit resources in different places
at the same time. They solved this problem by means of intrafamily division
of labour and intrafamily and interfamily cooperation as well as by some
automatic devices.

4. Any of their gathering techniques can be manipulated by a single person
or a family; the nature of techniques limits the scale of cooperation. Cooperation in gathering was usually between households in the same settlement.
No more than three households cooperated in any kind of gathering activity.

5. Staple food-stuffs of the Ainu were gathered from a relatively narrow
area surrounding their settlement and covering three ecological zones, i. e.
the river along which they settled, its river banks and river terraces. Main
hunting and fishing sites were fixed in location owing to the adaptability of
their techniques to migrative habits of animals. Under these conditions, the
Ainu were enabled to live in permanent settlement in spite of their depend-
ence upon gathering life. Settlements, however, were usually small in size
and were scattered along a river course in connection with the distribution
of the spawning grounds of dog salmon.

6. The Ainu maintained several categories of territories. The major category
was the territory of a river group which covered the valley of a river as
distinguished by the Ainu and was maintained throughout the four seasons.

The river valley constituted a unit area of resource distribution; the territory formed a nearly or completely self-contained unit of Ainu habitat. Within this were territories of minor categories which were seasonally maintained by such smaller groups as the local group, the cooperative group and the individual household. These might be hunting or fishing sites exploited by means of fixed devices or concentrations of certain specific resources which annually recurred at the same places.

7. The ecological system of the Ainu functions on adaptation of their techniques to the spatio-temporal structure of the activities of biotic species. The Ainu system of relationships in beliefs and ritual of man and nature is their own theory and practice for maintenance of the ecological system.

8. The Ainu system of social solidarity between man and nature was established on the principle of coresidence or local contiguity within a river valley as the territory of the river group. Ainu cosmology emphasized its component of spatial orientation; nature, i. e. *kamui*, was ordered on a local basis. The effective ritual relationship between those spatially oriented *kamui* and the Ainu was in the hands of the patrilineal kin group of males which was the basis of Ainu local organization.

Every organism leads its concrete life in a given environment; that no animal can function apart from its habitat is amply shown in animal ecology. It follows that when we look at man as a functioning organism and try to understand his group life as part of a living system, the relationship of the group with its habitat should be first examined. The present study shows that between the Ainu and their habitat there exist two systems of interrelations working on quite different levels: the first is an ecological system, i. e. a system of relationships through technological activities of man with habitat, and the second, a system of social solidarity between man and nature, i. e. a system of relationships through beliefs and rituals of man with habitat.

Significance of ecological factors relevant to group structure has been worked out by STEWARD (1938), EVANS-PRITCHARD (1940) and FORDE (1947) and the importance of the relationships through native beliefs and rituals between man and nature in connection with social organization has been shown by RADCLIFFE-BROWN (1952) and FORDE (1954), while the present study on the Ainu shows the reciprocal adjustment between the ecological system and the system of social solidarity between man and habitat and the group structure.

The present study leaves much unexplored owing partly to methodological limitations. It suggests sufficiently, however, that the influence of habitat upon the group life of a primitive people should be analysed not only through their technology but also through their cosmological view of habitat and ritual reaction to it and that in such an analysis it is important to examine the spatio-temporal structure of group life in relation to the nature of habitat, especially the ecology and ethology of the surrounding biotic species. It is hoped that quantitative analysis will be attempted to inquire further into the problem.

NOTES

Chapter I

(1) Population of the Ainu†

Date of Census			Number of Ainu Houses	Ainu Population	Average Inhabitants per House
1804	Hokkaido	East Ainu†† Territory	2927	12753	4.36
		West Ainu Territory	?	8944	
		Total		21697	
		Sakhalin	?	2100	
1822	Hokkaido	East Ainu Territory	2624	12028	4.58
		West Ainu Territory	2125	9121	4.29
		Total	4749	21149	
		Sakhalin	357	2571	7.20
1854	Hokkaido	East Ainu Territory	2280	10883	4.77
		West Ainu Territory	1127	5253	4.66
		Total	3407	16136	
		Sakhalin	373	2669	7.16
1873	Hokkaido	Ishikari†††	140	576	
		Shiribeshi	255	1005	
		Woshima	65	259	
		Ifuri	863	3537	
		Hitaka	989	5048	
		Tokapchi	275	1449	
		Kusuri	349	1576	
		Nemuro	120	480	
		Kitami	333	1393	
		Teshio	117	507	
		Total	3506	15830	4.52
		Chishima (Kurile Islands)	93	442	4.75

† Source: see following page.

†† For details on East and West Ainu Territories see Note 6.

††† Names of administrative divisions of Hokkaido established by law enacted in 1869.

Sources of foregoing figures, with notes (Hokkaido-chō, ed., 1937, Vol. 7, pp. 144-145 ; 148-149).

1804 : based on Ezo Zakki (Miscellanies on the Ainu). Under East Territory an addition was made of a certain number of houses with a population of 526 at six ' Basho' on the Kurile Isls. Surveys of West Territory and Sakhalin are extremely inaccurate ; figures for areas north of Rumoi seem to be mostly conjectural and below the actual numbers.

1822 : based on Ezo Kokō-hyō (A Table of Ainu House Distribution), Ezo Zakki and other books. No information is available for Matsumae clan territory. Incomplete figures for Shikotan Isls. in East Territory (houses, unknown ; population, 92) and Kamikawa in West Territory (houses, 75 ; population 527), have been omitted.

1854 : based on Ezo Kokō-hyō , Ezo Zakki and other books. Additions were made into East Territory of 96 houses with a population of 377 at six places on the Kurile Isls.

1873 : based on Kaitaku-shi Jigyō-hōkoku (the Business Reports of the Commissioner of Colonization).

(2) Monthly mean temperatures (C.) for 1921-1950 in different areas in Hokkaido (Tokyo Temmon-dai, 1954, Sect. Meteor., p. 8).

	I	II	III	IV	V	VI	VII	VIII	IX	X	XI	XII	Annual Mean
Hakodate	−3.4	−2.8	0.4	6.1	10.6	14.7	19.7	22.4	18.0	11.9	5.5	−0.7	8.5
Urakawa	−3.5	−3.2	−0.4	4.3	8.6	12.6	17.5	20.3	17.1	11.7	5.5	−0.8	7.5
Asahikawa	−9.4	−8.4	−3.6	4.0	10.7	16.0	20.9	21.2	15.5	8.6	1.4	−5.0	5.7
Obihiro	−9.8	−8.9	−3.2	4.3	10.0	14.0	18.8	19.7	15.6	9.0	2.1	−5.4	5.5
Kushiro	−7.1	−6.7	−2.5	2.8	6.8	10.7	15.4	18.2	15.2	9.7	3.5	−3.3	5.2
Suttu	−3.5	−2.8	0.5	5.5	10.1	14.2	19.1	21.2	17.9	12.1	5.3	−9.3	7.6
Sapporo	−6.6	−5.1	−1.4	5.3	10.7	15.3	20.1	21.7	18.4	10.2	3.6	−3.0	7.4
Uhoro	−5.7	−5.4	−1.8	4.3	9.3	14.0	18.8	20.7	16.5	10.6	3.8	−2.4	6.9
Wakkanai	−5.8	−5.8	−1.7	3.7	8.3	12.4	17.0	20.4	16.5	10.5	3.1	−3.3	6.3
Abashiri	−6.8	−7.3	−3.2	3.3	8.3	12.5	17.5	19.5	15.9	10.1	3.2	−3.3	5.2
Nemuro	−5.0	−5.7	−2.4	2.6	6.5	9.9	14.7	16.1	15.6	10.9	4.9	−1.4	5.5

(3) So far as the crown forests in Hokkaido are concerned which occupy a large part of the island, there usually occur at the foot of the mountains latifoliate forests; halfway up the mountains, mixed forests of latifoliate and coniferous trees, at a higher altitude coniferous forests and at an altitude of about 1000 metres above sea-level such flora as the creeping-pine (MIURA, 1933, p. 282). On Mt. Taisetsu, the highest mountain in Hokkaido, and other high mountains in the central highland, the upper boundary of the growth of

firs, Abies sachalinensis and Picea jezoensis, runs at an altitude of 1400 metres above sea-level, leaving the overlying zone to creeping-pines and grasses (INUKAI, 1943, p. 5).

(4) Kishida distinguishes two zoo-geographical regions in Hokkaido: the Highland and Lowland regions. The former is represented by the creeping-pine zone and one overlying it in the Taisetsu volcanic mountain range. The latter includes the whole lower regions in Hokkaido and the Kurile Islands south of Rasawo. The brown bear, Ursus arctos, is found in both of the regions, while the deer, Cervus nippon, is found exclusively in the Lowland region (KISHIDA, 1930, p. 372; KURODA, 1937, pp. 71-72 and 79). See also Note 3.

(5) The contact between the Ainu and the Japanese has taken different forms. The following is a summary made by the present writer from TAKA-KURA's study (TAKAKURA, 1942).

Before 1599, the contact must have been limited. In that year the Japanese Matsumae clan, which was subordinate to the Tokugawa Shogunate, was established with its headquarters at Matsumae in the southwestern end of Hokkaido and with adjacent area, Matsumae-chi, as clan territory. There no residence was allowed to Ainus except those who had been living in the area hitherto. At the same time Japanese civilians were prohibited to live outside the area, that is, in the Ainu territory. The Matsumae had exclusive trading rights with the Ainu and established trading and fishing posts along the coast. They traded rice, rice wine, tobacco, salt, pans, knives, axes, needles, threads, lacquer wares, trinkets and so on, in exchange for salmon, skins, craft objects, and certain other items brought over from the continent such as Manchurian trinkets and clothing. During this period the Ainu continued to retain their independence. But in 1799, this part of Hokkaido came under the direct control of the Tokugawa Shogunate for the purpose of protecting Japanese interests from the expanding Russian mercantile activities. In those days, foreign vessels, i. e. Dutch, Russian, English, and French ships for explorations, were often seen off the coast of Hokkaido, and the Russian colonization of the northern Pacific became active. As a result the Japanese trading stations were turned into military posts. The Japanese established a limited administrative organization over the Ainu territory but did little to interfere in their internal affairs except as requirements of defence dictated. Trading continued as before. In 1821 the Matsumae resumed the administration of the territory and continued the same policy. The Ainu were employed by the Japanese at those coastal posts. In 1854-67 the Matsumae-chi again came under the direct control of the Tokugawa Shogunate. It seems quite reasonable to state that until 1867 the Japanese had relatively slight effect upon

the life of the Ainu except through the distribution of Japanese goods among
them.

(6)   " Basho " or District System.
    The " basho " system came into being when the Matsumae clan, establish-
ing itself as a feudal clan under the Tokugawa Shogunate, claimed the " Matsumae clan territory " around the castle it built for its headquarters at the
tip of the Woshima peninsula in the southwest Hokkaido and divided part of
the Ainu territory on the island and the southern Kuriles into a number of
" basho " or districts as fiefs for its vassals (Hokkaido-chō, ed., 1937, Vol. 2,
pp. 102-103).   The result was a division of the Ainu territory roughly into
two sections, the east territory and the west, with probably either Kamui
Cape or Fuoi Cape as boundary (Note 1).   At the Kansei period (1789-1800)
there existed 43 " basho " in the east Ainu territory and 42 more in the west
(ibid., p. 359).   Down at the outset of the Japanese administration, that is,
immediately before the abolition of the system (1869), the number was 20 in
the east and about 25 in the west (ibid., Vol. 3, pp. 145-148).   The districts
varied considerably in area, their boundaries, it seems, being based on old
Ainu observances (ibid., Vol. 2, p. 105).
    Within the clan territory no Ainus were allowed to live except those
resident hitherto.   Nor in the earlier days were any Japanese permitted to
inhabit Ainu territory ; all they did with the natives was trading of goods
once every year at the coast of each " basho ".   In course of time, though
restrictions on Japanese residence continued, there emerged on the coast of
each " basho " a trading post, " unjoya ", to conduct periodic trading and
periodic shore fishing with employment of native labour (ibid., Vol. 2, pp.
105-108).   In " basho " with good fishing grounds a census-register was kept at
each trading post for the purpose of summoning interior Ainus to compulsory
service at the coast and calling out any surplus labour force from other
districts under the same contractor.   Some Ainus, however, who lived on the
upper courses of the larger rivers or in " basho " with poor fishing grounds,
were free from the service (TAKAKURA, 1942, p. 235).   Ainus employed at the
coast were mainly young and grown-up men, but sometimes women and even
young children were included (TAKAKURA, 1942, p. 289).   At the close of the
" basho " period (1854-1868) Ainus responsible for supporting a family were
exempted from shore service ; in absence of such in a family some one in his
place was chosen for exemption (ibid., p. 366).   The " basho " system was
abolished in 1869 by the Japanese Government shortly after the establishment
of the colonial government for development of Ezo Island.   The system was
temporarily replaced in some areas by direct government control and in others,
including Tokapchi, by the new system of " ryōba-mochi " (fishery holding)

whereby fishing in each district was consigned to some person who was placed concurrently in charge of the postal service in the area. In 1876 these temporary measures were formally all abolished, but a period of transition seems to have prevailed for some time afterwards (Hokkaido-chō, ed., 1937, Vol. 3, pp. 470–472).

(**7**) In 1868, with the establishment of the Japanese Government in place of the Tokugawa feudal government, Hokkaido came under the new Government. In that year the Government established its administrative headquarters and in the next year its colonial government, " Kaitaku-shi ", in Hokkaido. The Ainu were enrolled in the Japanese census registers by 1875 or 1876 (TAKA-KURA, 1942, p. 419). Their territory became Government property ; land laws were enacted for granting plots of land both to Ainu and Japanese settlers. While the Ainu were prohibited from fishing salmon and hunting deer and bears with poisoned arrows, the Government encouraged Japanese settlers to take up farming and keep cattle. Japanese fishermen and hunters came over with techniques superior to those used by the Ainu. Forestry and mining undertakings were set up. From 1883 onwards the Government encouraged the Ainu of Hokkaido to take up agriculture.

(**8**) Each Ainu household was granted a plot of land, given agricultural implements and seeds, and received technical instructions from specialist Japanese officials. This land allotment to the Ainu population with accompanying agricultural instruction began in 1883 in the Ashoro district in Hokkaido and spread gradually to other areas throughout the island (TAKAKURA, 1942, pp. 486–491) ; in the upper Tokapchi area the project was carried out in 1886 (YOSHIDA, 1955, p. 6) and in the Azuma area in 1888 (A Chronological Table of Azuma Village History, compiled by the village office). Even before this date the coastal Ainu and part of the interior Ainu had farmed by shifting cultivation, probably under Japanese influence (Note 39) but only on a small scale (p. 41). The practice of agriculture before the land allotment was actually observed in various places by MATSUURA, official of the Tokugawa Shogunate, on his explorations of the Ainu territory in Hokkaido in 1857-58 (Note 10).

The introduction of agriculture thus encouraged by the Japanese administrators after 1883 resulted in considerable displacement in the traditional territorial groupings of the Ainu which had been correlated to fishing, hunting, and collecting tracts rather than to any terrain suitable for farming (Note 10).

(**9**) The time horizon for the Ainu life as treated in the present study is roughly coeval with the final stage of the intermediate period (Notes 6-7),

during which the Ainu, especially those in the interior regions, still led their
social life of independence based on gathering activities, with a minimum of
intercourse with Japanese through trading and fishing labour. In Tokapchi,
for instance, which forms a main subject area for the present study and where
Japanese immigration and settlement came later than in other districts, practically no Japanese immigrants were found in ca. 1874 (Hokkaido-chō, ed.,
1937, Vol. 3, p. 299). It was in 1882-1883 when a small party of Japanese settlers called "Banseisha" came to settle near Obihiro on the middle Tokapchi
to open up the interior part of the river valley (Note 10). In the upper
Tokapchi surveyed by the author not a single Japanese settler was found
even at the outset of the land allotment and the agricultural coaching programme launched in that area in 1886 (Notes 8-10). As a result the Tokapchi
Ainu remained free in their gathering activities and from Japanese pressure
and influence till a comparatively later period. Hunting of deer in the entire
Tokapchi area was banned in 1879 to all except the local Ainu (TAKAKURA,
1942, p. 437); salmon fishing in the upper Tokapchi, which had been prohibited
in 1883, was released later to local natives alone (TAKAKURA, 1942, p. 486).

According to the author's informants' accounts of their experiences, the
contemporary social intercourse between the interior Tokapchi Ainu and
Japanese was as follows. (Conditions in the Azuma valley seem to have
been much the same.) Every year when it was spring, Japanese agents came
by boat to the interior Ainu settlements in order to hire natives for employment at coastal fishing grounds. The selection of the persons to go was
decided at the *ukosanio*, assembly of the headman and house-heads of the
local group. Such negotiations with Japanese were generally conducted by a
representative called "ottena", an old title conferred by the feudal clan on
native officers under the "basho" system and still used among the Ainu after
its abolition by the Japanese Government. Sometimes the title "ottena" was
held concurrently by the traditional headman himself, as at Nitmap and Pipaushi in Tokapchi (Note 23, N12 and P6); sometimes it was held by someone
else, as at Moseushi (Note 23, M3 and M14). Ainus hired for labour at the
fishing coasts were mostly young men but included some women. Work for
women, such as drying of sea-tangles, was sometimes over in a relatively
short period; but work for men, chiefly salmon and sardine fishing, usually
lasted well into autumn. On return home these men had immediately to go
hunting at their huts with fellow members (for examples see Note 41,
Shiokoro's and Shurunke's families). In reward for their service at the fishing coasts they received wine and foodstuffs, such as rice and salt. In spring
Japanese fur traders also came to their settlements to exchange deer and bear
skins, bark clothes and other products for articles of clothing, such as cotton
fabrics, articles of taste and food, such as wine, tobacco, rice and salt. The

southwestern and coastal Ainu, who had been in long and frequent contact with Japanese, were already in the initial stage of using firearms (matchlocks). The use, however, was still quite limited; on the upper Tokapchi, in parti cular, the native Ainu continued depending on their traditional hand- and spring-bows with accompanying poisoned arrows.

Chapter II

(**10**) Historical survey of size and distribution of Ainu settlements.—Reference
has already been made in Notes 8 and 9 in Chapter I to the agriculturalization policy for the Ainu adopted by the Japanese Government in its earliest
phase of Hokkaido administration (Notes 8-9). The policy was carried out
in the northeastern districts in 1883 starting with Ashoro, followed in 1884
by Shiranuka, Akan, Kawakami and Abashiri, and in 1885 in Kusuri (Kushiro),
Akkeshi and Shari ; for Hitaka district in 1885 in Saru (TAKAKURA, 1942, p.
487) ; for the Tokapchi district in 1886 (YOSHIDA, 1955, p. 6, from a publication
by Kasai Branch Office) and for the Azuma district in 1888 (A Chronological
Table of Azuma Village History, compiled by the village office).

Prior to this period the natives living near the coasts of the south-western,
north-western and south-eastern districts had grown millet and other cereals
subsidiary to their gathering. But their farming and the areas under cultivation were insignificant (p. 41). In fact, even those Ainus who practised some
farming lived in small settlements scattered over areas chosen for traditional
gathering, just as did non-agriculturist Ainus who lived more inland. With
many of them the first difficulty lay in finding necessary areas of arable land
near enough to their settlements. The consideration led the Government to
move those Ainus into more favourable areas as preliminary to enforcing its
policy. It was desired at the same time that the hitherto scattered Ainu
settlements be brought together into smaller areas which would be convenient for instruction in farming and supervision. Accordingly, the natives of
Ashoro, Tushipet and Rikupet were moved to Ashoro, those of Kushiro to
tributaries, those of Tokapchi into nine areas on the Tokapchi and three
other areas on the Tushipet. Even in fertile Saru there were large-scale
removals made by two or three settlements and minor ones by almost all the
others (TAKAKURA, 1942, pp. 487-491). On a field survey by the present
writer information was collected relating to some of those removals of settle
ments in the Shikot, Azuma, Nukapira and Tokapchi valleys as well.

Now the present study is concerned primarily with the Ainu settlements
as they had been prior to this redistribution period. Even before these move-
ments brought about by the agriculturalization programme, some changes had
taken place in Ainu settlements in relation to Japanese activities, namely, the
fishery development projects by the Matsumae feudal clan. In 1635, for instance, when the Matsumae government opened Kusuri (Kushiro) fishing
grounds, they looked for expedient supply of labour from the upper Kusuri
Ainu, whom they transferred en masse to the Kusuri coast (HABARA, 1939, p.

71). With the development of their administration and the expansion of trading and fishing under their direction, there grew up increasingly larger and more constant demand for workers of great variety for employment at the trading and fishing posts and the watchhouses belonging to the guards. At these places almost all menial work was done by Ainus—cooking, night-and farm-watch and lookout; charcoal making, firewood gathering and helping at smithy, carpenter's shop and stable. Ainus worked also as courier, maid to Japanese officials, transportation coolie, post-house driver, ferryman, etc. Some of the Ainus in regular employment at Japanese establishments eventually settled down around these posts in increasing number (TAKAKURA, 1942, pp. 236-246). The result in time was an emergence at coastal places of new-type Ainu settlements with life dependent on Japanese. The strikingly greater size generally of these settlements and the greater number of houses contained as compared with older-type settlements may be seen from the field surveys made by T. MATSUURA in 1857-1858 (MASAMUNE, ed, 1937). Except for these, few Ainu settlements were found on the coast. A *pishun kotan*, coastal settlement, whose inhabitants practised sea-fishing as voluntary occupation for subsistence, actually stood on river banks near the estuary and not by the seaside (WATANABE, 1954, p. 62). The fact is borne out by T. MATSU-URA in his record of the distribution of native settlements and his description about them which follows. " Formerly the natives always lived on river courses and never at the seaside. People say that it was only with the development of this district under Japanese management that the natives came to live by the seaside and at the ' unjoya ', Japanese fishing and trading posts, to be employed as fishing hands" (MASAMUNE, ed, 1937, Vol. I, p. 170). Although the Ainus of *pishun kotan* voluntarily practised sea-fishing, it seems almost certain from the field survey by the present writer that it was only secondary in their scale of economy, which was always predominated by river-fishing, hunting and plant-gathering almost as much as it was with the interior *kimun kotan* Ainu (WATANABE, 1954, p. 62).

Before the introduction of the land-allotment programme, in spite of such changes in coastal settlements due to Japanese influence and the serious effects in consequence on their ways of life, the majority of the Ainu continued their traditional life of gathering in their traditional settlements. The settling of Japanese in the interior areas dates back only to quite recent times.

In order to see where and when Japanese immigrants came to settle in the Ainu territory, information was collected from the census manuals for 1957 or 1958 of the local offices in the areas concerned. The results are tabulated as follows:

Tokapchi District (including Otopuke and Satnai valleys)

Area Number	Name of Area	Year	First and Early Immigration of the Japanese to the Area
1	Shintoku	1897	First immigrants: 2 men.
		1902	Immigrants: 9 families.
		1907	Sudden increase in immigrants owing to establishment of a railway communication.
2	Memro	1886	First immigrants: 3 men.
3	Obihiro	1882	First immigrant: a man (advance party).
		1883	First group immigrants: a party of 32 people.
4	Kamishihoro	1903	First immigrants: a party of 6 men.
5	Otopuke	1880	First immigrant: a man.
		1885	Agricultural instruction to the Ainu by the governmental officials started.
		ca. 1887	The Ainu of the area started, under governmental instructions, emigration to the new settlements in the Tokapchi valley.
		1896	Removal of the local Ainu to the allotted areas in the Otopuke valley.
6	Kasai	ca. 1895	First immigrants: a family.
7	Nakasatnai	1897	First immigrants; subsequently came from various parts of the Japanese mainland.
8	Honbetsu	1880	Only a few Japanese used to come for barter with the Ainu.
		1896	First immigrant: a man.
		1897	First group immigrants.
9	Ikeda	1879	First immigrant: a family.
		1880	Several hundred Japanese came to engage in deer hunting and barter, living in temporary huts and Ainu houses located near the junction of the Tushipet river.
		1882	The hunters and merchants dispersed away owing to a sudden fall in the number of deer caused by a heavy snow fall. Only a few remained to settle down.
		1885–1889	Some officials were sent to the area to give agricultural instruction to the local Ainu.
		1886–1892	Several immigrants (less than five).

Azuma River

Area Number	Name of area	Year	First and Early Immigration of the Japanese to the Area
10	Azuma	1800	Some officials of the Tokugawa Shogunate and the Nambu clan immigrated to the coastal area.
		1870	An immigrant to the coast.
		1881	First immigrant to the interior.
		1887	Second immigrant to the interior.
		1888	The Ainu in the area were brought together to live in a new settlement, given instruction in agricultural technique.

Mukawa River

Area Number	Name of area	Year	First and Early Immigration of the Japanese to the Area
11	Mukawa	1875	A family came to settle, engaged in fishing and running a hotel business.
		1882	First immigrants as farmers: some families.

Saru River

Area Number	Name of area	Year	First and Early Immigration of the Japanese to the Area
12	Hiratori	1870	First immigrants: 2 officials as agricultural instructors. Immigrants subsequently came after them.
		1880	Establishment of a public office at the coastal settlement, Sarufuto.
		1899	Japanese houses totaled 300 or more; total population of the Japanese immigrants about 2000.
13	Hitaka	1905	First immigrant; a man.
		1907	Second immigrants: 3 men.

For the size and distribution of Ainu settlements in the days of gathering activities, HABARA quotes from Hokkaido Kyu-Dojin (The Former Natives of Hokkaido) published by the Hokkaido Government: " The Ainu combine a few to a dozen houses in a settlement and live scattered over wide areas " (HABARA, 1939, p. 73). TAKAKURA remarks: " An Ainu community used to be extremely small-sized. Tokunai Mogami in Yezo Zōshi (A Story-Book of Yezo) (1790) writes: ' In Yezo a settlement is composed of no more than five to seven houses. Ten houses is considered a large one, which is very rare.' Yezo-Zakki Yakusetsu (Translations from Miscellaneous Foreign Works on Yezo, translated by Teiyu BABA at the order of the Naga-

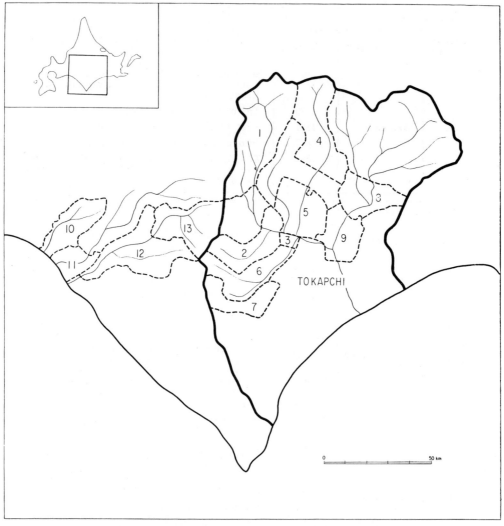

Reference Map for the Chart on Japanese Settlers.
The area numbers correspond to those given in the chart.

saki magistrate, published in 1809), vol. 2, contains a report of a Dutch
merchantship which touched Hokkaido in 1643 saying: 'A settlement of
twenty houses is about the largest I ever saw. Six or seven, even, eleven at
most, is the number of houses in a village. And these settlements lie far
between, seldom less than a mile apart'. In fact, according to records of the
Kansei and Kyōwa eras (ca. 1790 down to the later 1810's) when Japanese
influence first extended to these areas (Kondo Seisai Zenshu , Complete
Works of Seisai Kondo, vol. 1, p. 29), out of twenty-five settlements in six

' basho ' (districts) on Etorof of the Kurile Islands not one contained twenty houses. Only a few had a population of more than a hundred. In some cases a single house constituted a settlement " (TAKAKURA, 1942, p. 27).

For more concrete and comprehensive data on the size and distribution of Ainu settlements in those gathering days, reference should be made to T. MATSUURA, Yezo-Nissi-shū (Collected Diaries in Yezo, edited by A. MASA-MUNE, 1937). The book covers a series of explorations made in Ainu territories in 1857–1858 by Takeshiro MATSUURA, an official of the Tokugawa Shogunate. In spite of the extremely great value of the data it contains, the book has never received the wide utilization it deserves. Hence the data from his diaries have been tabulated by the present writer as follows:

Tokapchi River (in descending order of location)

Name of Settlement	Number of Ainu Houses	Number of Household Members in Each House	Remarks
Kamuiroki	1	4	
(No name mentioned)	2	5, 4 (the latter represented by an old woman).	Located near Satteki.
(No name mentioned)	2	2, 8	
Makunbetu	1	4	
Nitomafu (Nitmap)	3	23 in total	Arayok, the headman, and his lineage.
Okatomanai	3	2, 5, 7	
Hibaushi (Pipaushi)	2	(Number not stated)	
Chifuru	1	5	
Saoroputo	3	4, 5, 5	
Memroputu	2	4, 4	
Bibairuputo (Pipairuputu)	8	2, 2, 3, 4, 4, 6, 6, 7	
Obereberefu	2	4, 4	
Nubuka	4	(Number not stated)	
Hetchara	1	(Number not stated)	
Jiroto	5		
Horonokotcha	2		
Iikanhetu	10		
Kamokinai	4		
Yamwakkahira	Some		Some millet fields.
Furukeshi (Chiyota)	8		
Onnenai	2		
Tohioka	2		
Seyoi	4		
Tanneota	6		
Barautuka	2		

(The river forked here into two streams)

Name of Locality	Number of Ainu Houses		Remarks
Aneshum	6		
Nutabeto	3		
Urahoroputo	2		
Obekkohashi	9		
Betumoshiri	3		Being a ferry station at the river mouth.
Osaushi	11		Located by a Japanese seine-fishing ground.
Ootunai			A Japanese fishing and trading post near the river mouth.

Shikaripet River, a tributary of the Tokapchi

16 houses in total

Otopuke River, a tributary of the Tokapchi

21 houses in total

Tushipet River, a tributary of the Tokapchi

27 houses in total

Ashoro River, a tributary of the Tushipet

13 houses in total

Azuma River (in descending order of location)

Name of Locality	Number of Ainu Houses	Remarks
Ofumusenai	3	
Tonika	5	Plots cultivated by the Ainu.
Shiinai	5	
Kimunkotan	10	Many cultivated plots.
Funawatashi (named in Japanese meaning a ferry station)	3	The most downstream Ainu settlement located near the estuary.

Mukawa River (in descending order of location)

Name of Locality	Number of Ainu Houses	Remarks
Ninatumi	5	
Hattaruse	4	
(No name described)	6	

	Number	Remarks
Hohetufuto	15	Ainu houses continuously distributed crossing over small streams adjacent to each other, the Wennai, the Toyomanai, and the Yukoronai.
(No name described)	6	Located near Shufushinai.
Kaikuma	6	
Shittekinai (Ruheshihe)	4	
Kinaushi	8	
(No name mentioned)	2	
Ocharusenai (Ruheshihe)	3	
Ichimifu	6	Many plots cultivated by the Ainu.
Niwan	6	
Kinaushi	5	
Yukhetu	8	
Kirikachi	4	
Osannefu	1	
Moihetu	7	Many plots cultivated by the Ainu.
Kaanai	4	
Kenashoro	4	
Impoppe	6	
Chin	10	
Mukawaputo	4	Located near the estuary. A ferry- and rest-station along the coast-road linking Japanese fishing posts.

Saru River (in descending order of location)

Name of Locality	Number of Ainu Houses	Remarks
Horosaru (Porosaru)	22	Many plots cultivated by the Ainu.
Osatnai	20	
Penakori	11	
Kankan	3	
Bihaushi (Pipaushi)	15	Cultivated plots.
Nifutani (Niputani)	27	
Hiratori (Piratori)	31	
Saraha (Sarupa)	19	
Shumunkotu	30	Many cultivated plots.
Hitaraba (Pitarupa)	3	
Biraka (Piraka)	24	Cultivated plots. The most downstream settlement.

Nukabira River, a tributary of the Saru

Nukkehetu (Nukkipet)		House number not described.
Niyoi	9	
Shikerehe	5	

Ishikari River

The main stream (in descending order of location)

Name of Locality	Number of Ainu Houses	Remarks
Wenbetsu	5	
Asakara	1 (or 2?)	
Kinkushibetu	2	Each represented by an old woman.
Ochinkaba	1	
Mem	5	Each of two of the houses represented by an old woman.
Betchiushi	6	
Ijan	3	
Betubara	2	
Tokufuto	2	Cultivated plots.
Tuishikari	1 at least	Located by a Japanese fishing station " banya ".
Ishikari		Japanese fishing and trading post " unjoya " near the estuary.

Yuhari River, a tributary of the Ishikari

Taikeshi	3	Cultivated plots.
Tapkofu	1	Cultivated plots.

Shikot River, a tributary of the Yuhari

Osakmanai	5	
Nunnai	2	
Orokkochi	4	
Ruen	3	
Besa (Pesa)	5	
Rankoushi	3	
Chitose (name in Japanese)	15	An Ainu settlement by a Japanese fishing and trading post. Cultivated plots.
Osat	9	
Isarifuto	7	Located by a Japanese fishing station " banya ".
(Along the Isari, a small tributary)	9 in total	Many cultivated plots.
Shumamafuto	1	Situated near a Japanese rest-house.

Teshio River (in ascending order of location)

Name of Locality	Number of Ainu Houses	Number of House-hold Members in Each House	Remarks
The estuary			A Japanese fishing and trading post, " unjoya ".
Teutohitara	1	2	
Toinotafu	1	8	
Aheshinai	3	2, 3, 3	
Tonbeppo	2	6, 7	
Otoinefu	1	5	
Okurumatomanai	1	12	
Henkeniubu	2	2, 4	
Nayorofuto (Naibuto)	2	3, 5	At the junction of the Nayoro R.
(The river forked here into two streams)			
Main Stream:			
Kenefuchi	1	9	
Utu	3	4, 4, 4	One of the houses represented by an old woman.
Kunkattekkuru	3	4, 6, 8	
Sattekuhetu	3	3, 3, 4	
Nayoro River:			
Chirusushi	2	2, 5	
Henkekiushi-hitara	1	7	
Chinomi	2	2, 6	
Kamuicham	1	4	
Toushumakomanai	2	3, 5	
Shufunuto	1	7	

Kusuri (Kushiro) River (in descending order of location)

Name of Locality	Number of Ainu Houses	Remarks
Kutcharo	9	Located by Kutcharo Lake.
Teshikaka	8	One of them represented by an old woman.
Kumaushi	1	
Tohro	16	Located by Lake Tohro near the coastal plain.
Kusuri		A Japanese fishing and trading post near the estuary.

Akan River, a tributary of the Kushiro

Ikitaraushi	1	
Akihetu	3	
Soushi	3	
Fuushinai (Shitakaro)	4	2 houses were represented by an old woman respectively.
Shitakaroputo	5	The most downstream settlement. 2 houses represented by an old woman respectively.

(**11**) To quote from a report on the Saru Ainu: "The word *kotan* is used in two ways: as a residential area, and as a territorial group forming an integrated social unit. The *kotan* in the latter sense had an hereditary chief, called *kotan kor kur*". And again: "The two territorial groups (the two *kotan* of Panke-Pirautur and Penke-Pirautur), though distinct as residential areas, were socially and politically one Pirautur *kotan* ruled over by a single chief. So was Penakori; though divided now in two separate areas, it has always been a single *kotan* politically". (IZUMI, 1951, p. 33). No attempt, however, has been made to study more minutely the inner-structure and interrelationship of these two groups.

(**12**) For the kinship organization of the local group, a conclusion has already been offered by TAKAKURA on various historical documents, as follows: "Such *kotan* as came under our observation were more complex, embracing elements from other *kotan* besides their own kin: some of the larger *kotan* comprised a mixture of more than two kin groups. But the core and substance was an extremely narrow kin group" (TAKAKURA, 1942, p. 28). The chief of a *kotan* as kin group (*kotan koru kuru, kotan* owning man) was naturally the family head (*chise koru kuru*) of the head house (*porochise*) as well as the head of the kinsmen (*utarapake*) (ibid., p. 29). "In time the *kotan* came to embrace a number of non-consanguinity elements from other areas, but it was ruled out to receive any except through some kinship relations. A mere territorial relationship might mean a proximity of residence but little social integration" (Teikoku Gakushi-in, ed, 1944, p. 59).

A report by K. SUGIURA and S. IZUMI on a joint survey they made of the Saru Ainu in the summer 1951 fails to shed much light on the role of kinship in the Ainu local group. In fact, practically all they have to say on the subject is: "It is acknowledged by elders of the Saru basin that formerly some *kotan* were organized by the male members of the *shine* (one and the same) *itokpa*. But changes in the *kotan* in recent times make it extremely difficult for the writers to verify their view. As seen today, a *kotan* may embrace more than two *ekashi ikiru;* yet some *kotan* carry suggestions that

formerly one *kotan* represented one *ekashi ikiru* (SUGIURA, 1951, p. 19). Again:
"It (a *kotan* as social unit) has a *kotan* chief, *kotan koru kuru*. ....and its
people in many cases belong to families of the same blood (*ekashi ikiru*), rarely
to groups of different bloods" (IZUMI, 1951, p. 35). And: "The *kotan koru
kuru* is hereditary. In some cases his family is the oldest in the *ekashi ikiru*
of the *kotan*" (ibid.). For the related problem of how a newcomer is admitted
into *kotan* membership, see Note 14, especially its latter part.

(**13**) A definition and examples of *ekashi itokpa* are given by KŌNO (1934).
Some *ekashi itokpa* bear a design held by the Ainu to represent an animal,
or, more exactly, part of an animal: those given by KŌNO as actual examples
show the footprint of the brown bear, that of a bird whose name is unknown
and the fin of the dolphin (or grampus?) respectively (KŌNO, 1936). The fact
has been noted by some writers as evidence for a survival of a totemic custom
or totemism; but such a theory has not been accepted by others. The variety
of the *ekashi itokpa* among the Ainu inhabitants in the Saru valley in 1939 was
investigated by NATORI: the result shows a conformity of the marks among
the Ainu on the upper course and a diversity among those on the lower course
(NATORI, 1940; Note 8).

(**14**) Membership of local group.—Sugiura, on his survey of the Saru River
area, came on two conflicting sets of informants as to the membership formula
of the local group. According to one set "some *kotan* (local group as classified
by the present writer) were formerly composed exclusively of members of the
same *ekashi ikiru* group sharing the same *itokpa* (ancestral mark) and *pase
onkami* (ritual of some important *kamui*-spirit; properly called *kamuinomi
pase onkami*) in common. When such a *kotan* admits a member of another
kotan belonging to another *ekashi ikiru*, the person is required to give up
his old *itokpa* and *pase onkami* for those of the new *kotan* and become a member of the *ekashi ikiru*" (SUGIURA, 1951, p. 18.). According to the other set
of informants "it was thought too cruel to force the newcomer to accept the
itokpa and *pase onkami* of the new *kotan* and renounce his hereditary *pase
onkami*." (Ibid.) A case was brought to his notice in which "a male member,
on adoption or marriage into another family (but not on immigration), not
only received his new *itokpa* and *pase onkami* but retained his old ones as
well, which he handed down to his descendants" (ibid.).

Of these two conflicting formulas SUGIURA regards the first as norm and
the second as deviation. He remarks: "It might be assumed that some of
those newcomers retained their old *pase onkami* along with those of their
new village (*kotan*). The result was a confusion arising between different
itokpa ahd *pase onkami* which originally marked one *ekashi ikiru* from another.

The *ekashi ikiru*, instead of standing for a lineage in the strict sense of the word, tends to serve as a means of consolidating the *kotan* as a territorial group" (ibid.). While stating, however, that "the male members of the *kotan* constituted one or more patrilineal kinship groups, called *ekashi ikiru*," SUGI-URA makes no reference as to how an outsider might gain a membership of "a *kotan* with more than one *ekashi ikiru* group" (ibid.). For this point we must turn to IZUMI, who worked with SUGIURA on the same survey. Resting wholly on the first set of data without touching on the second which was regarded by SUGIURA as deviation from the norm, IZUMI gives the following remarks. "Usually, members of a *kotan* consist of families of one and the same family line (*ekashi ikiru*), and rarely of more than one.... Every stranger entering the *kotan* must be reported to the chief, *kotan koru kuru*.... The chief (after much deliberation) calls a village assembly, *ukoramkoru*, to ask for general consent.... If married, the newcomers receive permission to put up a temporary shed on the *kotan keshi*, lower outskirt of the village. If unmarried, the person is taken in charge of some willing household. These people are called *tomta ek kur* (newcomer) or *iyor un kuru* (hanger-on). They are not the members of the village so that they have difficulty in getting a living within the *iworu* (rendered 'arena of life' by IZUMI; p. 70 and Note 58) of the *kotan*. As a result, a bachelor will have to offer himself as servant to the household where he is staying, doing such work as is appointed by the master. A married couple have to sustain their lives by labouring in the service of the *kotan koru kuru* and some other person. At the end of a year or two the chief calls another assembly, at which, if there is no objection, a ritual called *tomta onkami* is arranged to take the newcomer formally into *kotan* membership. If, however, there are many objections, the person is driven out of the community.... If the newcomer is too young to know his *itokpa* (family mark) and *pase onkami* (*kamuinomi* ritual for some important *kamui*), or if he is marrying a girl of the *kotan* as son-in-law (*inau ramat*, heir), the person goes off his old *ekashi ikiru* and obtains new *itokpa* and *pase onkami* to become a member of the *ekashi ikiru*. This procedure is what is called *itokpa kikiraye*. If the village is composed of more than one *ekashi ikiru*, he goes into one or the other of the groups. An adopted son naturally goes into that group to which his adoptive family belongs. In all other cases it is usual for the newcomer, by means of *itokpa kikiraye*, to go into that of the household where he is staying as *iyor un kuru*. For married *tomta* who are familiar with their *ekashi ikiru*, its *itokpa* and *pase onkami*, the *itokpa kikiraye* is not so simple a procedure. If a *tomta* is thoughtful and is desirous of entering any one of the *ekashi ikiru* groups in the *kotan*, he must either entrust or contribute the best part of his treasures to the *kotan koru kuru* (if there is only one *ekashi ikiru* in the village) or to that *utaru pake*, head of an *ekashi ikiru*, who has approved of his *itokpa kikiraye* (if there are more than one)" (IZUMI, 1951, pp. 34–35). So far as the Tokapchi and Otopuke valleys before the land allotment are concerned, there is no evidence of a village assembly to assume such political functions in the days when the headmen swayed in the traditional way. Again, in these two valleys at least, *itokpa kikiraye* did not represent a transmission of an *itokpa* with associated ritual for affiliation into a local group. Instead, it is said to have meant an exchange of *ekashi itokpa* between two persons out of peculiar interest in the history of each other's *itokpa*, though detailed circumstances for such an action are not known. When such occurred, though very rarely with justification, it is said that the procedure required full sanction and directions from the headmen concerned.

Now the first question that arises will be about the relation between *utaru pake* (head of *ekashi ikiru*) and *kotan koru kuru* (head of local group). Concerning this point IZUMI remarks: " The *kotan koru kuru* is head of the *kotan* as territorial group; in case of a *kotan* of *shine* (one) *ekashi ikiru* he is at the same time *utaru pake*, head of the kin group that forms the *kotan*. Within a *kotan* with more than one *ekashi ikiru*, so views one informant, Hachiro Kurokawa of Nukipet, each *ekashi ikiru* had an *utar pake* of its own, that of the most influential acting as *kotan koru kuru* as well. In contradiction to the view another informant, Kunimatsu Nitani of Niputani, informs: ' The word *utaru pake* means, not "Zoku-chō" (*head of ekashi ikiru*), but a " big man " or " old man ". If you look for a word meaning "Zoku-chō" the word " *utaru koru kuru* " (person who owns people) would be more appropriate. *Utaru koru kuru* in this sense would then be synonymous with *kotan koru kuru*. However, even in a *kotan* with more than one *ekashi ikiru* the presence of an *utaru koru kuru* apart from the *kotan koru kuru* has never been heard of.' More extensive investigation seems necessary before anything can be said with certainty about which of these views is correct or if either view holds good in some particular localities...." (ibid. p. 35).

Regarding this conflict of information SUGIURA makes the following remarks. " However, when more than one *ekashi ikiru* groups formed a *kotan*, did only one head and no one else represent the *kotan* ?.... No evidence has been available to prove the theory that the *ekashi ikiru* formed a territorial group on the basis of the *kotan*, its chief (*utaru pake*) directing and controlling the male members sharing *shine* (one) *itokpa*. On the other hand it seems that there is not sufficient ground to deny the presence of the *utaru pake*. As far as is known today, the social life in the *kotan*, conducted chiefly on family basis, shows no sign of a strong solidarity worthy of an *ekashi ikiru*. The *pase onkami* mentioned above and the ancestor-ritual to be mentioned later are both apparently on a family level and not events for collec-

tive participation of the *ekashi ikiru*. Nor are there signs of the cooperation
of the *ekashi ikiru* as a whole for such economic purposes as ownership of
community property or cooperation in production and distribution. The
only exception is the reported presence in the field of politics of what is
called '*utaru pake*'; but what the post actually was remains unknown"
(SUGIURA, 1951, p. 20). At any rate, the relation between *kotan* (local group)
and *ekashi ikiru* (kin group) has never been made clear, and not without
reasons.

A perusal of the reports by SUGIURA and IZUMI makes one suspect that,
from the difficulty of securing competent informants, they could not obtain
any concrete data on the social activities of the Ainu as observed and participated in by the native informants themselves in the days before the introduction of land allotment with more or less universal redistribution in their
habitation and the destruction of their traditional group life. Another important factor accountable for their failure seems to be their regarding *ekashi
ikiru*, *itokpa* and *pase onkami* as mere symbols of the Ainu kin group, or as
mere criteria for distinguishing one group from another. The result was an
almost complete disregard of the inherent meaning and function of these
institutions. The term "*ekashi ikiru*", for instance, is treated as if it were an
everyday word for the patrilineal kin group of Ainu males as a mere social
unit. As used by the Ainu themselves, it meant the unit group that observed
kamuinomi rituals including *pase onkami*. Moreover, the word was exclusively
for use on the occasion of, and in connection with, *kamuinomi* rituals. Again,
itokpa, instead of being a mere family crest for showing lineage, was the
very mark of ancestry to be incised on such objects as the *inau* for offering
to *kamui spirits*. It also formed an essential item of the rites of *kamuinomi*.
The *itokpa* and *kamuinomi* through spatial orientation of the *kamui*, maintained an inseparable connection with the habitat of the Ainu. With these
rituals for cosmological adjustments, their technological adaptation to their
habitat was made complete. In a sense their social organizations were means
to maintain those relationships. Such, then, are some of the considerations
that are prerequisite to an understanding of the Ainu groups (Chapter IV).

(**15**) Obtaining new *ekashi itokpa*, patrilineal ancestor mark—cases and reasons.

TAKAKURA, on historical evidence, remarks: "Though the sharing of a
family mark in common was based on the fact of consanguinity, its use was
sometimes extended to those not related in blood. For example, a male servant from a different area living with a family might be favourably admitted
and made a sharer of the mark of the family" (Teikoku Gakushiin, ed., 1944b,
p. 57).

In 1939 NATORI made investigations among the living Saru river Ainu concerning the relation between the patrilineal descent, *ekashi ikiru*, and the pattern of the *ekashi itokpa*, patrilineal family mark for carving on the *inau*-offerings used in all *kamuinomi*-rituals and also on *kikeushi pashui*, the special libation-wand for rituals of some important *kamui*. His report (NATORI, 1940) contains several cases, with respective circumstances furnished, of the *ekashi itokpa* of one male line being handed down to another along with its *pase ongami* (or *onkami*) ritual for some *kamui* of special importance. The cases cited below, referring to *ekashi itokpa* engraved on the *kikeushi pashui* and not on the *inau*, will give, though vaguely, some hint and verification on the relation between the *itokpa*, the *ekashi ikiru* and the local group.

Case 1. Porosaru settlement today contains three distinct patrilineal Ainu families of long standing—those of Yukashite and Hoshipi, both originally from Tokapchi, and that of Rikizo, known to have lived in the Saru valley from time immemorial. Of the *ekashi itokpa* in use there is only one common to all, that of Rikizo handed down for generations among the Saru people (NATORI, 1940, pp. 207-208).

Case 2. Except Nukipet on the uppermost Nukapira which is tributary to the Saru, the six settlements on the upper Saru—Nioi, Shikerebe, Porosaru, Okotnai, Osatnai and Penakori—all share for the males of their old patrilineal families one *itokpa* inherited from the old Saru natives regardless of their origins (ibid., pp. 204-212).

Case 3. Onnep, grandfather of old Tekkerikin of Okotnai settlement, was of a male line of Shikoma on the Shibichari river. He was adopted by a family of a former Saru *kotan* Okotnai and inherited the *kamuinomi* of his adopted *kotan* with its *itokpa* (ibid., pp. 209-210).

Case 4. All the eight families now inhabiting Penakori settlement are of the same blood and share the same *itokpa*. When traced back along male lines, they resolve into two lineages, five related with Tadao's who descends from a headman of the former *kotan* of Penakori and three others related with old Sanouk. One of Sanouk's patrilineal ancestors came from Tokapchi; the mother of Ekoroekun, fifth on Tadao's male line, and the mother of Itoman-guru, fifth on Sanouk's male line, were sisters. The relationship led Itoman-guru to be adopted into Penakori settlement, making the two families sharers of one *itokpa* (ibid., p. 210).

In the above case of Penakori and those of other settlements further up-stream, the new *itokpa* inherited displaced the old one, at least, on the *kikeushi pashui*; nevertheless, the *pase ongami* ritual, ritual to *kamui*-spirit of special importance, and its worship attendant on the old *itokpa* were kept intact. On the other hand, at Niputani and other lower settlements the new *itokpa* as well as the old sometimes became composite in the carving of, at least, the *kikeushi pashui*.

Case 5. Yaibaro, ancestor of Isonoashi, an old man of Niputani, ran away from his home on the lower Saru. Arriving at the former *kotan* of Niputani, he met Pikun, who found him a promising youth and married him to a daughter of a relative, thus making him sharer of the *shine* (one) *itokpa* with himself (ibid., p. 213).

Case 6. Kenkichi, an inhabitant of Niputani, is descended by male line from Hao who came from Nioi, the former *kotan* on the upper Saru, to Niputani, the former *kotan*, on the middle reaches. His *itokpa* is a composite of the *itokpa* common in all the upper settlements including Nioi and that of Matsuji's family living in the present Niputani, descendants by male line of an inhabitant of the former Niputani *kotan* (ibid., p. 213).

Case 7. Arikate, father of Isonoashi, is a brother of Ukarikun, father of Matsuji, a descendant by male line of a member of the former *kotan* of Niputani. For certain reasons he was adopted by Pirakane, a member of Piraga, a lower Saru *kotan*. As he inherited the *kamuinomi*-ritual of his adoptive family, his *itokpa* represents a composite of his old one similar to Matsuji's and that of Pirakane's lineage (ibid., p. 214).

Case 8. Sueki is a son of Akchainu of the former *kotan* of Piratori by a Piraga girl named Chishiruye and not by his wife. He inherits the *itokpa* of his mother's father of Piraga and not his father's (ibid., p. 226).

Another report by INUKAI and NATORI gives the following as an indication of the relation between the *ekashi itokpa*, the family line, and the local group as existed among the Tokapchi Ainu.

The fifth ancestor by male line before Furukawa, Ainu resident of a Tokapchi settlement, Fushiko, came from the former *kotan* of Bebet on the Ishikari to Tokapchi, where he married a local woman and settled down. Thus Furukawa possesses two *ekashi itokpa*. One is called *Bebet un itokpa*, *itokpa* at Bebet, and is for most *kamuinomi*-rituals he observes. But the most important of all the *inau*, *pakkai inau* for supporting the bear's head in the bear festival, carries *Shupsara un itokpa*, Shupusara being the name of a former Tokapchi *kotan* near where now stands Fushiko (INUKAI and NATORI, 1940, p. 81).

(16) When Kazari, my informant from Otopuke, lived at Rucha settlement, a sister of her father, who had married into Shikaripet in Tokapchi, came

home to Rucha with her husband, a Tokapchi man, and their children and, after staying for about four years at a house of their building close by Kazari's, went back again to their area.

An ancestress five generations before Kazari, who came from Arumoisan, or Kitami as it is now called, was turned out of home by her husband who was also of Arumoisan. Crossing the mountains with an infant boy, she came over to Otopuke seeking help. Here, after working for some time as *ussiu*, servant, to the then headman of Naitai, she was remarried to an Otopuke man; her son when grown up married a local daughter and settled down as a regular member of the local group.

A few more examples follow which are related to the *anun utari* that came to the Tokapchi river area from the Ishikari. An Ishikari married couple came across the mountains with two sons called Ukachipi and Kotumiseainu, a daughter called Shureshu and an unmarried young man. They came to Nitmap *kotan*, whose headman—by what process or circumstances no one now knows—arranged for them eventually to build a house at Penke Pipaushi, and lived there. Whether the man and woman went back to Ishikari or not is unknown; when Ushino, my informant from Nitmap, knew, they had both already died. Their children who had come to Tokapchi when very young grew up there. Ukachipi married an elder sister of Ekarison of Sanenkoro *kotan* (Genealogical Chart 5, S 11), Kotumiseainu married a woman of Shupusara *kotan* on the middle Tokapchi and Shureshu, the daughter, became wife of Hontomoainu of Kumaushi *kotan* (Genealogical Chart 4, KM 29). The young man brought with them from Ishikari afterwards went home, where he married a local woman; later he came again with his wife to live in Tokapchi and there begot a son. But later he again went back to Ishikari.

There were two families who had come to Tokapchi from Chikapuni in Ishikari where they were to return after a few years. They were Tamanipeki (Genealogical Chart 2, N3) and her husband and Tuapanu (Genealogical Chart 5, S7) and her husband with their young daughters Returen and Tukisamat and son Yaitekka. Little is known about what circumstances or relationship had brought them where they were; but at any rate Inautakaainu (Genealogical Chart 6, M3), who married a woman from Kuttarashi and lived at Moseushi, and his sister Wenshiko (Genealogical Chart 2, N7), wife of Arayok of Nitmap, were Tamanipeki's children by her first husband; Kotanumat (Genealogical Chart 7, ST9), wife of Mauekainu of the Satnai area, was her child by her second husband that came with her to Tokapchi. Tukisamat (Genealogical Chart 5, S17), first daughter of Tuapano, was also married to Opittakoro of Sanenkoro *kotan* in Tokapchi.

There is no doubt about these children of Tamanipeki and Tuapano having married before their parents went home to Ishikari, but little can be known as to when and how their marriages came about. When Tamanipeki and Tuapano went home, Wenshiko and her husband Arayok with another man saw them part of the way. On their way back, in a border mountain of Ishikari and Tokapchi, a bear attacked them and killed the two men. The women escaped and came back to Tokapchi, where they settled down. Tamanipeki was old; she remained a widow all her life. Tuapanu was re-married to Shunkran of Kuttarashi (Genealogical Chart 5, S8).

(17)   The formation of a kind of corporate group by a number of local groups whose cores were patrilineally related, has already been suggested by TAKA-KURA on historical documents, although no discrimination was made between settlement group and local group. He states: " This fact (supreme importance being attached to family lines) made even a *kotan* chief to obey in reverence the head house of the mother *kotan*. The result was a number of chiefs who exercised a vast influence over several *kotan* as masters of head houses.... Among the best known of such chiefs in history were Shakshain of the Shibichari, Obinishi of the Saru, and Hankase of the Ishikari, each of whom was not only head of a single *kotan* but also a big chief controlling several *kotan* in their areas. Actually, however, there were few occasions for co-operation between several *kotan*, so that, save for joint ritual observance and adjustment of inter-settlement disputes, those big chiefs remained as mere head of the *kotan* under their direct control. The *kotan* was for the Ainu the unit of social life") TAKAKURA, 1942, pp. 29-30). Again, he notices the presence of a (patrilineal) kin group with a common family mark (*itokpa*), a common deity (*paseonkami*) and deriving, in the belief of the Ainu them-selves, from a common male ancestor (*ekashimoto*); and this he terms "uji-zoku" (clan) (TAKAKURA, in Teikoku Gakushi-in, ed., 1944, pp. 57-58). He concludes that though its functional characteristics are unknown, the 'clan' in olden times had apparently a joint responsibility in matters of offence and retaliation; that the largest possible of all Ainu kinship organizations was the (patrilineal) 'clan' or 'federation of clans' organized on occasions against some common enemy (ibid. p. 58). No reference is made to the relationship between the 'clan' or 'federation of clans' and the territorial groups.

The existence of the terms denoting the upper group, *peni un utaru*, and the lower group, *pana un utaru*, on a river, or the upper, the middle and the lower group of a river, has been pointed out by KINTAICHI with regard to the Ishikari River (KINTAICHI, 1937, p. 109), by IZUMI with the Saru River (IZUMI, 1951, p. 31), and by SUGIURA with the Shibichari (K. SUGIURA's oral information to the writer). It remains to be proved, however, if the larger categories each stood for a corporate kin group in any sense. In the upper Tokapchi area there are found two terms *peni un utaru* and *petomun utaru* denoting upper-stream people living in Sanenkoro and *kotans* above it, and lower-stream people living in Chirokto and *kotans* below it, respectively. The term to denote the people of the middle course was not kept in memory by my informant Ushino. The first at least, it seems, indicates the extreme upstream *shine itokpa* group, but nothing definite can be known.

(**18**)   The presence of a territorial group based on the unit of a river valley, already suggested by NATORI (NATORI, 1940), and TAKAKURA (TAKAKURA's oral information to IZUMI in IZUMI, 1951, p. 30), has been confirmed by IZUMI on his survey of the Saru River (IZUMI, 1951).   That on the Saru as elsewhere the territorial group represented a kind of corporate group might be inferred from IZUMI's account of joint actions in time of disputes with other river groups, of joint ritual observance praying against tidal waves and landslides, and of repelling trespasses of other river members on their areas.   At any rate little has been made clear about the relationship between this and various smaller territorial groups.   Nor has the fact ever been noticed that the inhabitants of the larger river systems such as the Tokapchi, instead of forming a single river group, constituted more than one on the basis of each "river" as distinguished in the Ainu classification.

(**19**)   Concerning the *Huchi Ikiru*.

An aged Tokapchi informant says: "A *shine huchi ikiru*, when three generations back, goes out of memory and little can be known about it".

A certain female informant was able to name 35 women of her *shine huchi ikiru* within a depth of six generations (SUGIURA, 1951, p. 209).   Another woman is said to have as many as 20 living female relatives of her *huchi ikiru* (SEGAWA, 1951, p. 251).

It is assumed by SUGIURA that a *huchi ikiru* group was symbolized by one and the same form of the *upshoru kut*, chastity belt (SUGIURA, 1951, pp. 3 and 21). Doubt may be raised, however, as to whether so many different forms existed; in fact, the possibility is that some same forms, like some family names, might have found wide distribution beyond the sphere of a single kin group, in the present case, a *huchi ikiru* group.

Inherent difficulty has impeded any satisfactory investigation on the various forms of the *upshoru kut* and their relation with the *huchi ikiru*. SEGAWA, in her studies on Ainu beliefs about it and related Ainu ideas and attitudes, states as follows.

"It is affirmed by every Ainu that there was slight difference in the braiding of cords attached to the *upshoru kut* or in their number according to different *shine huchi ikiru*. But it is unthinkable that so great a variety of forms as generally suggested could have existed. Some information has been

obtained that difference in forms might correspond to different social status of
the ancestry, different characteristics of the *kotan*, and different river courses
and districts. It is also suggestive of the presence of a place of origin to
each matrilineal ancestress and of difference in rank of each *huchi ikiru* line.
At any rate, if *shine upshoru* relationship has perpetuated itself through cen-
turies (meaning perhaps that the forms of *upshoru kut* have been handed
down from generation to generation matrilineally), a very small variety of
ancient *upshoru kut*, originated by a few ancestresses, must have come down
ever spreading without people's knowing" (SEGAWA, 1951, p. 69).

As is pointed out by SEGAWA, the secret nature of the *upshoru kut* barred
female members themselves from a direct and actual knowledge of girdle
forms worn by other members. It is noteworthy that actual identification of
female members of a *shine upshoru* was made, not by different forms of the
upshoru kut, but after all by tracing female forebears back along the matrilineal line, that is, the line of the *shine huchi ikiru*. In short, even if the
members of a *shine huchi ikiru* shared one form of *upshoru kut*, it may not
follow that bearers of one form belonged all to one *huchi ikiru* membership.

For forms, beliefs, myths and other ideas and practices relating to the
upshoru kut see reports by KŌNO and NATORI (KŌNO, 1931; NATORI, 1945,
pp. 91-112 and pp. 185-201). It should be also mentioned that MUNRO gives
new important information of various girdles attributed to various *kamui*
(MUNRO, 1962, pp. 142-3).

(**20**)   The practice of avoidance in marriage, since it was more aversion than
prohibition, was susceptible of evasion in compelling circumstances. If need
be, man and woman of the category were enabled to marry by going through
a ritual procedure: the woman concerned went through a ritual known as
upshoru kikiraye, at which she changed her *upshoru kut*, the girdle she wore,
made for her by a woman of her proper *huchi ikiru*, usually her grandmother
or mother for another *upshoru kut* prepared by a woman of the other *huchi
ikiru*. There is no evidence of her marriage then requiring any sanction of
the whole *huchi ikiru* group. It seems that it could take place simply at her
parents' discretion and with due ritual observance at their hands.

(**21**)   They were usually her matrilineal close relatives such as her mother,
sisters and/or daughters who could conveniently come to her. Only when
they failed, any woman related to her by *huchi ikiru* kinship would be called
instead. There also could be and actually were some women of the same
huchi ikiru who knew one another only by their names but had never met
together. SUGIURA reports an interesting case of a woman, Teki, from
the Atsuga valley who married a man in a distant *kotan* in the Saru

valley. The only woman of her *huchi ikiru* in her husband's *kotan* has been her mother's mother's mother's sister's daughter's daughter's daughter, Hatu. Teki became intimate with her after this woman came to marry in the *kotan*. Since then, Teki has been assisted by Hatu in childbirth and illness and has counseled with her in such private matters as would be secret to other persons (SUGIURA, 1951, p. 206).

(22) Intermarriage and "basho" or district system.—On the evidence of an old document from a trading post, TAKAKURA points out a custom among the Ainu formerly of aversion against marriages between people of different "basho" or districts (TAKAKURA, 1942, p. 336; for "basho" see Note 6).

  The area occupied by the four river groups of Shipet, Otopuke, Satnai and Tushipet living on the main and tributary waters of the Tokapchi river system and walled on three sides by the great divide of Hokkaido and its branches, constituted the Tokapchi "Basho". Among the Ainu on the upper Tokapchi, the Satnai and the Otopuke at least, as described in the text, there seems to have been a strong tendency to intermarriage within the area, i. e. the Tokapchi Basho, which appears to be in agreement with TAKAKURA's account. It is questionable, however, whether or not the sphere of intermarriage always corresponded in extent with the "basho" as in the case of Tokapchi. It is not known on what basis and in what manner the demarcating line of a "basho" was drawn; but it is said that "it seems to have been based on the boundary of the headman's sphere of influence, that is, the boundary of the hunting and fishing grounds of the 'ujizoku' (clan) or 'buzoku' (tribe) concerned" (Hokkaido-chō, ed., 1937, Vol. 2, p. 105).

  HABARA (1939, p. 131), TAKAKURA (Teikoku Gakushi-in, ed., 1944b, p. 55) and NATORI (1945, p. 123) have come to one and the same conclusion that the Ainu formerly practised endogamy within the group of patrilineal kinsfolk. It is called "ujizoku" (clan) by HABARA (1939, p. 131) as well as TAKAKURA (Teikoku Gakushi-in, ed., 1944b, pp. 55 and 57); however, the Ainu term for it is unknown. HABARA gives no definition of his term "ujizoku", stating merely that it is divided into one to several sections each belonging to a *kotan* (HABARA, 1939, p. 209). TAKAKURA's definition of the "ujizoku" (clan) is given in the following statement: "the clan the members of which believe themselves to have branched from a common male ancestor, *ekashimoto*, have a common family mark, *itokpa*, and a cult of a common principal deity, *paseonkami*" (Teikoku Gakushi-in, ed., 1944b, p. 57). In this description, the relationship of the 'clan' with the territorial group remains unexplained; however, it is suggested in his statement quoted in Note 17. There he points out that the 'clan' seems to have been the basis on which the sphere of intermarriage among the Ainu was determined (ibid., p. 57). NATORI makes another

important point that "the sphere of their intermarriage was formerly prescribed by both the family mark indicating their patrilineal descent and the
type of the chastity belt indicating their matrilineal descent" (NATORI, 1945,
p. 124), though no further details on this point have been given by the same
author. For *upshoru kut* (the so-called chastity belt) exogamy see Note 19.

(**23**) Explanation of the genealogical charts concerning the local groups of
the upper Tokapchi valley.
Kuttarashi (K) Eight houses; of which seven were inhabited each by a
simple family and the remaining one by the househead (K29) and his widowed
mother (K12). No one of the eight male house-heads was from other districts.
Three of them (K20, 21 and 22) were sons of a man (K7) from the Ishikari
river area who settled down in marriage; another (K29), a patrilineal relation
to P15, was descended through males from an Ishikari man who came to live
here some generations before. The remaining four house-heads (K17, 18, 28
and 33) were originally descended through the male line from Tokapchi Ainus;
the then headman of Kuttarashi (K17) and his younger brother (K18) among
the rest were patri-kin of the headman of Nitmap (N12) actually linked lineally
to him; so was K28, though of less distinct line of descent.
  1. Native of Nitmap; came to live at Kuttarashi and here gave birth
     to children.
  2. Came as bride from Asahikawa on the Ishikari.
  3. Patrilineally related to the headman of Nitmap (N12), sharing with
     him the *shine itokpa*, same male ancestor mark.
  4. Closely related to P15 through male line; descended patrilineally
     from an Ishikari man.
  5. Native and inhabitant of Kuttarashi.
  6. Came as bride either from Memroputu or Pipairu.
  7. Came from Asahikawa and settled down in marriage.
  8. Native of Kuttarashi.
  9. Native inhabitant of Kuttarashi.
  10. Claimed relationship to N8, late headman of Nitmap. Died from a
      blow received from her husband; she left a will by which her young
      son (K28) was taken in charge of N8.
  11. Native inhabitant of Kuttarashi.
  12. Native of Kuttarashi. Had for some time been a widow; her
      daughters had all married and she lived with her eldest son (K29).
  13. Late headman of Nitmap; of genuine descent from Tokapchi Ainus.
  14. Later went to Moseushi in Shikaripet; at the date still unmarried.
      It is not known with whom she stayed.
  17. Then headman of Kuttarashi.

20. Male; his spouse and that of his brother (K22) were sisters.
23. Was named Pashuikokit; of unknown origin.
28. The only son of K10, brought up by N8; when grown up went home to his father. In all later years, whenever he had game, took some to N8 living at Nitmap leaving Kattarashi before daybreak. On these occasions N16, who was my informant's mother and N8's daughter, and some others gave him clothing and baskets of their making. See K10.
30. Came as bride from Shikaripet.
33. Blinded when young by a blow from a bear.
34. Native of Kuttarashi and inhabitant of Moseushi.
35. Native of Kuttarashi and inhabitant of Kumaushi.
36. Native of Kuttarashi and resident of Moseushi.

Nitmap (N) Seven houses; of which one was occupied by a widow (N16) and her unmarried children, another by an unmarried woman living alone (N20), and the rest each by a simple family. Except N15 who is a man from the neighbouring Satnai river area, all the male house-heads were brothers, their line of descent through males representing that of Nitmap headman.
1. Male; native of Nitmap descending through males from ancient Tokapchi Ainus.
2. Male; native of Tupet on the Ishikari and former husband of N3.
3. Female; also native of Tupet. Went with N4, her later husband, to Tokapchi, where they stayed about two years. On their way home to Ishikari a bear fell upon them and killed her husband. She escaped and went back to Tokapchi. Too old to marry again, she remained a widow until she died. See S7.
4. Male; native of Pepet on the river Ishikari.
5. Male; native of Nitmap.
6. Female; native of Tokapchi.
7. Female; native of Asahikawa, Ishikari; came as a bride to Nitmap.
8. Late headman of Nitmap.
9. Male; native of the Satnai river area.
10. Native of Shikaripet; went in marriage to Satnai, where she lost her husband (N9). Then went to live at Shikaripet with her young children (N15 and M6).
12. Then headman and "ottena" of Nitmap. See Note 9.
14. Came in marriage from Perutnai on the Shikata near the Tokapchi coast.
15. Native of Satnai, grew up at Shikaripet. Came to Nitmap and got married. Died while my informant, his fifth child, was very young.

16. Female; her father (N8), who had only two daughters, was "loath to give her away" and she remained at Nitmap after her marriage. A widow now, she lived with her unmarried children.
19. Came from Kuttarashi as bride.
20. Remained a spinster all her life. At the time was living alone. For some time a man (ST25) was staying at Nitmap with an intention of taking her to wife; somehow he changed his mind and went away to Otopuke, where he married a local woman. The situation is ambiguous. Refer to ST25.

Pipaushi (P)   6 houses; of which one was occupied by an old widow (P8) and her unmarried daughter (P18), another by a young unmarried man (P19) and his two sisters; the rest were occupied each by a simple family. Two of the male house-heads (P7 and P15) were descended through a male line from Asahikawa people on the Ishikari. P7 in particular came from Asahikawa to Pipaushi himself and married a local woman. Of the other male househeads P9 was a descendant through the male line from an ancient Pipaushi native. The headman at the date was P6, a son of a man (P1) who came to live at Pipaushi, a brother of the fomer Nitmap headman (N8).

1. Came from Nitmap; former headman of Pipaushi.
2. Native resident of Pipaushi; descendant through males of an ancient inhabitant of Pipaushi. Patrilineally related with S2; probably his elder brother.
3. Native of Pipaushi.
4. Came from Asahikawa to Pipaushi, got married with a local woman and had lived here since.
5. Came from Asahikawa as bride. Younger sister of the Chikapumi (Asahikawa) headman's wife.
6. Native of Pipaushi; its headman and "ottena" at the date. See Note 9.
7. Native of Asahikawa; came to Pipaushi, got married with a local woman and had lived here since.
8. Native of Pipaushi; widowed, she lived with her unmarried daughter (P18).
10. Native of Pipaushi; went to Sanenkoro, where he lived with a local woman he took to wife.
11. Native of Pipaushi; went to live at Kumaushi, where he married a local woman. After their daughters' marriages, moved again to Perutnai (the river Shikata) near the Tokapchi sea-coast and was not at Kumaushi at the date.

13. Native of Pipaushi; a bachelor. Was living at the time at another settlement Kumaushi where his sister (P12) had her home.

14. Native of Pipaushi. As reported, was married to a Kuttarashi man.

16. P15's first wife from Sanenkoro. Was drowned in a river. After her children had grown up, her husband took a second wife (KM26).

18. Unmarried last daughter living with her mother. After her mother's death, continued to live alone.

19. Unmarried young man. He and his two younger sisters lived by themselves away from their father (P15) and his second wife (KM26) "because she was not their real mother."

Kumaushi (KM) 8 houses in all; of which one was occupied by a bachelor (P13; KM14) living alone, another by a widower (KM27) also living alone and yet another by a widow (P12) living together with her eldest son (KM20) and his wife and children. Of all the house-heads only two (KM10 and KM14, or P13) had come from other settlements to live at Kumaushi during their lifetime. The headman was KM22; his ancestor (KM5) two generations before him through males had come from Nitmap and he was a patrilineal relative of its headman (N12). The three house-heads (KM27, 28 and 30) were brothers with K35 for their father, who came from Kuttarashi and married a local woman. These, together with the headmen of Nitmap (N12), Pipaushi (P6) and Kuttarashi (K17), are regarded as descendants through males from an ancient Tokapchi Ainu. As for the other house-heads, little is known about their ancestries except that KM6's father and KM2's father's father were both natives of Kumaushi.

1. Male; native of Asahikawa. On his way from Ishikari to Tokapchi he was drowned while crossing a river carrying his young daughter on his back. The child was rescued by Kuttarashi people.

2. Wife of KM1, a native of Asahikawa in Ishikari. Her husband (KM1) went to Tokapchi leaving her at home. When he died and their daughter survived she went to live at Kuttarashi, where she was remarried to K1.

3. Male from Kumaushi.

4. Came as bride to a Kumaushi man. Native of Asahikawa in Ishikari but was brought up at Kuttarashi in Tokapchi.

5. Male; native of Nitmap. Patrilineal relative to N12.

6. Native of Kumaushi and its resident.

7. Came as bride from Perutnai (the river Shikata) near the sea-coast of Tokapchi.

8. Wife to a Kumaushi man.

9. Went to Shikaripet as bride.

10. Male; native of Memroput. Married a Kumaushi woman and lived there. His mother lived at Memroput; his father had been killed by a bear. Had two sisters Enkoashi and Tutanomat; the latter was married to N12, the headman of Nitmap.

11. Native of Kumaushi. Went to live at Penke Pipaushi in Shikaripet where, as he said, there were plenty of deer to hunt. Father to Imonkuk.

12. Wife; native of Shikaripet.

13. Native resident of Kumaushi. Had been dead for some years; his wife (P12) lived with their eldest son (KM20) and his family.

14. Native of Pipaushi; a bachelor.

15. Male from Kumaushi.

16. Native of Kumaushi; was married to a Pipaushi man but lived at Kumaushi.

17. Female; native resident of Kumaushi.

19. Went in marriage to the Satnai river area.

21. Young man; was away at some Japanese fishing grounds.

25. Native of Kumaushi; went in marriage to Sanenkoro.

26. Native of Kumaushi.

27. An eldest son; bereaved of his wife, was living alone.

28. Native of Kumaushi.

29. Native of Asahikawa; came from Penke Pipaushi as bride. See note on S11.

Sanenkoro (S) 4 houses; each occupied by a simple family. Of the 4 male house-heads 3 (S13, 14 and 18) were natives of Sanenkoro and 1 (P10) a native of another *kotan*, Pipaushi, who came to Sanenkoro, got married and became a resident. S18 was a patrilineal kinsman of the Nitmap headman (N12) with whom he had a common ancestor mark, *shine itokpa*. The father of S18's father (S2) and P10's father, it is reported, were siblings. The headman at the date was S13; he and S14 were sons of a man from the Ishikari river area (S1) who came here, married a local woman and settled down. A similar case concerning headmen will be seen with M3 of Moseushi.

1. Male; native of Ishikari.

2. Probably brother of P2; though full tracing of his lineage is difficult, was descended through male line from a common ancestor with the Nitmap headman, with whom he stood in a true (i. e. not by adoption) *shine itokpa* relationship.

4. Female; native of Sanenkoro.

5. Male; native of Asahikawa in Ishikari. Had lived at one time at Pipaushi and died young. For his spouse and children see ST16.

6. Male; native of Asahikawa in Ishikari and former spouse of S7.

7. Female; native of Asahikawa in Ishikari. Went on a visiting trip from Ishikari to Tokapchi in company with her husband (S6), their unmarried 3 daughters (S16, 17 and Yaitekka) and a married couple (N3 and 4). On their way back a bear fell upon them, killing S6 and N4. The women and the children survived and went back to Tokapchi. S7, still young enough, was remarried to S8 and lived at Sanenkoro, where her daughters also grew up.

8. Native of Kuttarashi.

10. Was linked in patrilineal kinship to the headman of Nitmap.

11. Native of Asahikawa on the Ishikari; grew up, got married and lived at Penke Pipaushi in Shikaripet. When very young, he and his younger sister (KM 29) were brought by their parents migrating from Ishikari to Tokapchi. They came to Nitmap as strangers and went to the headman for help. After certain procedures they settled down at Penke Pipaushi.

12. Native of Sanenkoro. Went to Penke Pipaushi as bride. Had four children. While gathering wild grass, *trep*, was killed by a bear.

13. Native of Sanenkoro; the headman.

16. Native of Asahikawa; a first daughter; grew up at Sanenkoro. Went to Asahikawa as bride.

17. Native of Asahikawa; grew up at Sanenkoro.

18. Native of Sanenkoro; the only surviving male at the date of S10's children.

Moseushi (M) 11 houses; of which one was inhabited by a widow (M10) living alone, another by an old widower, the headman (M3), with whom lived his son (M14) with wife and children. The remaining 9 houses were occupied each by a simple family. Those houses, belonging to the local group collectively called Moseushi, stood scattered at long intervals along the river Shikaripet. Farthest upstream near Sarunnai stood M7's house; about 2 miles lower came M9's; about 2 miles farther down, the 3 houses of M14, his sister Aresam and her spouse, and another sister of his and her husband (M8). Then at Moseushi, about 100 to 130 yards yet farther down, came the remaining 6 houses. 7 male inhabitants of 6 out of the 11 houses (M3, 14, 17, 19, 7, 8 and 9) were linked by patrilineal kinship, being all descendants through males from Asahikawa natives on the river Ishikari. The remaining 3 househeads (M21, 22 and 25) were descended through male lines from an ancient Tokapchi Ainu and were sons of two brothers who had come from Kuttarashi to Moseushi, where they married local women. The Moseushi headman at the date was M3, a native of Asahikawa, the only information about whom is as follows. There was at Moseushi a native headman who died without any brother or son to succeed him. Then M3, who had come from Asahikawa and married here, was made *utaru sapaha*, head of the people on account of his wisdom and personality.

1. Either the man himself or his father was native of Asahikawa in Ishikari and came migrating to Tokapchi and married a Moseushi woman. He and N1 were patrilineally related.

2. Female; native of Moseushi.

3. Native of Asahikawa. The then headman. Came to Tokapchi, married a Kuttarashi woman and then became headman of Moseushi. His wife having already been dead, lived with his son (M14). Patrilineal relative of M5 and others. See N3.

4. Female; native of Kuttarashi.

5. An eldest son; native of Shikaripet; had lived from infancy at Asahikawa. Detailed circumstances not known.

6. Female; native of Satnai and grew up at Shikaripet. For more information see note on N15.

7, 8 and 9. All native residents of Shikaripet.

10. Female; native of Moseushi. Married to K34, a man from Kuttarashi. Widowed, she now lived alone in a separate house by her son's.

11. Female; native of Shikaripet. Married to a man from Kuttarashi (K36) and lived at Moseushi.

14. "Ottena" in charge of negotiation with Japanese authorities. See N9.

15. Went as bride to the neighbouring Otopuke river area.

18. Went from Shikaripet to be wife of a Kuttarashi man (K18). Her father (M5), as reported, had lived from infancy at Asahikawa; but it is not known whether he later came back to Shikaripet or not.

20. The only one of her siblings that married.

23 and 24. Both brothers married women of Memroput on the middle Tokapchi and lived there; 25 alone was at Moseushi.

(24) Explanation of the genealogical chart concerning the Satnai river area.

Three local groups, each forming a single settlement group, made a corporate *shine ekashi ikiru* or *shine itokpa* group. Nupokomap contained 9 houses, Urekarip 3 and Munhunki 3. Four house-heads out of nine of Nupokomap (ST10, 18, 29's husband and 30's), one out of three of Urekarip (ST13's husband) and one out of three of Munhunki (ST27) were patrilineal kin descending from a common ancestor from Satnai. All the headmen in the Satnai river area were drawn from these particular kinsmen, those of Nupokomap, Urekarip and Munhunki being ST10, ST13's husband and ST27 respectively.

1. Male; native of Asahikawa on the Ishikari. A relative of N2, another Asahikawa man.
2. Female; native and resident of Asahikawa.
3. Male; native of Urekarip. Son of a man from the area of the Tottapet, tributary of the river Satnai.
4. Female; native of Satnai.
5. Son of a man from Tottapet in Satnai.
6. Came as bride from Fushiko.

7 and 8. Both natives of Asahikawa; the man and wife came originally with ST9 as escorts and helpers when she came as bride from 'far-off Shikaripet' to Satnai. They remained and settled down by the side of ST9's.

9. Came from Shikaripet as bride. For reasons not known, went back to Shikaripet, where she died.
10. Male; had always been in Satnai. Reported as the then first headman in all the Satnai area.
12. Came as bride from Perutnai on the Shikata near the Tokapchi seacoast. She was first married to ST11, on whose death she went home to Perutnai taking her children. When she returned to Satnai, was wife of ST31.
13. Female; native of Satnai.
14. Male; probably from Pipairu.
16. Went to Pipaushi as bride. On her spouse's death at Pipaushi, came home to Satnai with her two children (ST33 and 34) and lived at Nupokomap. At the date was living by herself.
17. Male; had always been in Satnai; resident thereof.
19. Male; had always been in Satnai.

20 and 21. Probably natives of Pipaushi, with homes there.

23. Male from Fushiko.
24. Native of Satnai.
25. Soon after marriage moved with his wife to her home, Otopuke, at about the time when Ushino, my informant, also moved from Nitmap to Kene, at the outset of the farming-land allotment programme for the Ainu.
26. Female; came as bride from the Otopuke river area.
28. Went to Fushiko on the middle Tokapchi as bride.
29. Came as bride from Shikaripet.
30. Came as bride from Perutnai near the coast of Tokapchi.
31. An only child.
34. Native of Pipaushi; his father having died in his infancy, grew up in Satnai which was his mother's home, and married there. Changed

wives. Several times came to Nitmap to join bear ceremonies but his *kotan* is not clearly identified.

35. Eldest of brothers and sisters. Went in marriage to the Otopuke area and died young. Was outlived by 3 brothers, Ikuchishi, Fushine and Irusanke, who were all unmarried at the date.
36. Had always been in Satnai.
37. Came as bride from Chirokto on the middle Tokapchi.
38. Male; had always been in Satnai. He and ST37 were brothers. Having lost one child, lived childless.
39. Came as bride from Fushiko on the middle Tokapchi.
40. Probably native of Pipaushi. Siblings unknown. Had 6 daughters and 1 son.
41. Female; native of Fushiko.
42. Male; native of Satnai.
43. Female from Fushiko.
44. Female; native of Satnai.
45. Came from Fushiko as bride.

Chapter Ⅲ

(**25**) The Ainu months. — On either the Tokapchi, the Otopuke ior the
Azuma, the Ainu had twelve successively named months covering the four
seasons of the year: *shune an chup, kuekai chup, zuurup chup, toetanne
chup, haprap chup, kiuta chup, shikiuta chup, momauta chup. shimauta chup,
moniorap chup, shiniorap chup* and *urepok chup*. That the divisions seem to
have been common to all the Hokkaido Ainu is indicated by information compiled by TAKABEYA (TAKABEYA, 1941, pp. 147-9). At least with the upper
Tokapchi Ainu it seems that the custom was to begin with *shune an chup;*
however, it has not been verified yet in any other area. The Ainu months
have been correlated by some students of the Ainu to the twelve months of
the Japanese lunar calendar (ibid., pp. 147-9). Both the above-cited material
and that of the present writer indicate that *shune an chup* corresponds to
the tenth month of the Japanese system and *urepok chup* to the ninth; by
the solar calendar, *shune an chup* corresponds roughly to November and *urepok* to October.

(**26**) The cherry salmon, Oncorhynchus masou, which resemble O. kisutch,
silver salmon or coho, which abound in the North Pacific and North America,
are peculiar to Japan and its neighbouring waters. In Hokkaido especially
they are found in such abundance that they come only second in importance
after the dog salmon, O. keta (HIKITA, 1956, p. 33).
       Generally speaking, cherry salmon in Hokkaido begin to run for spawn-
ing in early May, with of course some difference in different rivers (SANO,
1950, p. 16; IGARASHI, 1946, p. 13). In most of the Hokkaido rivers the fishing
season lasts from June till September (HIKITA, 1956, p. 34; MIHARA et al.,
1951, pp. 34-35) and passes into the dog salmon season that follows (ŌYA,
1954). In the Tokapchi today the season lasts from early June till late August,
while that of the dog salmon extends from early August to late December
(MIHARA, 1951, pp. 34-35). As for the height of the season no reliable information is available except ŌNO's, which gives it as from July to September
(ŌNO, 1933, p. 24). A journal kept by a group of the earliest settlers on the
middle Tokapchi (HAGIHARA, ed., 1937) records in effect that in the 1883 season the first cherry salmon were taken in July (ibid., p. 134) and in the 1884
season in June (ibid., p. 137); in both seasons the runs and the landing were
largest in August (ibid., pp. 135 and 170). From the start of their run or
arrival to their spawning, cherry salmon have a longer period to live in
rivers than dog salmon (SANO, 1950, p. 16), their spawning period beginning

in August (HANDA, 1933, p. 16; ŌNO, 1933, p. 17) or early September (SANO, 1950, p. 16) and ending around October (HANDA, 1933, p. 16; ŌNO, 1933, p. 17). After entering rivers, cherry salmon continue their runs feeding and growing until they become full spawners, so that they go scattering into all tributaries, large and small (IGARASHI, 1946, p. 13) and spawn in the upper reaches (ŌNO, 1933, p. 17; SANO, 1950, p. 16) or uppermost reaches of the streams (HANDA, 1933, p. 16). There is no running up into the glens in the upper reaches of the rivers until breeding begins (oral information from the Chitose Branch, Hokkaido Salmon Hatchery, 1957). For the spawning behaviour of cherry salmon, which resembles that of O. keta (SANO, 1950, p. 19), see description in Note 28.

(27)   The importance of the dog salmon as food for the Ainu may be illust- rated by a record of about 200 Ainus dying from starvation in Ishikari during the winter of 1725 and the following spring after disastrously short salmon runs in the river Ishikari during the autumn (Hokkaido-chō, ed., 1937, Vol. 2, p. 301 and Vol. 7, p. 56). Another record shows that in 1884 salmon runs in the middle course of the Tokapchi were so small that the Ainu in that area were on the verge of starvation in February of the following year (HAGIHARA, ed., 1937, pp. 171 and 188).

(28)   Concerning spawning behaviour, spawning-beds and spawning grounds.
     The spawning behaviour of the dog salmon as described by SANO and NAGASAWA (1958, p. 12) may be summarized as follows. When salmon run- ning in shoals reach favourable spots, they disperse to mate for spawning. The female digs out a cavity in the river bed, while its mate goes round on patrol to keep off any invading males, at times going some distance in driv- ing them off. In about an hour the spawning cavity is ready, and the pair nestle down in it and emit spawn and milt. This over, the female covers up the spawn laid with some gravel from the river bed and finishes the whole work. The covering takes about two hours, during which time the male stays by the bed to protect it from digging by any other individual. Spawning, however, seldom finishes in one place; soon after one spawning many in- dividuals begin preparing for another. A second spawning, if any, is per- formed by the same pair of fish in a place not far from their first spawning- bed. When everything is over, the female stays about its bed, becoming gradually emaciated until finally it dies.
     Observations in the Shiraoi indicate that the parent fish lie in hiding in bank-side deeps during the daytime and come out for spawning between nightfall and daybreak. Unless when running in large shoals or pressed for immediate spawning, they generally spawn by night, most actively near day-

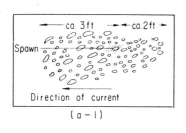

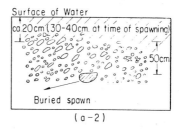

A

Fig. A. Spawning-bed. (a-1), ground plan; (a-2), cross section.
(Shiraoi Jigyō-jyō, 1956, p. 6).

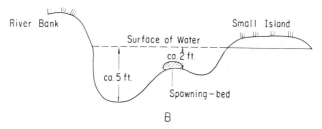

B

Fig. B. Cross section of a spawning-bed in Area B in the
Shiraoi. (Shiraoi Jigyō-jyō, 1956, p. 4).

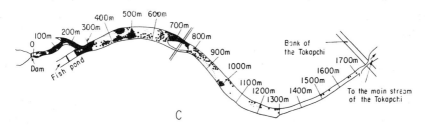

C

Fig. C. Distribution of natural spawning-beds and spawning
grounds in a small tributary of the Tokapchi. (Sano and Nagasawa, 1958, p. 3).

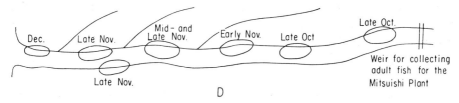

D

Fig. D. Distribution of the spawning areas or grounds as related
to the time of their occurrence. (Mitsuishi Jigyō-jyō, 1956).

break. In fact, any species of fish, whether spawning or not, behaves more actively by night than by day (Shiraoi Jigyō-jyō, 1956, p. 4; oral information obtained from Chitose Branch of the Hokkaido Salmon Hatchery in 1957).

An individual spawning-bed may be readily detected by the presence of a number of relatively large pebbles showing in one spot. An example of the form and size of the bed is shown in Fig. A (Shiraoi Jigyō-jyō 1956, p. 6).

A marked tendency is that the dog salmon spawns generally in a relatively shallow place where gravel and underwater springs concur (SANO and NAGA-SAWA, 1958, p. 4). The same tendency is reported from Shiraoi, as will be seen from Fig. B (Shiraoi Jigyō-jyō 1956, p. 4). Accordingly, spawning-beds in any stream are distributed in some particular areas or grounds, in groups or concentrations of different sizes and densities. Fig. C illustrates the dis-tribution of spawning-beds and spawning grounds observed and recorded in the Mem, a small tributary of the Tokapchi (SANO and NAGASAWA, 1958, p. 3). Natural spawning grounds or concentrations of spawning-beds annually recur in practically the same sites (Shiraoi Jigyō-jyō, 1953, p. 3).

The time of spawning is influenced primarily by the temperature of the river water; the higher the temperature, the longer the period needed for the salmon to grow into full spawners in any particular stream. Shoals, there-fore, running earliest in season have to ascend farthest upstream before they can spawn, while those running later as the water becomes colder have less to travel; the last spawning-beds of the season in Hitaka, for instance, occur at 2-3 km. from the river mouth (oral information obtained from the Chitose Branch of the Hokkaido Salmon Hatchery in 1957). The distribution of the spawning areas or grounds as related to the time of their occurrence in the Mitsuishi in 1956 is shown in Fig. D (Mitsuishi Jigyō-jyō, 1956).

Observation and recording of the actual conditions of natural spawning-beds in the Hokkaido rivers, however, began only in 1956 (Hokkaido Sake Masu Fuka-jyō, 1956). As a matter of fact, every river ascended by the dog salmon in Hokkaido today has some governmental installations near its mouth and/or on its lower course for capturing parent fish to yield spawn for artificial incu-bation. As a result, only a small number of individuals now spawn naturally, while those running and spawning above the installations are few in the extreme (SANO and NAGASAWA, 1958, p. 2; NISHINO, 1958, p. 51). Investiga-tions by the present writer indicate that before the general opening up of the island by the Japanese dog salmon had always swarmed the upper reaches of the rivers, that large-scale spawning grounds had been distributed along the river courses and that they had great influence on the distribution of Ainu settlements. The distribution of spawning grounds as Ainu local group territories will be shown in the text (pp. 60-62) and their more detailed loca-tion is described elsewhere (WATANABE, 1963).

(**29**) The fishing season among the Ainu of dog salmon, in either the Tokapchi, the Otopuke or the Azuma, covered the following three months; *urepok chup, shune an chup* and *kuekai chup* (p. 53). That these months correspond approximately to October, November and December has been explained in Note 25.

The fishing season in the Tokapchi is from early September till late December (MIHARA et al., 1951, pp. 34-5), and at the governmental fishing installation at Chiyota, located 40 kms. up from the river-mouth, several fishes per day begin to be caught in early September and the landing falls off in late December (Tokapchi Shijyō, official catch register for 1933-1955; oral information from the Branch in 1959). The run into the Tokapchi is so checked by a dam at Chiyota and the fishing installation lying lower that the number of fish running farther upstream is estimated to have decreased by 70 to 80 per cent (SANO and NAGASAWA, 1958, pp. 2 and 6). Apart from the situation, it is reported that in the Mem, a minor tributary on the middle course, the run occurs in late September and ends in early November; however, rumours point to fairly large runs seen formerly in December and even in January (ibid., p. 6). It is recorded in the diaries of first group settlers " Banseisha ", immigrated to Obihiro on the middle Tokapchi in 1882-3 that in 1882, 1883 and 1885 dog salmon appeared in the area in October and ascended in increasing numbers in December, while in 1884 they appeared in small quantity in September, with runs still small even in October and falling off in December; that the runs ceased at last in January in each of the years mentioned and the fish seen in that month were old ones such as were caught by few people (HAGIHARA, ed., 1937, pp. 106, 136-7, 167, 170-1, 188 and 191).

(**30**) *Meorun chep* regarded as the silvery salmon.—Night-fishing with torchlights was a practice among the Ainu of the anterior generation on every river course during the latter part of the dog salmon season. On any river course of the upper Tokapchi, the Otopuke and the Azuma as well as other rivers investigated by the present writer, the torchlight-fishing began in *shune an chup*, the month to start fishing with *shune*, the torch. The month approximately corresponds to November (Note 25). The beginning of the fishing season was marked in every river course by the arrival of a specific variety of dog salmon. This variety was what the Ainu called *meorun chep* in the main Tokapchi and the Otopuke areas, or *mata chep* in the Azuma, Mukawa and Shikot areas, meaning by *me* 'cold', by *mata* 'cold season' and by *chep* 'fish'; although these later runs were of special significance to the natives, no reference seems to have been made except by BATCHELOR. The *meuren chep* and *mat chep* referred to by him shows every indication of identity with our variety. He writes: "Meuren-chep, n. Silver salmon. Same as Mat-chep" (BATCHELOR, 1926, p. 283); "Mat-chep, n. Silver salmon. Oncorhynchus kisutch (Walb)" (ibid., p. 278). The silver salmon, O. kisutch, also known as 'coho,' occurs in great quantity in the area extending from the North American coasts to Alaska, but it seldom appears in the territorial waters of Japan (ŌSHIMA, 1940, p. 249). It is a very rare species in Japan and has been caught only several times so far in the rivers of Hokkaido (HIKITA, 1956, p. 31). The *meorun chep* or *mata chep*, then, seems a different variety from the silver salmon but may be identified as the 'silvery salmon' on the following evidence. The *meorun chep* or *mata chep* was distinguished by the natives by its silvery colour as against the spawning colour appearing on the common dog-salmon, by its smaller size generally and its arrival with the cold season, that is, late in the period of dog salmon run. It will be seen that all these features are in agreement with those of the variety known in Japan as 'silvery salmon'. The latest researches indicate that the silvery salmon, or 'ginke-sake' as it is called in Japan, is also known as 'mejika', 'ginpika' or 'gira'; it arrives at the end of Oncorhynchus keta's runs in all the rivers in Hokkaido and other regions of Japan ascended by O. keta; the majority found are not full-grown but are fairly small-sized; it undergoes no change of colour for spawning but retains its silvery colour into maturity; finally, its arrival signifies the end of O. keta's runs (SANO, 1947, p. 43). Inference is made that the variety is of the same species as the common dog-salmon but that some physiological variation has brought out the apparent difference (ibid., p. 44). *Meorun chep* is regarded likewise by the Ainu as the same kind as "*shiipe kamuichep*" with the runs that precede it. In the river Chitose or Shikot today at least, the silvery salmon arrives each season mingling with the common dog-salmon and then gradually increases in number till it predominates at the end of the season (SANO, 1946, p. 40), though the ratio of mingling and the time of its appearance varies in different rivers (SANO, 1947, p. 41). For the other Hokkaido rivers no report is available; only it is informed that in the Tokapchi in ca. 1946 a fairly large amount of 'mejika' or silvery salmon were witnessed ascending during December and January in the area around the Chiyota salmon fishery. Such runs were known as "last catch"; but in recent years they have almost ceased to be seen (oral information obtained in 1959 from the Tokapchi Branch, Hokkaido Salmon Hatchery).

A case of night-spearing by torchlight employed for a specific species of salmon is found also among the Klallam Indians on the Northwest Coast of North America. The Indians use this method for silver salmon that run from October till December and not for dog-salmon and other species that run earlier (GUNTHER, 1927, pp. 198 and 201). No further details are made known.

(**31**) The deer, Cervus nippon, drops its white spots in autumn and turns its coat into winter fur. The change completes itself, in Japan proper at least, between late September and mid-October, the older the individuals the earlier. The mating period extends from early October to late December with the height in mid-October to early November, at which time males bell most (IMAIZUMI, 1949, p. 139, cited from NAKAJIMA). In Hokkaido the mating time is said to cover the period from late September to October (INUKAI, 1952, p. 41).

(**32**) Seasonal migration of the deer.—It is noticed in a report by INUKAI, (1952), a zoologist, that, apart from and parallel to local migrations of deer between their wintering quarters on the hills and the lower plain within the same river valley, there occurred others on a larger scale extending over different river valleys, and that this habit (latter migrations) of the game was turned to account in some districts by Ainu hunters.

"The wild deer of Hokkaido fed on wild plants of almost every kind. ....Leaves of bamboo-grass, grazed in all seasons, were their chief winter food....

"Formerly (i. e. before the opening up by the Japanese Government got under way, that is, before the 1880's), while each summer lasted and food was plentiful everywhere, small herds of deer could be seen scattered all over the island. Late in autumn every year, before winter came with deep snow which buried all food plants, the deer of Teshio, Ishikari and Shiribeshi migrated in large flocks to Ifuri, Hitaka, Tokapchi, Kushiro and Nemuro. Far more flocked to Hitaka and Tokapchi than elsewhere, making these excellent hunting grounds for the Ainu.

"Before its opening up, the whole island was covered with dense forests; deer roamed about by trails known as 'deer paths,' reputed to have been so well beaten that they looked like human ways. These tracks they followed in their seasonal migrations in spring and again in autumn. When their way came to large rivers such as the Ishikari, they always swam across at the same points, thus affording ideal sites for Ainu hunters lying in wait, as has already been stated..." A similar description is given by BATCHELOR (of the deer of the west crossing rivers on their way to Ifuri in the east during September and October)...."In spring when it thawed, deer went back by the same routes from their wintering in Hitaka and Tokapchi. And this they had repeated year after year until they became scarce. Then they ceased to move on any large scale but stayed the whole year in their winter quarters in Hitaka and Tokapchi. They no more had need to venture a long way from these wintering areas where they could find plenty of food plants to support their small herds" (INUKAI, 1952, pp. 14-16).

(**33**) About the wintering quarters of the deer.—Any Ainu informant from any district will testify that wintering quarters of the deer, of which there were many sizes, were found not on the level plain but on the hills, generally in places sheltered by evergreens, mostly firs, where the snow was never so deep as to make it difficult for the animal to find bamboo-grass and other food during winter; that Ainu huts for deer-hunting were erected near those wintering quarters. It must be noted, however, that not all their huts and their hunting grounds occurred near those specific quarters which bore the title. It seems that *rikoruya* or *yuk ria ushi*, as some wintering centres were specifically named, were relatively large-scale. Apparently, there were not many in any river valley. The Ainu word '*rikoruya*', meaning 'wintering place of deer', is preserved to this day in some place-names (INUKAI, 1952, p. 10).

The writer's investigation shows that on the upper Tokapchi there existed five such named wintering places; two on the Panke Nikoro glen (*Panke Nikoro opashi an rikoruya* and *Panke Nikoro okimun an rikoruya*), two others on the Penke Nikoro glen (*Penke Nikoro opashi an rikoruya* and *Penke Nikoro okimun an rikoruya*) and another on the Pennai (or Penkenai) glen (*Pennai an rikoruya*). These five were the deer-hunting grounds of the people of Kuttarashi, the uppermost settlement on the river course. The huts for mountain hunting of deer in winter belonging to the cooperative groups of Nitmap, were found in the Shintoko, Penke Otash, Panke Kinaushi and Penke Kinaushi glens, all situated near wintering centres. But of all these only Penke Kinaushi and Panke Kinaushi, where there were dense growths of firs, had each a *rikoruya*, there being none in the other dales more sparsely wooded by the trees. On the Otopuke there could be identified only three '*yuk ria ushi*', named *Nukanan etoko yuk ria ushi*, *Kumaneshiri ebakike yuk ria ushi* and *Seta etoko yuk ria ushi*, respectively. All these were in the hills thickly wooded by firs. As there were no other hills to speak of, people of the whole river course, as it is said, went for deer hunting in the hills mostly in these areas. It seems, however, that of these three the uppermost Kumaneshiri shows no trace of having been developed by any other group than that of the uppermost settlement. In fact, there were other nameless centres utilized along with the so-called '*ria ushi*' as in the Nukapira glen. The examples given above will be sufficient to show that Ainu huts and grounds for deer hunting were never restricted to the major wintering quarters specifically titled '*rikoruya*' or '*yuk ria ushi*', but that they were established in nameless centres near each settlement as well, so long as they could satisfy the need of the group concerned.

(**34**) Other methods of deer hunting. — That the commonest method of deer hunting was by use of arrows poisoned with aconite, whether for hand-bow or spring-bow, is confirmed by a study of INUKAI (INUKAI, 1952). He reports also of a mass technique employed by hunters working together, or driving a deer herd by using dogs down a precipice and then clubbing them to death, and another of capturing the game after driving them into a lake or the sea. Setting the noose on a trail was also practised in some areas, but this does not seem to have been common.

(35)   The species Ursus arctos is distributed over Hokkaido, the Kurile Islands excluding the middle part, Sakhalin, Kamchatka, the Maritime Provinces, northern Manchuria, Siberia and even Europe.   Some of the brown bears in Hokkaido reach as large as 2 ms. or more in length and 300 to 400 kgs. in weight (INUKAI, 1933, p. 57).

(36)   Ursus arctos of Hokkaido.—Its ethology and ecology concerning Ainu hunting will be summarized from zoological descriptions given by HATTA (1911) and INUKAI (1933 and 1934) as follows.

   a)   When the snow on the lower damp places begins to melt and the surface of the ground begins to appear in spring, bears come out of their dens one after another even though the snow still remains on the mountains. There are some fluctuations in different areas and in different years; however, in any case, they begin to leave their hibernation dens in late March and are mostly out already by the end of May (HATTA, 1911, p. 34) or by mid-May (INUKAI, 1933, p. 63). At about that time their winter fur turns into summer fur (ibid.).

   b)   When the base snow reaches 2 or 3 inches deep, every bear retreats into a den.   In most years and areas, the base snow forms in Hokkaido between mid-November and mid-December (HATTA, p. 35).   It is also reported that most bears start hibernation in November and there is a tendency of bears with cubs or in pregnancy retreating earlier than others (INUKAI, 1933, p. 59). INUKAI states that their winter fur begins to turn into summer fur about mid-May and the summer fur back into winter fur in November (ibid., p. 63).

   c)   Bears, excluding cubs, usually hibernate each in a separate den (HATTA, 1911, p. 36; INUKAI, p. 63).   The cubs are born in the dens in January (ibid., p. 37) or during the period from January to March (INUKAI, 1933, p. 64).   In most cases, the number of cubs at one birth is 2 (HATTA, 1911, p. 37) or 1-2 (INUKAI, 1933, p. 64).

   d)   Usually the dens are natural caves.   However, holes under the roots of big trees, or under rocks, or in the earth are also utilized (HATTA, p. 35). There is also contrary information that most bears dig the holes themselves though some make use of natural caves or holes (INUKAI, 1933, p. 59).

Dens in very good conditions are used again in the following season by the same individuals, or sometimes by different individuals even two or three years later. For this reason, the Ainu regard the bear's den as something like a property (ibid., p. 63).

e) Place of hibernation and seasonal migration.—The bear is an animal which takes its abode in the mountain forest; however, owing to the food condition, it performs fairly constant migration. At the end of the autumn, it comes down from the mountains in search of food considerably near to human habitation and then begins hibernation. Coming out of its den in spring it goes back again to the interior (INUKAI, 1933, p. 58). In the mountain and forest district of Akan which retains more primitive conditions than other districts, according to the Ainu informants, a good many of the bears hibernate in the environ of Mt. O-akan which is rich in rock-caves suitable for their purpose. Part of those bears migrate toward Mt. Me-akan in early spring (INUKAI, 1934, p. 32).

(**37**) MATSUURA's diary of his geographical exploration in 1857–1858 in the Ainu territory in Hokkaido (MASAMUNE, ed., 1937) contains some information on the local distribution of Hokkaido bears which supports the generalization from the writer's own data. The areas described by MATSUURA as abounding with bears are all river-source areas (ibid., pp. 148, 156, 417 and 627), and the bear hunting grounds of the Ainu he incidentally recorded are all distributed in the source areas of rivers (ibid., pp. 284, 667 and 678). Regions recorded in connection with the deer are in every case distinct from these areas, places noted for abundance of the animal occurring invariably on level plains or hill skirts (ibid. pp. 134, 244, 273, 275, 365, 396, 415, 417 and 663).

(**38**) The scientific names here mentioned have been taken, for Nos. 9, 10 and 17, from MURAKOSHI and MAKINO's Manual of Flora in Japan (MURAKOSHI and MAKINO, 1956) and, for the remainder, from MAKINO's Manual of Flora in Japan (MAKINO, 1951) by referring through their Japanese names to CHIRI's dictionary (CHIRI, 1953). The places of occurrence or habitat are cited from the bulletin of the Experimental Farm of Hokkaido (Hokkaido Nōji Shiken-jyō, ed., 1931), with some modifications suggested by Dr. Hiro KANAI, of Botanical Institute, Tokyo University; reference was also made to The Hokkaido Government's Report (Hokkaido-chō, ed., 1917), and to MAKINO's Manual of Flora in Japan (MAKINO, 1951). For detailed information on the cultural meanings and the uses of plants utilized by the Ainu, see CHIRI's dictionary (1953).

(39) Origin of plant cultivation among the Ainu.—According to the latest research by TAKAKURA, the oldest literature on Ainu farming is contained in Recorded Talks on the Ainu written by Kanzan MATSUMIYA who visited Hokkaido in 1710 in company with the administration inspector of the Tokugawa Shogunate (TAKAKURA, 1957). It is a simple description of the farming conducted by natives in the vicinity of the Matsumae Area or clan territory. Then comes a more detailed account in an official document of the Matsumae feudal clan dated 1715, A Report submitted by Matsumae Shimanokami in the Fifth Year of Shotoku. The conclusion drawn by TAKAKURA is that even before 1715 small-scale farming had been practised by the Ainu in south-west Hokkaido but that no definite evidence is yet available to prove its introduction from the Japanese (ibid., p. 15). A History of Hokkaido states more definitely that, in spite of its obscurity of origin, Ainu farming may be safely regarded as modeled on Japanese farming in view of the crops grown and the extent and the methods of cultivation. Millet, Deccan-grass and turnips were about all the crops raised, and their cultivation, according to the Matsumae report of 1715, seems to have been confined to the area between Shiraoi in the east and Shikotan and southward in the west. There are, however, indications that some farming was practised also in Tokapchi and at Shiranuka in Kushiro (Hokkaido-cho, ed., 1937, Vol. 2, p. 215). Takeshiro MATSUURA, an official of the Shogunate who explored the Ainu territory in 1857–58, recorded his observations of cultivated plots found all over the areas he visited except the depths of such great rivers as the Ishikari, the Tokapchi and the Teshio (Note 10). The old Ainu agricultural implements and techniques are described in detail in HAYASHI's article (HAYASHI, 1958).

(40) A generalized statement regarding the stability of Ainu settlements on Hokkaido may be found in HABARA's quotation from The Aborigines of Hokkaido published by the Hokkaido government. " Nomadic habits are unknown to the Ainu ; however, they have not infrequently moved for reasons such as pressure from other settlements or facilities found in a new site.... The great majority, however, have lived for generations in the same places " (HABARA, 1939, pp. 73–74). The other quotations cited by HABARA from old documents in discussing this problem and the interpretations of, and reconstructions on, those documents offered by him, seem to impress the reader as if the Ainu in general had a moving or migratory habit (ibid., pp. 107–112). But as far as the inland Ainu surveyed by the present writer were concerned, there is not the slightest evidence of a general habit of frequent migrations, although at times some individual families moved for hunting purposes or went on a visit to distant relations and, on rare occasions, might even have stayed over several years, as seen in Notes 16, 24 and 25. Nor is

there any proof of nomadic wanderings without fixed habitation, although they had the habit of seasonal migrations from fixed homes to fixed huts for hunting or fishing. As regards seasonal migrations among the Ainu, an inference has been made of those between inland dwellings for summer and seaside dwellings for winter (ibid., pp. 112–113); a report has been made also of migrations of male members of each family in the home settlement to mountain huts in winter, to seaside huts in summer and to riverside fishing-huts in autumn (IZUMI, 1951, pp. 214 and 229). In either case, no attempt was made to analyze the mechanism of migrations or the relationship between them and the community activities in general.

In the earlier stage of his field survey the author made a report that, as far as the inland Ainu were concerned, there is no trace of seasonal migrations ever taking place between the inland and the coasts except for labour migrations by some to Japanese-owned fishing grounds (Notes 6 and 9) and seasonal visitings for trading purposes; that, shortly after the land allotments, some male members of certain coastal settlement families migrated in spring and autumn to their seaside fishing huts in order to occupy themselves exclusively in stretch-rope fishing (WATANABE, 1955; Note 53). Later investigations have increasingly convinced the writer that, save for the labour migrations to Japanese fisheries, no seasonal migrations to the coasts were attempted by inland Ainus. As for the coastal Ainu, on the other hand, only fragmentary information has been obtained for the period subsequent to the land allotments. As regards the inland Ainu at least, their seasonal migrations to fishing huts on the inland waters were in no way a general phenomenon. In the upper Tokapchi area, for instance, a section of the family members of its settlements had a habit of migrating each summer to huts for cherry salmon fishing on one of the tribulets (p. 27); but no such group habits are observable among the neighbouring lower settlement group or any of the upper Otopuke or upper Azuma settlement groups. Again, in dog-salmon fishing, usually practised in the main streams near each settlement, there is no instance from any river valley of regular group migrations to such fishing sites and of erection there of fishing huts to pass the season in. Huts were sometimes built in relation to their fishing activities in main streams; however, those were usually for the purpose of taking rest or warming by turns on weir fishing or net-trap fishing which was usually done at night. In fact some members of certain individual families made fishing expeditions going a long distance from their settlement and staying the season out. But those are exceptional cases as far as dog salmon fishing is concerned (p. 64). It might be concluded that seasonal migrations common to all the inland Ainu groups investigated by the present writer were only those undertaken by certain members of families to their hunting huts in the hills and mountains.

Chapter IV

(**41**) Information concerning member families of Nitmap local group and co-operative activities among them.

Shiokoro and his family.—Shiokoro was an old man; he no longer went hunting bears himself, because his sons had all grown enough to do that for him and themselves. Nor did old Shiokoro play an active part in deer-hunting as did his younger brothers and his sons. All his sons were good bear-hunters, Itomochara, the second, being the best. As some of them were every year drafted in service at some Japanese fishing grounds on the sea-coast from about May to early October and soon after their return went for bear hunting, deer-hunting on the fields was operated by the remaining male hands with their home as base, so as to carry on dog-salmon fishing side by side. Their deer-fence was accordingly built within half a mile of their settlement, on a level hill on the way to Shintoku on a smaller scale. But after their return from bear hunting they went deer-hunting in the hills and got sufficient amount of deer. The children being all grown up, Shiokoro and his family built their own cherry-salmon weirs in the main stream and the glens.

Shurunke and his family.—Shurunke, a traditional headman of a *kotan* and formerly a great bear-hunter, was now too old to go hunting the beast. But his eldest son Sankur was one of the best bear-hunters of Nitmap and his second, Usareta, was another fine hunter. The third and the fourth, though always following their brothers on bear-hunting expeditions, had never killed a bear themselves yet. Sankur, like Shiokoro's sons, had to be away during summer for service at the coast; immediately on his return he entered the mountains to chase bears. Deer hunts in autumn fell largely on Shurunke and his son Usareta, who like Shiokoro's family set up their deer-fence less than a mile and a half from their settlement, on a level height on the way to Pekerepet, and there chased deer of the plain. Their daily routine was to go round the fence during the morning and bring back spoils killed with hand-bows, spending the rest of the day in catching dog-salmon. In spring Sankur and Usareta always went together for bear-hunts; in autumn Sankur alone went because there were deer-hunting and dog-salmon fishing going on concurrently which needed hands. The building and use of the cherry-salmon weir in the main stream was a joint enterprise with the families of Shukemon, Kapkotuk and Osareainu; for the cherry salmon weir and the fishing hut on the glen they cooperated with the two families of Shukemon and Osareainu.

Zarashi and his family.—Zarashi and his first son Konishikupa were both
superior bear-hunters; his second son Zanrura and the third Repani also
hunted bears, though the last-named was not very skilful in the art. They
formed a group of themselves for hunting both bears and deer. For deer-
hunting they went to stay at a hut at relatively distant Penkechin on the
Shikaripet and chased deer of the plain by means of a fence erected near-by,
while some of the male hands went to their mountain hut for bear-hunts.
There are indications, though not very definite, that during the deer season
in the hills some of Zarashi's sons went with those of Shurunke to the wintering centre of the animal on the Kinaushi glen. For the cherry-salmon weir-
fishing in the main stream they were joined by Retunun who lived alone;
for that in the glens they worked all by themselves.

Shukemon and her family.—Shukemon's husband had died when her children
were still very young. Her eldest son Aniainu, who had always followed
Sankur, eldest son of Shurunke, in his bear-hunts, had now become his fellow
hunter. Her second son Ukae had in a like manner become associated with
Itomochara, second son of Shiokoro. In the matter of deer-fence hunting her
family associated themselves with those of Kapkotuk and Osareainu, her sons
and daughters helping the others in building and maintaining the fence.
Actually her family seldom used the construction themselves; instead Kapkotuk and others brought to them a portion of their take. On such occasions
Shukemon's family offered some dog-salmon, saying that 'they must give
some fish in return for the flesh received.' In the weir-fishing of cherry salmon in the main stream they worked with the families of Shurunke, Kapkotuk and Osareainu; for that in the glens of the Sahorun they used to work,
while the children were young, with Shurunke's and Osareainu's families staying with them at a fishing hut. Since the children had grown up, they formed
a group by themselves with their own hut and weir. They built no peep-
fishing hut.

Kapkotuk and his family.—Kapkotuk, former associate of Osareainu in bear-
hunting, was too weak now to go hunting the beast. His only son Ukainotte
had become by his own request an associate of Sankur, the superior bear-
hunter. Kapkotuk himself, though he no longer hunted bears, did some deer-
hunting. In cooperation with Osareainu and his family, he and his children
occupied themselves busily with work at a deer-fence two miles and a half
long which it took them nearly a whole day to go checking round. Kaptotuk
speared fish as well as anyone in Nitmap and all his family were good at
fishing which they liked. For the weir-fishing of cherry salmon in the main
stream they worked with the families of Shurunke, Shukemon and Osareainu;

for that in the cherry salmon fishing on the Sahorun they and the Retununs formed a cooperative group.

Osareainu and his family.—Osareainu was known as a good bear-hunter but his young sons had had little more than two or three years of bear-hunting experience. For hunting deer they cooperated with Kapkotuk's family, staying all autumn at a hut in Penkechin by the Shikaripet working at the fence. Even when Osareainu was away, his sons did the work. For the weir-fishing of cherry salmon in the main stream they worked with the aforesaid two families and that of Shurunke; for cherry salmon fishing in the glens of the Sahorun they formed a cooperative group with the last-named and the Shukemons alone. Katunum, wife of Osareainu, was among the best women spearers of Nitmap, ranking with Retunun, Kasamushi, daughter of Shiokoro, and Inokare, daughter of Shurunke; in fact, her skill equalled many men's. Osareainu himself was not very enthusiastic; he never built a peep-fishing hut for catching dog-salmon.

(42) Information concerning cooperative activities among member families of Pipaushi local group.

Chiokatupa and his family.—Chiokatupa, a traditional headman and a great hunter in his day, was too old now to go hunting. His son Uturusote, who did some hill-hunting of deer in early winter, seldom went on an autumn bear-hunting expedition because he had to go to the coast for service at some Japanese fishing ground. But when he did, he went in company with Sayuturuk, son of Haukiainu. Chiokatupa's family never grew millet and other cereals; for trout-fishing in the glen, unlike other families, they all migrated to a fishing-hut on the Sahorun river.

Haukiainu and his family.—Haukiainu was a bear-hunter and the best hand at spearing in all Pipaushi. Sayuturuk, son by his former wife, also hunted bears.

Chipreka and his family.—Chipreka did no bear hunting himself; his only son had grown enough to hunt both bears and deer. Always cooperating with this family in hunting and fishing was his younger brother Kutsamainu; they formed a group independent of other families in Pipaushi. Kutsamainu lived alone at the next settlement Kumaushi where his younger sister Usashikun had a home. Usashikun's two sons, Ukanotte and Saimatte, and her daughter Sakemonka formed by themselves a bag-netting group. They often went cherry salmon fishing to glens of the Sahorun not far from Kumaushi, where parties from Pipaushi and Nitmap fished cherry salmon staying at fishing huts.

Isontomam and his family.—Isontomam, another bear-hunter, formed no hunting group with other families; he went alone on any bear-hunting expedition.
As far as my informant Ushino observed when at Nitmap, he was the only
man in all Pipaushi that captured and reared bear cubs. During summer,
when he was drafted at some Japanese fishing ground on the sea-coast, his
wife Ueashi and his children carried on cherry salmon fishing in the Sahorun
staying at a hut in company with Chiokatupa's family and building weirs
with them.

(**43**) Coastal people and coastal settlements.—Of the Ainu groups on the
Pacific coasts of Hokkaido surveyed by the present writer, the *pishun kotan*
(coastal settlements) were the only ones that voluntarily and regularly practised sea fishing (Note 53). The word *pishun* means 'being at the seashore'
but is here of nominal application. Like the *kimun utaru* of *kimun kotan*
(interior settlements), these people dwelled on river courses and their fishing
activities extending to the sea were oriented primarily to the river (WATA-
NABE, 1954).

The *pishun utaru* lived in groups in one or more settlements situated on
the lowermost reaches of rivers close to the estuary (Note 10). On the eve
of the farming land allotments there was a *pishun kotan* in the Azuma valley,
which formed itself a local group and *shine itokpa* group. Shortly after in
the Mukawa valley there were two *pishun kotan* local groups (Imoppe and
Chin) and in the Saru valley at about the same period there were three (Nina,
Sarupa and Piraga) at least which constituted a local group respectively.
The three *pishun kotan* in Saru and the two in Mukawa formed probably a
shine itokpa group respectively. Evidence shows that between the coastal and
the interior people in the same or adjacent valleys intermarriages took place
and through the affinal relations social intercourse was maintained on
private and family levels by reciprocating calls and sending gifts. No evidence is available to prove, however, that even in the same valley the local
group cores of the coastal and interior peoples ever represented the member
sections of one *ekashi ikiru*, patrilineal kin group of males. Nor is it clear if
local groups of the same river *pishun utar* ever formed more than one *shine
itokpa* group.

(**44**) 1) Japanese bush-warbler, Horeites cantans, appears in the plains in
early spring, migrating to hills in the breeding season from April to August;
in Hokkaido its warbling begins in about the last part of March (KIYOSU,
1952, Vol. II, pp. 250-2).

2) Himalayan cuckoo, Cuculus saturatus, crosses over to Japan in the

period from the middle part of April to the early part of May, migrating to the South to winter there (ibid., pp. 409-11).

3) Japanese cuckoo, Cuculus canorus telephonus, crosses over to Japan in the period from the middle part of May to the early part of June, migrating to Malay and New Guinea in winter (ibid., pp. 406-8). In Obihiro on the middle course of the Tokapchi the mean date of its first appearance is May 15th ; in 1958 it was May 21st (Obihiro Sokkō-sho, ed., 1959).

Chapter V

(**45**) Evidence for non-coincidence between the river group territory and the valley of the river.

Tokapchi.—Geographically, the river Sorapchi is a tributary of the river Ishikari and its valley a part of the valley of the Ishikari river system. Practically, however, the part of the Sorapchi river basin that lies above the line of the Nishitap glen that feeds it and the Numoppe glen that feeds the Nishitap, formed a portion of the Tokapchi river group's territory (Map 2). This means that Tokapchi territory extended in part over the intervening watershed into the Ishikari river basin. In this extension of territory the Tokapchi Ainu from at least the Kuttarashi and Nitmap local groups maintained hunters' huts, to which they came for bear hunts every season (p. 59). The area was also visited by collectors from Tokapchi who gathered bark for making textile material. For the fact of its belonging to the Tokapchi river group Ushino from Nitmap explains : " The upper Sorapchi runs parallel with the Sahorun that feeds the Tokapchi and points with it in the direction of Mt. Optateshuke, the ' head' mountain of the river Tokapchi. That is why the upper Sorapchi belonged to Tokapchi ". A similar reason is seen applied to the following other cases. The valley of the Shikaripet, tributary to the Tokapchi and inhabited by some of the member local groups of the upper Tokapchi *shine itokpa* group, belonged for the most part to the Tokapchi, or *shipet*, river group. But part of its lower region, that part of it on the Otopuke side which is bordered by the river's lower course from the mouth to the junction with the tributary Penkechin glen and then by the course of this glen, was included in the Otopuke river group territory (Map 2). The point was confirmed by my two informants, Ushino from Tokapchi and Kazari from Otopuke. Ushino explains that ' inasmuch as the Shikaripet flows out of one mountain with the Tokapchi, it belonged truly to Tokapchi.' Kazari on the other hand explains that the glens of the Shikaripet on its west side belonged to Tokapchi because they all point to the depth of Tokapchi, whereas those on its north side belonged to Otopuke because they point to Otopuke.

Otopuke.—The territory of the Otopuke river group stretched out again in part in its interior region into the geographical basin of the neighbouring Tushipet, extending the whole breadth between the Meto and Nukanan glens down to the Piripet tributary into which they flow, the three streams forming the boundaries on the Tushipet river group territory (Map 2). Of the territory of the Otopuke river group, that part of it which extended over the watershed into the Tushipet river basin was called *ekoipokun an (Otopue)* *iworu* (*iworu* in the east of Otopuke), while the aforesaid portion that bordered on Shikaripet was called *echupokun an (Otopuke) iworu* (*iworu* in the west of Otopuke); the geographical Otopuke river basin plus the above portions was known as Otopuke *iworu*. The reason given by Kazari for the two glens forming the territorial boundaries is that they run on the west side of Mt. Piripet where all the glens point in the direction and flow out of 'the true head mountain of the Otopuke' that lies deep in the most revered source of the main Otopuke. The glens rest on Otopuke and that is why their areas formed its *iworu*. On the other hand, the glens on the east side of the mountain point to the head of the Tushipet: they rest on Tushipet. That is why their areas formed the *iworu* thereof.

Tushipet.—Mention has already been made of the Tushipet river basin, home of the Tushipet river group, forming in part an extension of the neighbouring Otopuke river group area; into another part of the same basin there extended the Kusuri river group's territory adjoining on the other side. This was an area encircled on one side by the watershed draining on the Penke-sempiri side into the Ashoro, tributary to the Tushipet, on another side by the main course of the Tushipet above the end of the watershed and on another by the watershed that divides the Tushipet and Kusuri river basins.

Mukawa.—As Kashindeashi of Chin heard from people of the older generation who lived the traditional life, their hill hunting grounds for deer lay at the head of the Noyasube glen that feeds the neighbouring river Azuma. They were covered with a well-developed fir forest, affording fine winter quarters for the deer, and the hunters built their huts on the edge of the forest. Geographically, the place lies within the Azuma river valley, but it never belonged to Azuma *iworu* or basin as distinguished by the Ainu. Though the actual demarcation lines are not clear, the lower Noyasube which is tributary to the Azuma belonged, at any rate by Ainu distinction, to Azuma *iworu* and therefore to the Azuma Ainu. Nevertheless, the uppermost reaches of the glen alone belonged to the Mukawa Ainu. The reason, though vague, is given as below. Three glens flow out of the waterhead mountain—the Noyasube, the Irushikapet and the Moipet. Of these only the Noyasube flows on the side of Azuma; the other glens, running on the side of Mukawa, enter Mukawa *iworu* or basin. That is why the uppermost Noyasube, rising as it does with the others in the same mountain, belonged alone to Mukawa *iworu*.

Saru.—As Hachiro Kurokawa, son of the Nukipet headman's brother, heard from people of the older generation, the natives of the Nukapira, tributary to the Saru, went for bear hunts beyond the upper reaches of their river into those of the adjacent Nikap river. For the area on the Nukapira side that stretched between the Puirapet and Aipet glens, both tributary to the upper Nikap, was Nukapira territory, whereas the area lying opposite was Nikap territory and no Nukapira Ainu could cross the river Nikap without permission. This area on the upper Nikap which formed an extension of Nukapira territory apparently coincides with what has already been reported by IZUMI as a part of Saru *iworu* (IZUMI, 1951, p. 43). He ascribes the origin to a strife in which the area was taken by the people of Saru as prize from those of a neighbouring river area. As far as the author has examined, no information is available from any river valley to confirm such an origin.

These briefly are the evidences from which it might very roughly be concluded that there is no doubt about the Ainu conceptions of territory resting upon their cosmological theory on the relations between the river and the mountain and the actual demarcation being conditioned by that theory. The details will be given in Chapter VI.

(46) It may be assumed from what Hachiro Kurokawa of Nukipet, an old Ainu settlement on the Nukapira, tributary to the river Saru, a son of a brother of the Nukipet headman, heard from people of the elder generation who knew traditional life, that the natives living on the Nukapira river course—residents of Nukipet (a local group), Nioi and Shikerepe (both probably local groups) settlements—had been from old times a group by themselves distinct from any others living along the main Saru, or a distinct 'river group' as termed by the writer. By native distinction the river Nukapira, like the river Saru, formed a distinct *pet*, main stream or river, pointing to its own head mountain, Poroshiri. The two rivers were accompanied each by a river-spirit, *petorun kamui* of its own. The people of Saru observed their own ritual for the Saru river-spirit, *petorun kamuinomi;* those of Nukapira their own. On some necessary occasions the inhabitants of Nukapira conducted a group activity independent of the Saru people. "Members of the same river group could freely go gathering anywhere within their own river area, as did the Nukapira people. But the people of Nukapira were not to go fishing without permission in the Saru river area. In any area other than their own they could never act freely". This information, of which little more particulars are to be known, carries an impression that the people of Nukapira might have formed a different river group from those of Saru. IZUMI's report on the Saru Ainu as a territorial group makes no mention of these points but treats the natives of the Nukapira and the main Saru as belonging to the same river group. Apart from this, there is no available report relating to the matter.

(47)   About the territory jointly maintained by the local group. — Hokkaidō Kyū-dojin (The Former Natives of Hokkaido), published in 1911 by the Hokkaido government, states, " Although no definite boundary marked off one *kotan* territory from another, its area of fishing and hunting was apparently more or less clearly defined " (Quoted in SASAKI, 1927, p. 25). TAKA-KURA remarks that the *kotan* or a group of *kotan* had a hunting or fishing ground in common for all its members to utilize freely and that trespass by non-members was forbidden by penalty of atonement, *ashimpe* (TAKAKURA, 1942, p. 21). He also quotes an Ainu as saying, " Areas for deer and bear hunting as well as for fishing were marked off. Natives of a *kotan* were not to hunt or fish elsewhere than in their own area or territory. Anyone that dared to do so was punished immediately " (Ibid., p. 21). The last-cited information closely resembles the accounts heard by the present writer from a good many informants. Such, for example, was the abstract and generalized information picked up in the earlier stage of his interviews: " For both hunting and fishing each *kotan* had its own restricted area "; " Fishing grounds were customarily marked off for different *kotan*"; " In front of one's *kotan* was its fishing ground "; " Each *kotan* had its own area for deer and bear hunting "; " From the time of our great-grandfathers or great-great-grandfathers each *kotan* has had a dale of its own for bear hunting "; " Formerly each *kotan* had its own *iworu*, hunting ground "; " Bear hunters protected their respective *iworu* (p. 70; Note 58) as their own "; etc.

On further analysis of these generalizations in the light of both the habitat and the actual gathering activities performed in it, it will be seen that after all the word *kotan* is used in two ways: a local group as a whole in reference to a fishing ground and a cooperative group as a constituent unit of a settlement, *kotan*, in reference to a hunting ground. Actually, the fishing ground or territory for each *kotan* was the named spawning grounds of dog salmon maintained jointly by the local group (p. 59). Strangely, notwithstanding their extreme importance to Ainu life, spawning grounds as such have received no attention so far from students of the Ainu. The hunting ground of each " *kotan* " as called by the Ainu themselves means actually the bear or deer hunting territory maintained by a cooperative group of males from families usually belonging to the same settlement. For distinction and relationship between the *iworu* as simply an area around a stream and the *iworu* as a hunting territory, see Note 58.

Referring to the Saru valley Ainu, IZUMI reports as follows : " The *iworu* (i. e. territory of the Saru people), as the arena of their daily life, is divided among and occupied by a certain number of *kotan* (villages)....It is prohibited to enter the *iworu* of any other *kotan* than one's own without permission, except the *ru* (public way) " (IZUMI, 1951, p. 29 and Map 2 on p. 32). As investigated by the present writer, however, there is no evidence to show a division of the *iworu* as an entire river group territory into a number of sub-*iworu* each occupied by one of the constituent local groups and controlled for all exploitative activities conducted within the boundary, though it is certain that their gathering sites except bear-hunting grounds were concentrated around each *kotan*. MUNRO shows a diagram representing the principle of assigning fishing and hunting rights among the Saru Ainu (MUNRO, 1962, p. 156).

(48) The information was given by Kazari from Otopuke.

*The people of Opchapet and Ichanpet settlements, located between Wop and Nipushipet and both belonging to the upper local group, exploited the spawning grounds at the junctions of the Opchapet and Ichanpet glens respectively; but to all appearances the grounds had no specific names. Spawning beds there were so few and scattered that they went to the concentration or ground exploited regularly by the neighbouring Kamaune group or by permission to that of Nipushipet group farther downstream.

** The spawning ground at the junction of the Otopuke, Otopuke-*putu un ichanuni*, came off last in season in the whole river course (for the distribution of the spawning grounds as related to their time of occurrence, see Note 28). During the last week or so of the season, between the closing on the upper stream and that on the whole, this ground was exploited every year by people of the settlements lower than Nipushipet, i. e. the lower local group. They went there by night and speared by torch lights. In the daytime they found it difficult to spear the fish hiding in deep places. It must be noticed that customarily each family of the lower local group sent to each family of the upper local group a gift of one, two or three fish from out of their catch, according to the size of the recipient family.

(49) The information on the spawning grounds of the Memroputu group except those at Chepotpiuka, and of the Fushikopet, Furemem and Ponsatnai groups, was given by Ritu Yoshine from Fushiko, and that on the rest by Ushino from Nitmap.

* The spawning ground at Kapotpira was the territory of the Pipaushi group; it seems, however, that some members of the Nitmap group also came to fish there.

** The Sanenkoro group had only one spawning ground of their own on the main stream; they intensively utilized three other spawning grounds on the Sahorun, a tributary, claiming them as their fishing territory,

*** Ushino from Nitmap could name two other spawning grounds concerning the group: Shupusan-*putu un ichan* (ca. 100 yds) and Kiusan-*putu*

un ichan (ca. 100 yds). These relatively small spawning grounds on the Memro, a tributary to the Tokapchi, were exploited habitually by the Memro-putu group in time of a rise of the main stream; it is, however, not clearly known whether or not they had a claim to these.

(**50**) In regard to the Satnai, it is not known whether Munhunki group, a settlement and a local group, had any spawning ground of their own. My informant, Ushino, from Nitmap could not name any more spawning grounds on the Satnai than those mentioned in the text, which she actually visited in company with some of her kinsmen in Satnai, though to all appearances there were some more.

(**51**) The following information on the named spawning grounds on the lowest course of the Saru given by Mopi from Nina, one of the *pishun kotan* (p. 47) of the valley, is based on her direct observations and experiences in the period covering some years from the time of the land-allotment downward. There are some evidences that even in those days, at least these settlements and the local groups on the lowest course respectively remained in approximately the same area as before and continued to practise dog salmon fishing, controlling the spawning grounds by means of ritual observances similar to those described in pp. 72–73.

Named Spawning Grounds on the Lower Saru
(in descending order of location)

Name of Spawning Ground	Group Exploiting Regularly	Controlling Body
Panke-piraturu-putu Un Ichan*	Piraturu settlement group	Piraturu group as local group
Penke-nina-putu Un Ichan	Nina settlement group	Nina group as local group
Apka Un Ichan	Sarupa settlement group	Sarupa group as local group
Shira-putu Un Ichan**	„ „	(?)

  * The Piraturu group seems to have controlled several other grounds besides this, which was their best.

  ** This ground also seems to have been controlled by the Sarupa group, but it is not certain.

Chapter Ⅵ

(**52**) The category of supernatural beings that received the greatest emphasis among the Ainu is the *kamui*. Except for the Ainu culture-hero, *aeoina kamui*, all *kamui* are spirits of natural phenomena. In the supernatural world *kamui* take the form of Ainus. They have families, settlements, and even headmen. They may visit the land of the Ainu. When they do so, they disguise themselves by taking the form of some natural phenomena on earth, and bring something for the Ainu. When the material guise of the *kamui* was killed, the *kamui* departed for the *kamui*-land; its departure had to be marked with an appropriate ritual. It is for this reason that the Ainu dumped bones and skins as well as broken or used-up artifacts and even ashes from the fire-place in prescribed spots with due ritual (Fig. 1).

According to my informants the dead and *kamui* are different things. BATCHELOR (1901, pp. 567 and 569) and NATORI (1945, p. 150) describe an Ainu belief that the dead join company with their ancestors, *shinrit*, and live in the same way as in this world, even observing rituals for *kamui*. BATCHELOR (1901, pp. 568-9) and NATORI (1945, pp. 149-50) note the idea of dichotomy of their other world into the *kamui*-land which is the destination of the good and the under-land believed to be the destination of the bad. KUBODERA (1956, p. 6) states that the Ainu regard another world as existing under this world, and IZUMI (1951, p. 215) mentions that the other world of the Saru Ainu was believed to exist under the territory of the river group. My informants distinguish between the ancestor ritual, *shinnurappa*, and the ritual for *kamui*, *kamuinomi* and between the offering sticks to ancestors, *icharupa inau* or *shinnurappa inau*, and those to *kamui*, *kamuinomi inau*. The ancestor ritual was performed at a place different from that for the *kamui*-ritual.

The essential components of the ancestor ritual are shedding of wine and foods onto *icharupa inau* each to be offered to an ancestor or ancestress, and associated prayers which are different from those for *kamui*-deities, *kamuinomi inono itak*. The *icharupa* ritual was observed by men as well as women; however, it should always have been preceded by *kamuinomi* ritual the observance of which was exclusively in the hands of men.

It is said that a male Ainu worshipped male ancestors of his *ekashi ikiru* and a female Ainu female ancestors of her *huchi ikiru*. In practice, however, the ancestors to whom they directed the ritual and the generations which the ancestors covered seem to have been few. According to Kazari, my informant from Otopuke, those ancestors were usually patrilineal or matrilineal relatives of the observer of the ritual whom the observer had seen and

known well and by whom the observer was taken care of during their
life time. The ritual seems rather to have been a family affair. In both
Azuma and Otopuke, principal ancestors to be worshipped were ' *ekashi* and
huchi of the household ', that is father and mother of the male household-
head. In the days of their traditional life it was held on such an occasion
as the bear ceremony for which wine was brewed. It was usually carried out
by 'close relatives' who voluntarily came together to participate in it after
finishing the bear ritual. The social aspect of the ancestor ritual in the
traditional age still remains unexplained. KUBODERA (1951) and MUNRO (1962)
give some data on the subject in the later period.

(53) It seems certain—in fact, all informants agree on this point—that among
the *pishun utaru* (coastal people) the number of hunters specializing in bear
hunting, with grounds and huts mainly for that purpose, was very small in
proportion to that among the *kimun utaru* (interior people). As a matter of
fact, the *pishun utaru* also went hunting deer, and incidentally bears if any,
on neighbouring plains and hills. What characterized them most was, however, the practice of sea-fishing.

Reports have already been made with reference to the Saru valley on the
customary division of the fishing ground into sections with *kamui*-spirits
attributed to each (IZUMI, 1951, pp. 30-31). The same practice is found to
have prevailed in the Mukawa valley, where, it must be noted, the division
and the *kamui*-spirits attributed were in close relationship with the ecology
of the game and the methods of fishing employed by the Ainu.

Yanke tomari and *repun tomari*.—Of this only a small area near the river
mouth, known as *tomari*, was for actual exploitation. This was the area
where the outflowing river current kept the waters relatively free from wind
and waves. Here smaller fishes, such as dace and grey mullet, came together
and provided a favourable site for seining. At the Mukawa *tomari* only the
people of the river's *pishun kotan*, Chin and Immope, habitually went fishing
with seines, of which they possessed each a set in common. Measuring 22-
23 fathoms in length,* these nets of nettle fibre were made under the direction
of each headman from sections assigned to each family in the group. Except
in winter, seining was done occasionally whenever the people liked. It was
a day's work going out from the settlement and back. *Repun tomari* was
the zone of waters lying next to *yanke tomari*; here hinder mountain tops
could be seen above fore hills. This was the field of activity for *repun tomari
koru kamui*. In one area of the zone near Huihap Cape, which bordered on
the territory of the Saru river group, good fishing was made of rays and
plaices by setting stretch-rope hung with lines. The sea-bed there is said to
be favourable for the habitation of these fishes. Only a few families of the

---

* According to Ainu informants.

pishun utaru followed stretch-rope fishing: shortly after the land allotments, 2 families out of 10 – odd at Chin on the Mukawa and or 3 out of 14 or 15 at Nina on the Saru.

Each spring and again each autumn, for about a month while favourable weather prevailed for drying and storing away their catches, the males of these families went to stay at seaside fishing lodges, *haina koru kucha* or *pishun kucha*, and devoted themselves to fishing with the stretch-rope, 'haina', while their families remained at home. Information has it that about the same time there were 5 or 6 lodges belonging to the Saru group standing in cluster on their side of Huihap Cape.

Yanke sotki and repun sotki.—*Yanke sotki* was the area lying next to *repun tomari* and extending to where the hinder mountain tops were seen to disappear beneath the horizon. *Repun sotki* was the open sea lying beyond. The former was associated with *yanke sotki kor kamui* and the latter with *repun sotki kor kamui*. It is said that *yanke soti kor kamui* was the spirit of the younger killer whale and *repun sotki kor kamui* that of the elder killer whale. Little can be known about the probable connection between them and *repun kamui*, king killer whale or chief killer whale, referred to by all informants from interior settlements as a special *kamui* worshipped by *pishun utaru*, coastal people. It is also said that *repun kamui* was a brother to *metot ushi kamui*, chief of bears.

The above-mentioned two *sotki* provided the Ainu with fishing grounds for swordfish, *shirikap*. The subdivision of the area seems related with the habit of swordfish and its effect on the method of their fishing. The Ainu fished for them during summer when the fish swam round in groups of several near the sea surface. The fishermen chased them in *itaoma chip*, dugouts with broadened sides, and pierced them with harpoons, *kite*. Harpooning from small-sized dugouts on the open sea of this large fish held as ferocious as the spearfish, was regarded by the Ainu as an operation of as much special ability, both technical and ritual, as brown bear hunting. At the Mukawa shortly after the land allotments only 3 families from the Chin local group core followed swordfish harpooning. It was known that in some years the fish came nearer shore and in others they kept farther off shore. The boundary of *yanke sotki* represented the nearest approach line of the fish known by experience, and the off-shore boundary their farthest line of departure from shore. When the harpooning season came on, the *shirikap* fishermen could foretell the probable course of the fish, whether they would come the way of *yanke sotki* or that of *repun sotki*, by such signs as the high or low flights of fireflies. The coming of swordfish to *repun sotki* meant for the Ainu going out into the markless open sea; it was then that the Ainu became most particular on the observation of their ritual for *sotki kor kamui*.

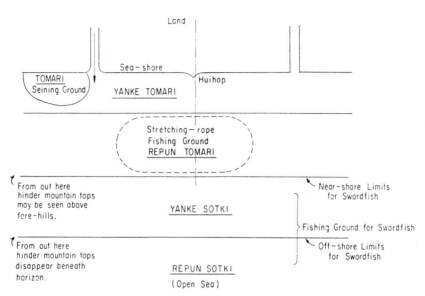

The operation was carried out with their settlements as base without using any special lodges. The fish caught was disposed in practically the same way as with the bear. Its head was set on an altar erected out of doors "so that it might return to the open sea with the *inau* and regain its original shape." The flesh was shared as *aeimek* among all the families in the local group and also relatives living outside.

(54) YOSHIDA was informed by an old Ainu that the Tokapchi, a male river, and the Ishikari, a female river, are a married couple whose children are the Otopuke and Satnai rivers (YOSHIDA, 1956b, p. 151). Another old Ainu informed him that the Otopuke is a son of the Tokapchi and the Satnai a daughter of it (ibid., p. 326).

(55) The dominance-subordinance relation between the *kamui* attributed to a river, *pet*, as distinguished by the Ainu and around which a river group has evolved, and the *kamui* attributed to each of the tributary streams of the river, has been given no attention in any published materials. For the Ainu belief of water spirits living in a large group with its chief or headman presiding over them, reference may be made to the following descriptions by KINTAICHI: "There are so many of these (water spirits) *kamui* that, when soliciting their help, the Ainus call a chief as (in this ritual prayer),

    0 *kamui*, who keep your eyes on the stream flowing down this village
        of Saru,

O *kamui*, who command a host of retainers of *wakka ushi kamui*, the
      kamui of water,
   To you we implore......" (KINTAICHI, 1944, p. 270).
   NATORI describes a mythical relationship between *Wakka ushi kamui*, the
kamui of a given main stream or river, for instance the Saru, and *Nai koru
kamui*, the *kamui* of a given glen or spring flowing into it (NATORI, 1941, p.
38). KINTAICHI cites *Pet koru kamui*, river owning *kamui*   (1944, p. 217).

(**56**) *Shi*-stream.—In CHIRI's explanation of the use and meaning of the affix
'*shi*' it is remarked that a number of streams into which the headwaters of
a river branch are regarded as parent and children and that the one thought
to be the main stream receives the affix to indicate its parentage: thus *Shi*-
Tokoro means the 'parent' Tokoro, i. e. the head of the main Tokoro (CHIRI,
1951, p. 34).
   Since geographically the headwaters of every river branch into a number
of streams, whether large or small, it might be supposed that all rivers have
their main stream affixed with '*shi*', but whether or not that is always the
actual case remains to be proved.   As a matter of fact, where the head-
streams are distinguished one from another, that one certainly carries the
affix which is regarded to be the true main stream.   The Satnai, however,
gives no indication of its main head-stream being specially distinguished as
shi-stream, because, as Ushino of Nitmap explains, the head of this river
never branches.   No investigation has been made for the river Azuma.

(**57**) *Iworu tapka* and the upper reaches of a river as the abode of nature
spirits.—In Otopuke the abode of the river-owning *kamui* was also oriented
to the *iworu tapka* of the river, i. e. the summit of Mt. Otopuke. In Mukawa,
the chief tree-spirit, *shirampa kamui*, as well as the chief bear-spirit, *metotush kamui*, and the river-spirit, *wakka ush kamui*, were believed to reside
in the highest mountains in the upper reaches of the river.   The land-*iworu*-
owning spirits of Tokapchi or Otopuke, *Tokapchi or Otopuke iworu koru kamui*,
the river-owning spirit, *petorun kamui*, of Tokapchi, and the river-spirit,
wakka ush kamui, of Azuma, were each held to live in the upper reaches of
the respective river.   The number and kinds of the land-*iworu*-owning *kamui*
could not be identified strictly; in regard to Tokapchi, the spirits belonging
to the category are *kotan koru kamui*, the *kotan*-owning *kamui*, i. e. the owl
spirit, *niyash koru kamui*, the spirit of a certain bird, and some others which
could not be named; concerning Otopuke, it is only informed that there were
six or seven *kamui* of the category, the names of which my informant could
not mention.   The author's attempts at reaching a clear definition of this
category have been fruitless.   It is identified by Hikoichiro Oyamada, of

Shikot, with *shiri koru kamui* and *wakka ushi kamui*, by Hachiro Kurokawa and Manjiro Hiramura, of Saru, with bear-spirits, and again by Kentaro Yoshimura, of Azuma, with bear-spirits and probably *wakka ushi kamui*. A published material refers to it as standing in Saru for *hashi inau koro kamui* (i. e. *kamui* in the shape of a certain bird) and *shirampa kamui* (NATORI, 1941, p. 77).

Referring to the dwelling place assigned to *kotan koru kamui* of village-owning *kamui*, YOSHIDA quotes an old Tokapchi Ainu as saying: " In Satnai (i. e. Mt. Satnai at the head of the river Satnai—present writer) and Nupkaushi (i e. Mt. Nupkaushi on the border of Otopuke *iworu*—present writer) there dwells in each a *kotan koru kamui*: in Satnai the *kamui* of the people of Satnai and in Nupkaushi that of the people of Otopuke " (YOSHIDA, 1956b, p. 154). An old Saru Ainu from Porosaru *kotan* informs that in his *kotan* " people offer *inau* and wine to Poroshiri (i. e. Mt. Poroshiri, recognized by Ainu as the head of the river Saru—present writer) as held to be the place where lives the *kotan koru kamui*" (YOSHIDA, 1957, p. 57). The only information available concerning the chief of water-spirits has been quoted from MITSUOKA in Note 59. For a belief in the guardian *kamui* of a district or land dwelling in the water-head mountain of a river along which the natives lived, see a quotation from YOSHIDA in Note 59.

(**58**) *Iworu* as a dale basin and the hunting territory.—The word *iworu*, rather than being a general term, is more usually a particular term to denote the basin of an actual river, *pet*, or dale, *nai*. As viewed by the Ainu, a river- or dale-basin has two aspects, as a geographical area and as a field of activity for associated nature-spirits. The designation of a river basin was made by the name of the *pet*, as, for instance, ' Otopuke *iworu* '. Similarly, when the term was applied to a dale basin, the name of the dale came first, as ' Wop *iworu* '. In practice the term was used in connection with hunting activities, as, for example, " I am going to Wop *iworu* ", " Deer are plentiful in Nitatnai *iworu* ", or " Wop *iworu hutne*, the narrows of the Wop valley ".

Many Ainus, when asked what the *iworu* is, answer that it is a hunting ground, for the following reason. Their hunting lodge, *iramande chise* or *kucha chise*, was invariably found in some dale, *nai*, with the whole of its upper area as *iramande* (hunting) *ushi* (site or place) or *ku ari* (set with bows) *ushi* of the occupants. It will be seen that their hunting ground lay always in some particular dale or *iworu*. In case of some hunting ritual or dispute with outsiders over a hunting ground, reference was made by the name of the representative (elder) of the hunting group concerned or by the name of the territorial group to which the hunting group belonged, as ' So-and-so's *iworu* ' or ' *iworu* under such and such people's control '. It must be noted

that the way of calling one and the same controlling body varied with varying situations, as when the addressed or the subject belonged to one's own
settlement, to another of the same river group, or to an entirely different
river group. To cite just an example, the *ku ari ushi* of a hunting group—
Zarashi and his sons—of Nitmap settlement belonging to the Tokapchi river
group, was known as 'Zarashi *koru (to own) iworu*', '*ku(I) kor iworu*', 'Nitmap (name of the settlement) *un (to be at) utar (people) kor iworu*', and
'Tokapchi (*shipet* name) *un utar kor iworu*'. It must be noticed that the last
name is identical with that of the *pet* area seen as the entire river group
territory. These names, then, all denoting the hunting grounds of a particular
cooperative group, stood for the dale area under its habitual control with
attendant ritual observance.

Here caution must be taken in discriminating between the *iworu* as a
river basin and the *iworu* as the hunting territory of a cooperative group.
Nor should the *iworu* in the latter sense be taken, when designated as aforesaid by the name of a settlement, as if standing for any territory jointly
controlled by the settlement group or local group.

PILSUDSKY reports that the Ainu of Sakhalin have from time immemorial
distributed all the streams among themselves as private property, and no one
but the owner has the right to hunt anywhere along the stream (PILSUDSKY,
1912, p. 136).

(**59**) The orientation scheme of the Ainu house has been referred by some
writers merely to the points of the compass, while a few have referred it to
the direction in which the house stands to the river flowing by the settlement.

YOSHIDA, who visited one of the Otopuke settlements in 1907, observed
that every house in the settlement invariably opened its door to the south,
that is, to the lower stream of the river Otopuke with one window facing
east and another facing north, the second being called *kamui puyara* because
it opened to the north where *kamui* dwells (YOSHIDA, 1956a, p. 11). He describes about the Ainu of the age before 1885 who lived in the vicinity of
Fushiko on the middle Tokapchi which he visited in 1907 and 1914 and where
he became a resident from 1916 to 1930, as follows. The native houses stood
along the bank of the river in the order from upper to lower positions with
each *kamui*-window opening to the waterhead mountain and each door to the
lower stream. Outside each house, toward the upper stream, there stood the
altar, between which and the window was erected the cage for the bear-cub.
The orientation scheme of the houses varys according to the direction in
which the river flows (YOSHIDA, 1955, p. 45). A generalization on the meaning
of positions is also made by him as follows: "In every district a position
in an Ainu house on the side of the upper stream is regarded as an upper

seat and one on the other side as a lower one; the house is so oriented in the belief that at the top of the head mountain in the direction of the upper side of the house there dwells the guardian *kamui* of the land" (YOSHIDA, 1958, p. 39).

MITSUOKA cites similar information on the Shiraoi Ainu in the Southwestern part of Hokkaido: "The first thing that strikes one from the mainland of Japan as strange is the regular orientation of all the houses in a (Ainu) settlement. Needless to say, ancient tradition rules out all free planning by individuals. Opening a door or window facing upstream is to be avoided in reverence to the many *kamui* or deities, such as *wakka ushi kamui*, that reside on the upper reaches of the river. Houses must face downstream, for human habitation is subject to privacy and uncleanliness which it is too awful to expose to the sight of the *kamui*" (MITSUOKA, 1941, p. 29).

HABARA quotes an Ainu writer, T. TAKESUMI, as saying, "The door of a house always faces downstream....; the window opening on the side of the upper stream...." (HABARA, 1939, p. 73).

HABARA, examining published materials, concludes: "Their (the Ainus') settlements are built in a uniform direction on the bank of a river or lake in order to meet the necessity of their economic life and the requirements of their religion born of such life" (ibid, p. 69).

Referring to a similar habit among the Orok of Sakhalin, NAGANE reports: "The settlement, of a scattered pattern similar to that described for the Ainus, contained five small huts. All faced in one direction and had two doors each, one for the mountain and the other for the sea. The door for the mountain seemed in everyday use. They were coastal houses, apparently after the style of winter houses" (NAGANE, 1925, p. 176).

(60) The use and significance of the sacred window.—On the basis of the data given by GREY and BATCHELOR, HALLOWELL pointed out the Ainu custom of taking any part of the bear, and on certain occasions other game or fish, into the dwelling through a special window (HALLOWELL, 1926, p. 143).

For the use and significance of the window an account is given by BATCHELOR (1901, p. 124). KINTAICHI states, "Implements of hunting and fishing are taken out of the house by this window, *kamui kush puyara*, window for *kamui*, and never by the ordinary doorway. Game brought home also enter by this and no other way. Right below it you see a space, called *moshkaru*, set apart for depositing the game. In Ainu conception game of all kinds are *kamui*; an animal or fish taken by a household master is a guest coming on a visit to the fire-spirit of the house. The belief is that when the game arrives, the fire-*kamui*, invisible to human eyes, is at the window to greet and show in the *kamui* of the game. Hence the great sanctity in which the window is held at all times and the taboo of peeping therein as a gravest violence." (KINTAICHI, 1937, pp. 118-9). The present writer also was informed of exactly the same ideas and practices concerning the window from Kazari, my informant from Otopuke. YOSHIDA gives the following information obtained from the Otopuke Ainu on his visit to Otopuke early in the 1900's: the window, *kamui puyara*, is faced towards the North or the upper reaches of the Otopuke river where *kamui* reside, and the *kamui* look into the Ainu house through the window (YOSHIDA, 1956a, p. 11).

Of the Sakhalin Ainu the sacred window of similar use and significance is reported. The name is *kamui kushi puyara*, window for *kamui* to pass through, or *inau kushi puyara*, window for the *inau*, one for taking out *inau*-offerings for the outdoor altar (NAGANE, 1925, p. 95).

Miss Gerda SMIDT of the National Museum in Copenhagen, called my attention to a fact that the Lapp house also has a special entrance for a bear killed.

(**61**) Spatial arrangement of the Ainu dwelling house, the associated structures and workshops.—Being inseparably connected with gathering activities, these structures and workshops, together with their traditional pattern of arrangement (Figs. 1 and 6; p. 9) were fast discarded in comparatively recent times with the conversion to agricultural life (Notes 7-8). Today what remains is a scrap of their names preserved in Ainu dictionaries and oral epics known as *yukar*. Nor is there literature referable on the spatial orientation of those structures and workshops that used to be annexed to the dwelling house of the Hokkaido Ainu. For the Sakhalin Ainu, information is supplied by YAMAMOTO concerning their dwelling house, food storehouse, dog-leashing poles, lavatory, bear-cub cage, altar, ash- and refuse-heaps, etc., all arranged on a prescribed pattern in their home settlement (YAMAMOTO, 1943, pp. 57-62).

The book indicates that the Sakhalin Ainu built their dwelling house, altar and bear-cub cage in a relative position identical with their Hokkaido Ainu counterparts as investigated by the present writer. The relative position of the ash-heap in either case is also roughly the same. Some of the storehouses were also in the same position. That the sacred window and the altar apparently formed an axis likewise pointing up the stream flowing past the settlement, may be inferred from a statement in the book that the Sakhalin Ainu settlement was originally located, with their doors opening on the sea and their backs to the mountain, on a seaside elevation near a river-mouth ascended by the dog- and cherry-salmon (ibid., pp. 45 and 57) and also from three accompanying sketch maps (ibid., pp. 55-56).

(**62**) Social aspect of the dog salmon ritual and of the rituals for other fishes.

—Little mention is found in published materials of the dog salmon ritual of the Ainu and much less has been made known about its social aspect. Something of the social context has been reported as follows: " The Shiraoi Ainu (a coastal group in southwestern Hokkaido), fishing mainly in the Nishitap river, observed their *kamuinomi*-ritual at the river's mouth every autumn before it was time for the first dog salmon to ascend the river. The event was known as *pet kamuinomi*, the river-spirit ritual, and the *inau*-offerings and the altar were prepared by male members from each family in the settlement." (INUKAI, 1954, p. 81.) " When dog salmon fishing started, the first fish, *ashichep*, was cooked....to be offered to the fire-spirit....and the house-spirit ....Offering was also made at the mouth of the river to the river-spirit as ' the first catch of the season ' ". (Ibid., p. 83.) Another report shows that almost the same pre-fishing and first salmon rituals were practised in Horobetu in Hitaka in the last part of the Meiji era (1868–1912) (CHIRI, 1959, pp. 259–60). According to CHIRI's description, the pre-fishing ritual, *pet kamuinomi*, i. e. the river-spirit ritual, was performed by males, one from each household, who solicited the river-spirit as the spirit of water at the spawning places for plentiful runs and spawning of the dog salmon. In all published material, description on the post-fishing ritual is lacking.

The collective activities at the dog salmon rituals as described in the text were easy of detection in the Tokapchi, Otopuke and Saru Valleys, whilst in the Azuma valley little could be known but that some ritual came off as joint activities of the local group. Owing to the death of one of my chief informants, Ushintasan from Tonika in the Azuma valley, the present writer failed to clarify the point. Nor was anything clear in the Shikot valley beyond that my informant from Rankoushi, H. Oyamada, had seen elders of the former *kotan* going to the river bank to set up *inau* there before dog salmon fishing started and that each family gave a ritual to offer their first fish to the fire-spirit of their household.

The natives of the Tokapchi, Otopuke and Tushipet areas at least had, besides the dog salmon rites, others for the first fish of the spring, *chirai* or Fucho perryi, and the cherry salmon that followed; however, there is no published material available on the latter rites.

Economically of less importance than the cherry salmon, the *chirai*, or *chirai kamuichep*, it seems, was ritually more important than the cherry salmon. In Tokapchi at least, the rituals for the fish, like those for the dog salmon, came on three occasions, on the eve of the ascent, on the first catch, and on the close of the runs. Extreme meagreness of data on the subject makes it doubtful whether or not they likewise came off as a joint enterprise of the local group. Perhaps all that has been made known is that the headman knew the approach of the runs by the waxing and waning of the moon;

that when the time came he went down to a certain place on a certain tributary, where he made *inau*-offerings in a ritual for the fish and then watched for their arrival. When they came, he had a number of his local group men visit the site daily to haul them by spearing. In either of the Tokapchi and Otopuke valleys, the rituals for the *chirai*, like those for the dog salmon, differed from the cherry salmon rites to be described below in that they involved a post-run or post-fishing ritual including the throwing of the mandible of the first-caught fish and the *inau* offerings into the stream.

The ritual for the cherry salmon, *ichaniu* or *ichanui* or *ichaniu kamuichep*, took place at the approach of the runs and was an observance on the level of the cooperative group as a unit. On the upper Tokapchi, on the bank of the main stream, close by the weir site, *tesh karu ushi*, shaved wooden sticks, *inau*, were set up by male members of the weir fishing group. The ritual over, the group immediately set to work together building the weir. In Otopuke where each local group was split into several minor *kotan* groups (p. 9), and each *kotan* group constituted a weir fishing group (p. 44), the eldest member of each *kotan* seems to have been in charge of the pre-fishing ritual. The practice of offering the first cherry salmon to the fire-spirit is known from Tokapchi, Otopuke and Tushipet at least. No post-fishing ritual was observed for the fish in either of the areas.

In Otopuke at least, *spun*, a kind of Tribolodon, was also called *kamuichep* and the first-caught fish of each family was offered to the fire spirit of their house. The fish was treated with neither a pre-fishing nor post-fishing ritual.

The cults for those kinds of fishes remain to be explored in further details.

(**63**) Chief of the bears and its subordinates.—The chief of the bears is represented by different names in different parts of Hokkaido. A few examples from a list of different *kamui* names relating to the bear ceremony (NATORI, 1941) are: *ponporokatok etok un kamui* (i. e. *kamui* in the depth of Ponporo-katok—Sorapchi area), *nupuri koru kamui* (i. e. mountain-owning *kamui*.—Mashike area), *nupuri noshiki un kamui* (i. e. *kamui* in the middle of the mountains.—also Mashike area). *kamui ekashi* (i. e. *kamui* old man—Yoichi area), *kimun kamui* (*kamui* deep in the mountains—Shiraoi area), *medotushi kamui* (i. e. *kamui* deep in the mountains—Saru area). Still another name collected in Azuma by the present writer is *kimerok kamui*, *kamui* sitting in the heart of the mountain.

As is well known, the Ainu view is that the world of bears has its chiefs and their family or subordinates and that the subordinates come as guests to the Ainu, who in due time send them back again to their chief. The view is clearly indicated, for instance, in the information collected by NATORI

(NATORI, 1941, p. 43) and the mythological stories collected by KINTAICHI (KINTAICHI, 1943, pp. 153-154; 176-177). Nevertheless, the Ainu view according to which they established a territorial ordering or grouping of bears is indicated only in the writings of INUKAI as follows: " the Ainu in this district (i. e. Otopuke) believe that just as they themselves have from generation to generation lived in such a way as not to disgrace their *kotan* and family names, so the bears of the mountains with their definite ancestry—e. g. the Bears of the Mountains of Akan (at the head of the river Akan in Kushiro) or the Bears of Mt. Optateshke (at the head of the river Tokapchi) coming down from respective forefathers—behave themselves alike not to disgrace their ancestors" (INUKAI, 1942, p. 143).

(**64**)   The river along which the Ainu settled, its source and the high mountain that harbours the source also played important parts in providing backgrounds for their mythology, as may be seen in KINTAICHI's material of myths collected in Saru (KINTAICHI, 1943, pp. 15, 66, 71, 88,89, 153-154, 172, 176-177). The material contains some myths which clearly indicate the relation existing between the mountain of *kamui*, the large house standing on its top and the chief of the bears who lives there (ibid., pp. 153-4; 176-7).

CHIRI remarks that the *kamui nupuri* or *kamui*-mountains rise as watersheds for most of the rivers and that they are associated with many legends of gardens for the *kamui* and mysterious lakes called *kamui to* on their summits (CHIRI, 1951, p. 11).

(**65**)   Return of the bear-spirit to the river source area.—In most of the writings hitherto published it is simply mentioned that the spirit of the ritually-killed bear goes back to the ' land of *kamui* ' or ' divine land ' where its parent or chief lives, no reference being made to the spatial orientation of nature spirits which is so charateristic of Ainu cosmology.   A survey guided in the light of the Ainu view of habitat unmistakably reveals the fact that the land so designated is not a mere divine land of imagination but an actual, spatially-oriented land of the chief of the bears.   The fact is also borne out by scattered information hitherto published, such as that of a Sakhalin Ainu headman who informs that " the bear ceremony is performed to send off the bear-spirit back to the mountain simply because that is where he came from and where the deity of the mountain lives " (INUKAI and NATORI, 1939, p. 254) or that from an Otopuke Ainu that " the *maratto* (the skull representing the spirit of the ritually-killed bear), guided by *niyash koru kamui* and *kotan koru kamui*, goes to the abode of *nupri koro kamui*" (i. e. mountain-owning *kamui*, chief of the bears) (NATORI, 1941, p. 63). Information similar to the last was collected by the present writer from Ushino, an informant from

Tokapchi. The Ainu belief that the spirit of the sent-off animal returns to the specific mountain at the head of a river that is regarded as the abode of the chief of the bears, is distinctively and minutely represented in some of their mythological stories (KINTAICHI, 1943, pp. 153-154; pp. 176-177).

The only available information that suggests a territorial ordering of bears as laid down by the Ainu will be found in a quotation from INUKAI at the end of Note 63.

In spite of all such information, however, no attention has ever been paid to the system of social solidarity, based on the territorial principle, which exists between the river group and the bears in the same river area.

(**66**) Season for the bear ceremony.—Different writers and informers give different times for the bear ceremony: September or October (HALLOWELL, 1926, p. 121); mostly between late November and January to February (INU-KAI and NATORI, 1939, p. 256); in and about Kutcharo at least, between December and January to February (SARASHINA, 1942, p. 126). The actual dates of the few festivals observed by Ainu hunters in recent times vary considerably as in the following cases: 25 November, 1939, for one performed by Oyamada at Rankoushi in Shikot (NATORI, 1941, p. 68); 16-17 December, 1939, for one observed by Ōno at Suwan in Kushiro (INUKAI and NATORI, 1940, p. 96); 29 January, 1940, for another again by Oyamada at the same place (NATORI, 1941, p. 68). It must be noticed, however, that in the days when the natives still lived in their traditional ways a limited period in winter was the only time for a whole settlement group to engage in festive activities which lasted for days or for any great number of people to come together from different settlements, as may be observed in the chart on p. 53 showing the cycle of gathering activities. A diary left by one of the earliest Japanese settlers on the middle Tokapchi (HAGIHARA, ed., 1937) records an invitation he received to a bear ceremony at one local Ainu household on 21 January, 1883 (ibid., p. 111) and another to one at a local headman's on 14 January, 1884 (ibid., p. 160). SARASHINA mentions that along the river Kutcharo or Kushiro bear ceremonies went round in succession from the upper to lower settlements (SARASHINA, 1942, p. 126; for a case of the ceremonies in modern times in the same area, see Note 67). Though no detailed information is available, such a custom appears to have been related in some way with the system described in the text by which a series of bear ceremonies were performed in sequence by different member local groups or settlement groups of each *shine itokpa* group.

(**67**) Social aspect of bear ritual.—The so-called bear ceremony of the Ainu in its traditional form is now only barely preserved among the small remnant of Ainu bear hunters, and even with those huntsmen the event has ceased to function socially as it did in the past. What has hitherto been described by various writers has been confined to its formal aspect, chief works dealing with which may be found in the bibliographies by HALLOWELL (1926) and INUKAI and NATORI (1939); more recently, minutely detailed reports have been published by INUKAI and NATORI (INUKAI and NATORI, 1939 and 1940; NATORI, 1941). For various reasons its social aspect has been virtually ignored in nearly all studies of the Ainu, and our knowledge of that aspect has remained little further than what was summarized by HALLOWELL, as follows: "In every case it is evident that the affair is communal in nature. Not only friends and relatives in the village but sometimes individuals from other settlements as well are invited by the owner of the bear, who is also the host" (HALLOWELL, 1926, p. 122). Only in a later report by INUKAI and NATORI (1940) on the formal aspect of the bear rite as it is observed today may one have fragmentary information regarding the subject—the relation between the rite and the participants. Here follows an excerpt from the above report referring to a bear festival which took place in the middle of December in 1939 at Suwan settlement in Kushiro, one of the older native *kotan* (INUKAI and NATORI, 1940, pp. 96-135).

In the spring of 1939 a bear cub was caught by Kawasaki, an old Ainu from Kutcharo settlement who lodged at the settlement of Suwan. The cub was taken over by Old Ōno, a descendant of Hashibami, elder of the former Suwan *kotan*, and it was kept in a cage built by the sacred window of his ancestral dwelling. The ritual killing of the bear was performed at an old altar left by the late Hashibami, about 40 metres from the cage.

The ceremony was attended by members of the three other settlements on the river, Kutcharo (the uppermost settlement), Tohro and Harutori (the lowermost settlement). The attendants from Harutori were all females. On this occasion at least, for reasons not known, no invitation was sent to the settlement but the women came to join the ceremony. It is informed that the bear festivals at Suwan had been attended by members of about the same four *kotan*. The main participants were: old Ōno, who had brought up the cub; old Kawasaki, who caught it, old Isosato, who was descended from a headman of the former Kutcharo; Tosa, an old member of Tohro; Yamanaka and Teshi, old members of Kutcharo. The main part of the bear ceremony consisted of a series of rituals, not only to the bear itself but also to other associated *kamui* groups. The essential element of the rituals is the offering of prayers and *inau*-sticks to the respective *kamui*. The performance of the rituals was allotted to the male participants who came from the aforementioned settlements, the important parts being taken by the elders whose names were previously mentioned. Now old Ōno was adopted into his family and he had been in Japanese service since an early age, which circumstance had made his knowledge of the bear rite insufficient for a chief priest. The duty on this occasion had accordingly been commissioned to Kawasaki who had caught the cub, but something or other prevented him from taking up the duty, which finally went to old Teshi of Kutcharo. Of all the eight *inau* offered to the bear-spirit the most important were the two fixed to the forked ends of the pole set up at the outdoor altar and supporting the bear's skull. These carried Ōno's ancestor mark, *ekashi itokpa*, which also marked two other of the remaining six set up on both outer sides. Of the rest two had the *itokpa* of Kawasaki and one that of Tosa. The person who offered the remaining one is not mentioned. NATORI did not give any information about the kinship relation between those persons who offered the *inau* and that between their *kotan*; however, it is interesting to see that the ancestor marks of all those persons share a common design element but differ from each other in the total pattern (ibid., p. 131, Fig. 39).

NATORI states that though presided over by a chief priest, the Ainu bear ceremony was no family affair but a joint observance of the whole local membership. In the days when the headman was the undisputed centre of authority, every bear cub taken was brought to him and every bear killed on a hunt received due rites in his presence (ibid., p. 131).

(68) INUKAI and NATORI are the only writers who have supplied information on the frequency of the bear festival, pointing out that in spite of many writers describing the ceremony as if it were a sort of calendar custom in the Ainu *kotan*, there can be no bear ceremony in a *kotan* in the year when no cub is taken; that since different households in the same *kotan* may capture cubs in different years, it is natural that different families perform the festival in different years; that in some years one family may ritually kill two or three cubs at a time (INUKAI and NATORI, 1939, p. 255). These points have been confirmed in his surveys by the present writer. Usually, a cub caught in the spring was killed at the ceremony early in the following year. Sometimes one was kept for two or three years before it was killed. The development of the bear-rearing custom among the Ainu as described above naturally had for its requisite more or less surplus production of food stuffs. The stability of the settlement should be counted among other factors.

(69) In the *kamuinomi*-ritual he was required to offer *ashimpe* to the *kamui* concerned. The *ashimpe* in this case might include, besides *inau*-sticks, some items regarded by the Ainu as the best of their treasures, *ikoro*, such as *tuki* and *shintoko*, lacquer wares imported from Japan. Such *ikoro* were offered to local *kamui* concerned also in case of getting permission in advance of

exploiting resources in the territory of a different river group. According to Kazari from Otopuke the *ikoro* received as *ashimpe* in relation to those activities was kept and stewarded by the headman and was called *kamui korube, kamui*'s property, as distinguished from Ainu's properties. TAKAKURA points out that *ashimpe* is not a mere fine but an offering to *kamui* or an act of giving which expresses one's apology (TAKAKURA, 1942, p. 39).

(**70**) The building up in this wise of a system of social relations between man and natural phenomena presents a marked contrast to that on the principle of origin or kinship as seen, for instance, in Arunta totemism. The Ainu system is related closely with their way of ordering nature in terms of spatial orientation. In this connection the present writer is deeply interested in the Northwest Coast Indians of North America. A comparison reveals a striking similarity between their beliefs concerning salmon (DRUCKER, 1950, p. 283) and those of the Ainu. Elements reported as native to the Northwest Coast such as 'the belief in the immortality of game' and 'the ritual requirement of honoring captured animals and of returning certain parts' (DRUCKER, 1955, p. 71) are common with the Ainu. The close similarity in form of belief and ritual may conceal a great difference in meaning and function. Yet the present writer cannot but wonder what parts are played in the system of social solidarity between the Northwest Coast Indians and their habitat by such spatial elements as, for instance, laying down the first-caught salmon with heads pointing upstream, throwing pieces of meat in prescribed directions, placing the bear head eastward (DRUCKER, 1950) and the esoteric formula spoken before various rocks and spots that mark the abodes of their spirits (GUNTHER, 1928, p. 143). It is also interesting to see that the Japanese and the Tungus are other peoples who emphasize the ordering of nature spirits on local basis and the establishment of the ritual relationship between man and nature on the principle of local contiguity (WATANABE, 1964).

REFERENCES CITED

BARTHOLOMEW, George A., Jr. and Joseph B. BIRDSELL. 1953. Ecology and Proto-hominids. American Anthropologist, Vol. 55, pp. 481–498.

BATCHELOR, John. 1901. The Ainu and Their Folklore. London.

BATCHELOR, John. 1926. An Ainu-English-Japanese Dictionary. Tokyo.

CHIRI, Mashiho. 1951. *Ainu Chimei Goi* (Ainu Topographical Terms). Kyōdo Kenkyū Sōsho, No. 1. Sapporo.

CHIRI, Mashiho. 1953. *Bunrui Ainu-go Jiten: Shokubutsu-hen* (A Classificatory Ainu Dictionary: Plants). Nihon Jōmin Bunka Kenkyū-sho Ihō, No. 64. Tokyo.

CHIRI, Mashiho. 1959. *Ainu no Sake-ryō: Horobetsu ni okeru Chōsa* (Dog Salmon Fishing of the Ainu: An Investigation in Horobetsu). Hoppō Bunka Kenkyū Hōkoku, No. 14, pp. 245–265. Sapporo.

DRUCKER, Philip. 1950. Northwest Coast. University of California Anthropological Records 9:3, Culture Element Distributions: XXVI.

DRUCKER, Philip. 1951. The Northern and Central Nootkan Tribes. Smithsonian Institution Bureau of American Ethnology, Bull. 144.

DRUCKER, Philip. 1955. Sources of Northwest Coast Culture. 75th Anniversary Volume of the Anthropological Society of Washington, pp. 59–81.

ELTON, Charles. 1953. Animal Ecology. London.

EVANS-PRITCHARD, E. E. 1940. The Nuer. A Description of the Modes of Livelihood and Political Institutions of a Nilotic People. London.

FORDE, Daryll. 1947. The Integration of Anthropological Studies. Journal of the Royal Anthropological Institute, Vol. 78, pp. 1–10.

FORDE, Daryll. 1954. Introduction to 'African Worlds. Studies in the Cosmological Ideas and Social Values of African Peoples,' Daryll Forde (ed.), pp. viii–xvii. London.

GUNTHER, Erna. 1927. Klallam Enthography. University of Washington Publications in Anthropology, Vol. 1, No. 5, pp. 171–314.

GUNTHER, Erna. 1928. A Further Analysis of the First Salmon Ceremony. University of Washington Publications in Anthropology, Vol. 2, No. 5, pp. 129–173.

HABARA, Matakichi. 1939. *Ainu Shakai-keizai-shi* (A Socio-economic History of the Ainu). Tokyo.

HAGIHARA, Minoru (ed.). 1937. *Tokachi Kaihatsu-shi* (A History of Land Development in Tokapchi). Tokyo.

HALLOWELL, I. 1926. Bear Ceremonialism in the Northern Hemisphere. American Anthropologist, Vol. 28, No. 1.

HANDA, Yoshio. 1933. *Sake Masu no Hanashi* (On the Salmon). Keison Ihō, Vol. 5, No. 1, pp. 14–17. Sapporo.

HATTA, Saburo. 1911. *Muma* (The Bear). Tokyo.

HAYASHI, Yoshishige. 1958. *Ainu no Kōun Gijutsu* (Cultivation Techniques of the Ainu). Hoppō Bunka Kenkyū Hōkoku, No. 13, pp. 175–203. Sapporo.

HIKITA, Hirochika. 1956. *Hokkaido-Engan oyobi Kasen de torareru Taiheiyō Keison-rui* (Pacific Salmon, Genus: Oncorhynchus, known to occur in Coasts and Rivers of Hokkaido). Hokkaido Suisan Fuka-jyō Shiken Hōkoku, No. 11, 25–44. Sapporo.

HITCHCOCK, Romyn. 1891. The Ainus of Yezo, Japan. Report of the U.S. National Museum for 1890, pp. 429–502.

Hokkaido-chō (Hokkaido Government) (ed.). 1917. *Nopporo Kokuyū-rin Yasei Shokubutsu Chōsa Hōkoku-sho* (Scientific Report on Wild Plants in the Nopporo National Forest). Sapporo.

Hokkaido-chō (ed.). 1937. *Hokkaido-shi* (A History of Hokkaido). 7 vols. Sapporo.

Hokkaido Nōji Shiken-jyō (Experimental Farm of Hokkaido) (ed.). 1931. *Hokkaido ni okeru Shokuyō Yasei Shokubutsu* (Edible Wild Plants in Hokkaido). Hokkaido Noji Shiken-jyō Ihō, No. 52. Sapporo.

Hokkaido Sake Masu Fuka-jyō (Hokkaido Salmon Hatchery). 1956. *Sake Masu Tennen Sanran Jyōkyō Chōsa Keikaku-sho* (Scheme for Survey of Natural Spawning-beds of Salmon). Official Circular.

IGARASHI, Shin'ichi. 1946. *Sakura-masu no Chikuyō Saijuku* (Short-Term Rearing for Maturation of Cherry Salmon). Hokkaido Suisan Fuka-jyō Shiken Hōkoku, Vol. 1, No. 1, pp. 13-18. Sapporo.

IMAIZUMI, Yoshinori. 1949. *Nihon Honyū-dōbutsu Zusetsu. Bunrui to Seitai* (Illustrated Manual of Mammals in Japan. Taxonomy and Ecology). Tokyo.

INUKAI, Tetsuo. 1933. *Higuma no Shūsei ni tsuite* (On the Habits of the Brown Bear). Shokubutsu oyobi Dōbutsu, Vol. 1, No. 1, pp. 57-64. Tokyo.

INUKAI, Tetsuo. 1934. *Akan Kokuritsu Kōen Chitai no Dōbutsu* (Fauna in the Area of the Akan National Park). Hokkaido Keishō-chi Kyōkai. Sapporo.

INUKAI, Tetsuo. 1942. *Tensai ni okeru Ainu no Taido* (Ainus' Attitudes towards Natural Disasters). Hoppō Bunka Kenkyū Hōkoku, No. 6, pp. 141-162. Sapporo.

INUKAI, Tetsuo. 1943. *Hoppō no Fūdo to Dōbutsu* (Land and Animals in the North.) Sapporo and Tokyo.

INUKAI, Tetsuo. 1952. *Hokkaido no Shika to sono Kōbō* (On the Deer in Hokkaido, its Decrease and Coming Back). Hoppō Bunka Kenkyū Hōkoku, No. 7, pp. 1-45. Sapporo.

INUKAI, Tetsuo. 1954. *Ainu no Sake-ryō ni okeru Matsuri-goto* (The Salmon Ceremonialism among the Ainu). Hoppō Bunka Kenkyū Hōkoku, No. 9, pp. 79-90. Sapporo.

INUKAI, Tetsuo and Takemitsu NATORI. 1939. *Iomante* (Ainu no Kuma-matsuri) no Bunka-shi-teki Igi to sono Keishiki, I (On the Significance of the Bear Festival, *iomante*, in Ainu Culture and its Local Forms, I). Hoppō Bunka Kenkyū Hōkoku, No. 2, pp. 237-271. Sapporo.

INUKAI, Tetsuo and Takemitsu NATORI. 1940. *Iomante* (Ainu no Kuma-matsuri) no Bunka-shi-teki Igi to sono Keishiki, II (On the Significance of the Bear Festival, *iomante*, in Ainu Culture and its Local Forms, II). Hoppō Bunka Kenkyū Hōkoku, No. 3, pp. 79-135. Sapporo.

IZUMI, Seiichi. 1951. *Saru Ainu no Chien Shūdan ni okeru Iworu* (The *Iworu* and the Territorial Group of the Saru Ainu). Minzokugaku Kenkyū, Vol. 16, No. 3/4, pp. 29-45. Tokyo.

KINTAICHI, Kyōsuke. 1937. *Saihō Zuihitsu* (Miscellanies on Field Studies). Kyoto.

KINTAICHI, Kyōsuke. 1943. *Ainu no Shinten* (A Collection of Ainu Myths). Tokyo.

KINTAICHI, Kyōsuke. 1944. *Ainu no Kenkyū* (Studies on the Ainu). 3rd ed. Tokyo.

KISHIDA, Hisakichi. 1930. *Nippon Hokutai no Mammal Fauna ni tsuite* (On the Mammal Fauna in the Northern Zone of Japan). Dōbutsugaku Zasshi, Vol. 42, pp. 372-373. Tokyo.

KIYOSU, Yukiyasu. 1952. *Genshoku Nippon Chōrui Dai-zukan* (Illustrated Manual of Birds in Japan). 3 vols. Tokyo.

KŌNO, Hiromichi. 1931. *Ainu no Shita-obi* (The Waist Girdle of the Ainu). Hoppō Jidai, Vol. 2, No. 5, pp. 1-6. (An offprint.)

Kōno, Hiromichi. 1934. *Ainu no Inau Shiroshi* (*Inau Shiroshi* of the Ainu). Jinruigaku Zasshi, Vol. 49, No. 1, pp. 12-24. Tokyo.

Kōno, Hiromichi. 1936. *Ainu to Totem-teki Ifū* (The Ainu and a Totemism-like Custom). Minzokugaku Kenkyū, Vol. 2, pp. 45-53. Tokyo.

Kubodera, Itsuhiko. 1951. *Saru Ainu no Sorei Saishi* (Ancestor Cult of the Saru Ainu). Minzokugaku Kenkyū, Vol. 16, No. 3/4, pp. 46-61. Tokyo.

Kubodera, Itsuhiko. 1956. *Hokkaido Ainu no Sō-sei—Saru Ainu wo Chūsin to shite* (The Antiquated Funeral Customs of the Hokkaido Ainu with special reference to the Saru Ainu). Minzokugaku Kenkyū, Vol. 20, No. 1/2, pp. 1-35. Tokyo.

Kuroda, Nagamichi. 1937. *Sekitsui-dōbutsu Taikei. Ho'nyu-rui* (An Outline of Vertebrates. Mammals). Tokyo.

Makino, Tomitaro. 1951. *Nippon Shokubutsu Zukan* (Illustrated Manual of Flora in Japan). Tokyo.

Masamune, Atsuo (ed). 1937. *Takeshiro Ezo-nisshi-shū* (A Collection of Takeshiro's Diaries in Yezo). 2 vols. Tokyo.

Mihara, Tateo, Shigeru Ito, Toshio Hachiya and Miyoe Ichikawa. 1951. *Hokkaido ni okeru Keison Gyokyō no Hendō ni kansuru Kenkyū* (Studies on the Change of Fishing Conditions of Salmon in Hokkaido), I. Hokkaido Suisan Fuka-jyō Shiken Hōkoku, Vol. 6, No. 1/2, pp. 27-133.

Mitsuishi Jigyō-jyō (Mitsuishi Plant, Hokkaido Salmon Hatchery). 1956. Official Report submitted to the Chitose Branch of the Hatchery.

Mitsuoka, Shin-ichi. 1941. *Ainu no Sokuseki* (Footsteps of the Ainu). 6th ed. Shiraoi, Hokkaido.

Miura, Ihachiro. 1933. Ringyō (Forestry). Chiri Kōza, Nihon-hen, Vol. 1 (*Karafuto oyobi Hokkaido*), pp. 275-290. Tokyo.

Miyaji, Denzaburo and Shuichi Mori. 1953. *Dōbutsu no Seitai* (Ecology of Animals). Tokyo.

Montandon, George. 1937. La Civilisation Ainou. Paris.

Munro, Gordon N. 1962. The Ainu. Creed and Cult. London.

Murakoshi, Michio and Tomitaro Makino. 1956. *Genshoku Shokubutu Zukan* (Illustrated Manual of Flora in Japan). Vol. 2. Tokyo.

Nagane, Sukehachi. 1925. *Karafuto Dojin no Seikatsu* (Life of the Sakhalin Aborigines). Tokyo.

Natori, Takemitsu. 1940. *Kezuri-bashi Soin Sokei Sogen oyobi Shushin yori mitaru Saru Kawasuji no Ainu* (The Genealogy of the Ainu in the Saru Valley). Jinruigaku Zasshi, Vol. 55, pp. 203-229. Tokyo.

Natori, Takemitsu. 1941. *Saru Ainu no Kuma-okuri ni okeru Kamigami no Yurai to Nusa* (The Origin of Gods and the *nusa*, cluster of *inau*, in the Bear Festival of the Saru Ainu). Hoppō Bunka Kenkyū Hōkoku, No. 4, pp. 35-112. Sapporo.

Natori, Takemitsu. 1945. *Funka-wan Ainu no Hogei* (Whale Hunting among the Funka-wan Ainu). Sapporo.

Nishino, Kazuhiko. 1958. *Hokkaido no Sake Sanran Kasen ni okeru Hyōshiki Hōryū Shiken* (Chum Salmon Tagging Experiments in Spawning Streams in Hokkaido). Hokkaido Sake Masu Fuka-jyō Kenkyū Hōkoku, No. 12, pp. 51-61. Sapporo.

Obihiro Sokkō-sho (Meteorological Station of Obihiro)(ed.). 1959. *Tokachi Kishō Yōran* (Manual of Climate in Tokapchi). Obihiro.

Ōno, Isokichi. 1933. *Hokkaido-san Sakura-masu no Seikatsu-shi* (Life History of Cherry Salmon in Hokkaido), I., Keison Ihō, Vol. 5, No. 2, pp. 15-26. Sapporo.

Ōshima, Masamitsu. 1940. *Sekitsui-dōbutsu Taikei. Sakana.* (An Outline of Vertebrates. Fishes). Tokyo.

OYA, Yoshinobu. 1954. *Kasen-kan no Sake Sojyō Keitai no Ruijisei ni tsuite* (The Affinity of the Spawning Type of Salmon, O. keta Walbaum, which are found in the Rivers of Hokkaido). Hokkaido Suisan Fuka-jyō Shiken Hōkoku, No. 9, pp. 113-126. Sapporo.

PILSUDSKI, Bronislaw. 1912. Materials for the Study of the Ainu Language and Folklore. Crakow.

RADCLIFFE-BROWN, A. R. 1952. Structure and Function in Primitive Society. London.

SANO, Seizo. 1946. *Soka Sake ohū Tsūshō Ginke-sake ni kansuru Chōsa, Yohō* I (Investigations on the So-called Silvery Salmon among the Run Salmon. Preliminary Report I). Hokkaido Suisan Fuka-jyō Shiken Hōkoku, Vol. 1, No. 1, pp. 39-43. Sapporo.

SANO, Seizo. 1947. *Soka Sake chū Tsūshō Ginke Sake ni kansuru Chōsa Yohō* II (Investigations on the So-called Silvery Salmon among the Run Salmon, II). Hokkaido Suisan Fuka-jyō Shiken Hōkoku, Vol. 2, No. 1, pp. 41-45. Sapporo.

SANO, Seizo. 1950. *Sakura-masu no Seikatsu-shi* (Life History of Cherry Salmon, O. masou). Sakana to Tamago, No. 2 (February), pp. 51-22. Hokkaido Suisan Fuka-jyō. Sapporo.

SANO, Seizo and Ariaki NAGASAWA. 1958. *Tokachi-gawa Shiryū Memugawa ni okeru Sake no Tennen Hanshoku* (Natural Propagation of Chum Salmon, Oncorhynchus keta, in the Mem River, Tokapchi). Hokkaido Sake Masu Fuka-jyō Kenkyū Hōkoku, No. 12, pp. 1-19. Sapporo.

SARASHINA, Genzo. 1942. *Kotan Seibutsu Ki* (Ethnobiological Notes on an Ainu Settlement). Sapporo.

SASAKI, Chozaemon. 1927. *Ainu no Hanashi* (A Lecture on the Ainu). Asahikawa.

SEGAWA, Kiyoko. 1951. *Saru Ainu Fujin no Upshoru ni tsuite* (On the Waist Girdle, *upshoru kutu*, of Ainu Women in the Saru Valley). Minzokugaku Kenkyū, Vol. 16, No. 3/4, pp. 62-70. Tokyo.

Shiraoi Jigyō-jyō (Shiraoi Plant, Hokkaido Salmon Hatchery). 1956. *Shiraoi-gawa ni okeru Sake Shingyo Tennen Sanran-shō Chōsa* (The Survey of Natural Spawning-beds of Dog Salmon in the Shiraoi). Official Report submitted to the Chitose Branch of the Hatchery.

STEWARD, Julian H. 1938. Basin Plateau Aboriginal Sociopolitical Groups. Smithsonian Institution Bureau of American Ethnology, Bull. 137.

SUGIURA, Ken'ichi. 1951. *Saru Ainu no Shinzoku Soshiki* (Kinship System of the Saru Ainu). Minzokugaku Kenkyū, Vol. 16, No. 3/4, pp. 3-28. Tokyo.

TAKABEYA, Fukuhei. 1939. *Ainu Jyūkyo no Kenkyū* (Studies on Ainu Dwellings). Hoppō Bunka Kenkyū Hōkoku, No. 2, pp. 1-124. Sapporo.

TAKABEYA, Fukuhei. 1941. *Ainu Minzoku no shiyō-shitaru Keiryō no Tan-i* (Studies on Units of Measures used by the Ainu). Hoppō Bunka Kenkyū Hōkoku, No. 4, pp. 113-200. Sapporo.

TAKAKURA, Shin'ichiro. 1942. *Ainu Seisaku-shi* (A History of Ainu Policies). Tokyo.

TAKAKURA, Shin'ichiro. 1957. *Meiji-izen no Hokkaido ni okeru Nō-boku-gyō* (Agricultural History of Hokkaido before the Introduction of European Techniques). Hoppō Bunka Kenkyū Hōkoku, No. 12, pp. 13-41. Sapporo.

Teikoku Gakushi-in (Imperial Academy of Japan) (ed.). 1944a. *Tōa Minzoku Meii* (Names of Eastern Asian Peoples). Tokyo.

Teikoku Gakushi-in (ed.). 1944b. *Ainu* (The Ainu). Tōa Minzoku Yōshi Shiryō, No. 2. Tokyo.

TOKACHI Shijyō (Tokapchi Branch, Hokkaido Salmon Hatchery). Official Catch Register for 1933-1956.

Tokyo Temmon-dai (Astronomical Observatory of Tokyo) (ed.). 1954. *Rika Nempyō* 1955 (Science Tables for 1955). Tokyo.

WATANABE, Hitoshi. 1951. *Saru Ainu ni okeru Tennen-shigen no Riyō* (Utilization of Natural Resources by the Saru Ainu). Minzokugaku Kenkyū, Vol. 16, No. 3/4, pp. 71-82.

WATANABE, Hitoshi. 1953. *Ainu ni okeru Yumi* (Bows among the Ainu). Jinruigaku-kai Minzokugaku-kyōkai Rengō Taikai Kiji, 6th Session, pp. 129-132. Tokyo.

WATANABE, Hitoshi. 1954. *Ifuri Ainu ni okeru Suisan Shigen no Riyō* (Utilization of Aquatic Resources by the Ifuri Ainu). Jinruigaku-kai Minzokugaku-kyōkai Rengō Taikai Kiji, 7th Session, pp. 43-48. Tokyo.

WATANABE, Hitoshi. 1955. *Kisetsuteki Ijyū Gijutsu Shigen. Ainu ni okeru Seitaiteki Ichi-sokumen* (Seasonal Migration, Technology and Natural Resources. An Ecological Aspect of the Ainu). Jinruigaku-kai Minzokugaku-kyōkai Rengō Taikai Kiji, 8th Session, pp. 62-63. Tokyo.

WATANABE, Hitoshi. 1963. *Ainu no Nawabari to shiteno Sake no Sanran-kuiki* (Spawning Grounds of Dog Salmon as the Territory of the Ainu Local Group). Minzokugaku Note (Oka Kyōju Kanreki Kinen Ronbun-shū), pp. 278-297. Tokyo.

WATANABE, Hitoshi. 1964, *Ningen to Shizen no Shakai-teki Ketsugo Kankei. Ainu Nihon-minzoku Tungus no Kyōtsūsei* (Social Solidarity between Man and Nature. Features common to the Ainu, the Japanese and the Tungus). Nihon Minzoku-gaku-kyōkai Kenkyū Taikai, 2nd Session (1963), Proceedings (in print).

YAMAMOTO, Yūkō. 1943. *Karafuto Ainu no Jyūkyo* (The Dwellings of the Sakhalin Ainu). Kenchiku Shinsho 10. Tokyo.

YOSHIDA, Iwao. 1955. *Higashi Hokkaido Ainu Koji Fudoki Shiryō* (Ethnographical Materials on the Ainu in Eastern Hokkaido). Obihiro-shi Shakai Kyōiku Sōsho, No. 1. Obihiro.

YOSHIDA, Iwao. 1956a. *Higashi Hokkaido Ainu Koji Fudoki Shiryō* (Ethnographical Materials on the Ainu in Eastern Hokkaido). Obihiro-shi Shakai Kyōiku Sōsho, No. 2. Obihiro.

YOSHIDA, Iwao. 1956b. *Tsue no Mitama: Tokachi-Ainu Korō Danwa Kiroku* (Ainu Ethnography as told by Six Old Tokapchi Ainus). Minzokugaku Kenkyū, Vol. 19, No. 3/4, pp. 135-156. Tokyo.

YOSHIDA, Iwao. 1957. *Higashi Hokkaido Ainu Koji Fudoki Shiryō* (Ethnographical Materials on the Ainu in Eastern Hokkaido). Obihiro-shi Shakai Kyōiku Sōsho, No. 3. Obihiro.

YOSHIDA, Iwao. 1958. *Higashi Hokkaido Ainu Koji Fudoki Shiryō* (Ethnographical Materials on the Ainu in Eastern Hokkaido). Obihiro-shi Shakai Kyōiku Sōsho, No. 4. Obihiro.

A Short History of Ainu Studies

The aim of this postscript is twofold : to trace briefly the historical development of social and cultural studies of the Ainu, and at the same time to make a parallel introduction to basic literature concerning the subject. For reasons of space, reference will be made only to the Ainu in Hokkaido and to a selective bibliography thereof, with the result that much relevant literature will have to be overlooked.

No history of Ainu studies should ignore those admirable reports and records from the Tokugawa period which, with all their weaknesses in methodology, were nevertheless based on actual explorations and travels in the island then called Yezo. Only a few will be mentioned here.

HATA, Kusumaru (ed.), rev. and enl. by MAMIYA, Sōrin. 1823. *Yezo Seikei Zusetsu* (An Illustrated Book of Yezo Life). 8 vols.

MATSUURA, Takeshiro. 1937. *Takeshiro Yezo Nisshi* (Takeshiro's Collected Diaries in Yezo). 3 vols. Tokyo.

————. 1855–58. *Tōzai Yezo Sansen Chiri Torishirabe Kikō* (A Record of Geographical Explorations in East and West Yezo). 22 vols. Woodcut printing.

For convenient reference to literature from pre-Meiji periods, the following works are extremely helpful :

TAKAKURA, Shin'ichiro. 1936. *Ainu Bunken Kaidai* (Expository Bibliography on the Ainu). Hokkaido Daigaku Shinbun, May 19, 1936, and subsequent issues. Sapporo.

————. 1942. *Ainu Seisaku-shi* (A History of Ainu Policies). Tokyo. See especially the bibliography on old literature on the Ainu, and the notes.

————. 1953. *Kyōdo Kenkyū Series* (Local Study Series), No. 3. Sapporo.

————. 1953. *Yezo Fūzokuga ni tsuite* (On Pictorial Representations of Ainu Life). Hoppō Bunka Kenkyū Hōkoku, No. 8, pp. 1–67. Sapporo.

Beginning early in the Meiji era, when the Japanese Government installed its first Commissioner of Colonization for the administration and development of Hokkaido, the native Ainu and the Japanese entered on a new phase of direct and intensive intercourse such as had never been seen before. As a result the Ainu became a serious administrative problem. Before the mid-Meiji period, or more exactly, around the years 1884–85, the natives, breaking off rather precipitously from their traditional mode of life, turned to a life based on farming. It appears that both the rise of general interest in the race and the earliest studies and research on them date from about the same period ; these include :

HIZUKA, Takamasa (ed.). 1882. *Yezo Fūzoku Isan* (A Miscellany on Ways and Customs in Yezo). 20 vols. Woodcut printing, Kaitaku-shi (Office of the Commissioner of Colonization).

SAKAI, Tadafumi. *Hokkaidō Junkō-ki* (A Record of Official Tours in Hokkaido). 3 vols. MSS. Written by a clerk in the Kaitaku-shi. See particularly Vol. 3, which contains some diaries on the natives.

It must be remembered, however, that for the introduction of scientific research on the Ainu and the arousal of worldwide interest in them, the credit must go to a handful of Europeans who came over to Hokkaido during that period. Some of them published reports on language, ' material culture ', manners and customs, and physical characteristics ; others wrote on travels they made among the natives :

CHAMBERLAIN, Basil Hall. 1887. *The Language, Mythology, and Geographical Nomenclature of Japan Viewed in the Light of Ainu Studies.* Tokyo.

HITCHCOCK, Romyn. 1891. *The Ainus of Yezo, Japan.* Report of the U.S. National Museum for 1890, pp. 429–502.

LANDOR, A. H. S. 1893. *Alone with the Hairy Ainu.* London.

RITTER, H. 1874. *Über eine Reise in Südwestlicher Theile von Yezo.* Mitteilungen der deutscher Gesellschaft für Natur und Völkerkunde Ostasiens, Bd. 1, Heft 6. Yokohama.

SCHEUBE, B. 1882. *Die Ainos.* Mitteilungen der deutscher Gesellschaft für Natur und Völkerkunde Ostasiens, Bd. 3, Heft 26. Yokohama.

SIEBOLD, Heinrich von. 1881. *Ethnologische Studien über die Aino auf der Insel Yesso.* Zeitschrift für Ethnologie, Supplement. Berlin.

STAR, Frederick. 1904. *The Ainu Group.* Chicago.

Of these Europeans, the most remarkable was BATCHELOR, whose ethnological contributions, especially in the fields of language, religion, and folklore, deserve special mention. Representative among his many works are :

BATCHELOR, John. 1889. *An Ainu-English-Japanese Dictionary and Grammar.* Tokyo.
———. 1892. *The Ainu of Japan.* London.
———. 1901. *The Ainu and Their Folk-lore.* London.

This pioneer research by Europeans served as a timely stimulus to the then rising tide of anthropological interest in academic circles in Japan. In time there appeared Ainu studies by Japanese anthropologists, beginning with inquiries into the racial and ethnological origins of the native people. Those early studies came out chiefly in the *Journal of the Anthropological Society* of that time.

TSUBOI, Shōgorō. 1886–ca. 1910. Various articles in the *Journal of the Anthropological Society.* Tokyo.

YOSHIDA, Iwao. 1910–18. Articles in ibid.

Also carried by the journal were numerous other articles on the Ainu, which cannot be listed here.

Ainu studies by Japanese thenceforth developed in three main directions, namely, physical anthropology, language, and ' material culture '. Some mergings occurred as, for instance, between the studies of language and ' material culture ' in the area of religion; and some new developments took place, such as in the direction of mythology and folklore :

CHIRI, Mashiho. 1936–37. *Ainu Minzoku Kenkyū Shiryō* (Research Materials for Ainu Ethnology). Attic Museum Report, No. 8. Tokyo.

———. 1954. *Ainu no Shin'yō* (The Sacred Verses of the Ainu). Hoppō Bunka Kenkyū Hōkoku, No. 9, pp. 1–78. Sapporo.

KINDAICHI, Kyōsuke. 1931. *Yūkara Kenkyū* (A Study of Yūkara, the Ainu Epics). Tokyo.

———. 1943. *Ainu no Shinten—Ainu Rakkuru no Densetsu* (The Sacred Book of the Ainu —The Legend of Ainu Rakkuru, the Culture Hero). Tokyo.

———. 1944. *Ainu no Kenkyū* (A Study of the Ainu). 3d ed., Tokyo. See particularly Chs. 7 and 8.

The following studies of Ainu religious beliefs and rituals may be regarded as an outcome of this trend of interest :

CHIRI, Mashiho. 1952. *Jushi to Kawauso* (The Shaman and the Otter). Hoppō Bunka Kenkyū Hōkoku, No. 7, pp. 47–80. Sapporo.

KUBODERA, Itsuhiko, and CHIRI, Mashiho. 1940. *Ainu no Hōsō-shin Pākorokamui ni tsuite* (On Pakorokamui, the Ainu Smallpox Deity). Journal of the Anthropological Society of Nippon, Vol. 55, pp. 125–28, 169–99. Tokyo.

Studies in the field of ' material culture ' developed in conjunction with studies of religion ; in other words, Ainu ' material culture ' was studied with religion as the background. This tendency was helped by a recognition of the fact that the Ainu tools and techniques were inseparably linked with their beliefs and rituals. Writings on Ainu ' material culture ' throughout the long years are found in great numbers in the *Journal of the Anthropological Society of Tokyo* (now known as *of Nippon*), *Hoppō Bunka Kenkyū Hōkoku* (Reports on Northern Culture Studies), and so on. Notable among these many studies made in connection with religion are those by KŌNO, INUKAI, NATORI, CHIRI, and others, some of whose representative articles are as follows :

INUKAI, Tetsuo. 1954. *Ainu no Sakeryō ni okeru Saiji* (The Salmon Fishing Rites among the Ainu). Hoppō Bunka Kenkyū Hōkoku, No. 9, pp. 79–90. Sapporo.

INUKAI, Tetsuo, and NATORI, Takemitsu. 1939. *Iomante (Ainu no Kuma-matsuri) no Bunkashi-teki Igi to sono Keishiki*, I (On the Significance of the Bear Festival, Iomante, in Ainu Culture and Its Local Forms, I). Hoppō Bunka Kenkyū Hōkoku, No. 2, pp. 237–71. Sapporo.

INUKAI, Tetsuo, and TAKEKASA, Kōzō. 1958. *Ainu no Marukibune no Sakusei* (Canoemaking among the Ainu). Hoppō Bunka Kenkyū Hōkoku, No. 8, pp. 117–84. Sapporo.

NATORI, Takemitsu. 1941. *Saru Ainu no Kuma-okuri ni okeru Kamigami no Yurai to Nusa* (The Origin of Gods and the *Nusa*, Clusters of *Inau*, in the Bear Festival of the Saru Ainu). Hoppō Bunka Kenkyū Hōkoku, No. 4, pp. 35–112. Sapporo.

Some of these studies have been made available in separate book form. The most outstanding are :

CHIRI, Mashiho. 1953. *Bunrui Ainu-go Jiten, I: Shokubutsu-hen* (A Classificatory Ainu Dictionary, I : Plants). Attic Museum Report, No. 64. Tokyo.
———. 1954–55. *Bunrui Ainu-go Jiten, II : Ningen-hen* (A Classificatory Ainu Dictionary, II : Man). Attic Museum Report, No. 68. Tokyo.

NATORI, Takemitsu. 1945. *Funka-wan Ainu no Hogei* (Whale Hunting among the Funkawan Ainu). Sapporo. A collection of his articles.

The dictionary by CHIRI is quite unique in its presentation of data. Volume I may be described as a study on ethnobotany which also incorporates linguistics. Together with Vol. II, it forms a truly epochal piece of work. It should also be noted in this connection that an attempt has been made to record Ainu life in an ethnozoological and ethnobotanical way :

SARASHINA, Genzo. 1942. *Kotan Seibutsu Ki* (Ethnobiological Notes on an Ainu Settlement). Sapporo.

The work by NATORI mentioned above is really a collection of diverse research papers including some notable studies on material life viewed from a religious standpoint. The book also reports significant research on the same subject with consideration of its sociological aspects. A few other writers may also be cited as proving the significance of studies based on this method :

KŌNO, Hiromichi. 1931. *Bohyō no Katachi yori mitaru Ainu no Shokeitō* (Different Stocks of the Ainu as Viewed from the Type of Grave-Posts). Yezo Ōrai, No. 4, pp. 101–21. Sapporo.

NATORI, Takemitsu. 1940. *Kezuri-bashi Soin Sokei Sogen oyobi Shushinki yori mitaru Saru Kawasuji no Ainu* (The Genealogy of the Ainu in the Saru Valley). Journal of the Anthropological Society of Nippon, Vol. 55, pp. 203–29. Tokyo.

The study of Ainu ' material culture ' has a long history of its own, apart from that of language and religion.   Of the great many writings on this subject, the following two clearly show a high level of scholarship, based on long years of accumulated labours :

SUGIYAMA, Sueo. 1941–43.   *Ainu Geijutsu* (Ainu Arts).   3 vols. Tokyo.
TAKABEYA, Fukuhei. 1946–48, 1950.   *Ainu Jyūkyo no Kenkyū* (Studies on Ainu Dwellings).
Hoppō Bunka Kenkyū Hōkoku, Nos. 1–3 (1946–48) and 5 (1950).   Sapporo.

As regards comparative studies, the mainstream so far has focused on individual culture elements rather than on complexes of various elements or on the Ainu culture as a whole.   This makes all the more memorable the classic work by STERNBERG :

STERNBERG, Leo. 1929.   *The Ainu Problem.*   Anthropos, Bd. 26, pp. 755–99.

It will be clear from what we have seen so far that, although much has been studied and written by Japanese Ainu scholars, most of their studies have tended to be ' monographic ' or confined to one or another single aspect or element in Ainu life ; very little has been done on the level of comprehensive ethnography covering broad aspects of the Ainu way of life.   For this reason, the work of KŌNO to be mentioned below, recording as it does the general life of the people and based on actual field surveys, is still very important.   It is also significant in this connection that in comparatively recent years a number of ethnographical studies, made jointly by a group of scholars on the Ainu, have been published by the former Imperial Academy.   As a study made on the same lines by a European, following in the footsteps of HITCHCOCK, that of MONTANDON should be mentioned.

Ainu-Bunka Hozon Taisaku Kyōgikai (Association for the Preservation of Ainu Culture) (ed.). 1969.   *Ainu Minzoku-shi* (Ainu Ethnography). 2 vols. Tokyo.
Imperial Academy Ethnographic Survey of Far Eastern Peoples (ed.). 1944.   *Ainu : Tōaminzoku Yōshi Shiryō*, 2 (The Ainu : Ethnographic Materials on Far Eastern Peoples, No. 2). Tokyo.
KŌNO, Tsunekichi. 1911.   *Hokkaido Kyū-dojin* (The Aborigines of Hokkaido).   Hokkaido Government Office, Sapporo.
MONTANDON, George. 1937.   *La Civilisation Ainou et les Cultures Arctiques.*   Paris.

Another European who, after BATCHELOR, spent many years in Hokkaido studying the Ainu was MUNRO ; he worked in cooperation with C. G. SELIGMAN, then a professor at Cambridge. Through direct observations and other information MUNRO successfully made a detailed ethnographical study of the Ainu people.   After his death and SELIGMAN's, his vast and valuable collection of photographs and his manuscripts were put in the keeping of the Royal Anthropological Institute in London.   These manuscripts were recently published in book form :

MUNRO, Gordon N. 1962.   *Ainu Creed and Cult.*   London.

Now, it will be noticed that all the studies that I have mentioned so far are characterized by the ' culture-historical method '.   Their concern has been mainly the comparison of individual culture elements and the problem of the origins, diffusion, and development of these elements ; very little has been written about the society in which those elements occur.   The result is that the sociological and economic side of Ainu life has been largely neglected.   In saying this, however, I do not mean to overlook some valuable historical studies in the field of the socio-economic organization of the Ainu :

HABARA, Matakichi. 1939.   *Ainu Shakai-keizai-shi* (A Socio-economic History of the Ainu). Tokyo.   See particularly Chs. 5 (Village Forms), 6 (Social Organization), and 7 (Economic Life).

TAKAKURA, Shin'ichiro. 1942. *Ainu-Seisaku-shi*, cited above, p. 164. Tokyo. See particularly Ch. 1, Sec. 2, where an attempt is made at a reconstruction of the Ainu social life of the Tokugawa era; other chapters provide historical introductions to socio-economic life in various periods. See also the bibliography, which includes a number of historical documents.

The above book by TAKAKURA in particular provides important data for studying exterior factors that worked on Ainu culture, i.e. the influence of the Japanese. His book also contains some valuable bibliographical and historical data on the study of Ainu social and economic organization. Another book should be mentioned as one dealing with the Ainu in relation to the general history of the Japanese in Hokkaido from ancient times down to the present:

Hokkaido Government Office. 1936–37. *Shinsen Hokkaido-shi* (A New History of Hokkaido). 7 vols. Sapporo. See particularly Vol. 2, which deals with the periods from ancient times to the late Tokugawa era; there the Ainu ways and customs are viewed through their intercourse and in relation with the Japanese. Volume 7 contains chronological and statistical tables.

After the end of World War II a new attempt was made in the study of the old Ainu social organization. Whereas the earlier sociological studies were largely on historical lines with old documents as the principal data, the new development was characterized by ethnological field work. Moreover, it was made significant by the functional method it employed in considering relationships with whole aspects of Ainu life; again, it was also new in that it took the form of a joint project conducted by a number of researchers. The work extended over several years; however, only the first part of the official reports has so far been made available:

Reports on Joint Research on the Saru Ainu. 1952. Minzoku Kenkyū (Journal of the Ethnological Society of Japan), Vol. 16, Nos. 3/4, pp. 1–101. Tokyo. Among the reports contained are: K. SUGIURA, Kinship Organization; S. IZUMI, The *Iwor* and the Territorial Group; I. KUBODERA, The Worship of the Ancestral Spirits; K. SEGAWA, On the *Upshor*; H. WATANABE, On the Exploitation of Natural Resources. These are reports on the results of the first season.

This approach implies a number of difficulties: in the first place, Ainu society as an autonomous entity no longer exists; the Ainus' traditional mode of life underwent a radical transformation through intercourse with the Japanese, especially during the mid-Meiji period. Thus, there is only a small remnant of natives who remember their old ways. One further report related to this research project was a study of the Ainu ecosystem by WATANABE, which constitutes the text of the present book:

WATANABE, Hitoshi. 1964. *The Ainu: A Study of Ecology and the System of Social Solidarity between Man and Nature in Relation to Group Structure.* Journal of the Faculty of Science, University of Tokyo, Sec. 5, Vol. 2, Pt. 6, pp. 1–164.
————. 1966. *Die sozialen Funktionen des Bärenfestes der Ainu und die ökologischen Faktoren in seiner Entwicklung.* Anthropos, Bd. 61, pp. 708–26.

Ecological research on the Ainu has been extended to include the field of comparative ecology so that such studies concerning population history and prehistory as the following have been published:

WATANABE, Hitoshi. 1964. *Ecology of the Ainu and Problems in Prehistory in Japan.* Journal of the Anthropological Society of Nippon, Vol. 72, No. 740, pp. 9–23.
————. 1968. *Subsistence and Ecology of Northern Food Gatherers with Special Reference to the Ainu.* In: R. B. Lee and I. DeVore, eds., Man the Hunter, pp. 69–77. Chicago: Aldine Publishing Co.
————. 1969. *Famine as a Population Check: Comparative Ecology of Northern Peoples.* Journal of the Faculty of Science, University of Tokyo, Sec. 5, Vol. 3, Pt. 4, pp. 237–52.

The studies briefly surveyed above were all concerned with reconstruction of the traditional life of the Ainu or with the past of the people. In the future, the most urgent studies will be those made on the Ainu as they exist today—an ethnic minority group living in Japanese territory. The Ainu are not yet completely extinct; moreover, they present an unsolved mystery to the scientists of the world.